George Barnes Hall

Historical sketches and events in the colonization of America

And the outgrowth of our country

George Barnes Hall

Historical sketches and events in the colonization of America
And the outgrowth of our country

ISBN/EAN: 9783337152697

Printed in Europe, USA, Canada, Australia, Japan

Cover: Foto ©ninafisch / pixelio.de

More available books at **www.hansebooks.com**

HISTORICAL SKETCHES
AND
EVENTS IN THE COLONIZATION
OF
AMERICA
AND THE OUTGROWTH OF OUR COUNTRY
ILLUSTRATED.

The Discoveries by Columbus and other Navigators.
LANDING OF THE PURITANS AND NUMEROUS OTHER COLONIES.

A Portrait Gallery of our Great Rulers and Men
WITH BIOGRAPHICAL SKETCHES

AN ENCYCLOPEDIA OF INFORMATION CONDENSED; HISTORICAL AND
STATISTICAL TABLE OF THE UNITED STATES OF NORTH AMERICA;
THE DECLARATION OF INDEPENDENCE AND ITS FRAMERS;
DELEGATES TO THE FIRST CONGRESS; THE CONSTITU-
TION; WHO DID AND WHO DID NOT SIGN THE
ARTICLES EMBRACING THE CONSTITUTION;
DATE OF RATIFICATION OF THE CONSTITUTION BY THE THIRTEEN
ORIGINAL STATES.

OUR NATIONAL GOVERNMENT
AND HOW IT IS ADMINISTERED IN THE DIFFERENT DEPARTMENTS.

*Washington at Newburg; Benedict Arnold's Treason; Capture
and Execution of Major Andre; Sketch of the Schuyler
Family and their Historical Mansion; also the
Van Rensselaer Manor House.*

**THE ELECTION, POLITICS, MAJORITY, AUTOGRAPHS, PORTRAITS AND BIO-
GRAPHICAL SKETCH OF ALL OUR CHIEF RULERS TO THE PRESENT TIME.**
A POLITICAL COMPENDIUM.

The First Steam Navigation and First Railroad. A Chronolgical Statistical
Discussion of our Population and Area from 1790 to 1880.
The Territories and their Capitals.

Arnold's Address to the American People, Attempting to Vindicate his Treason;
A Historical Treasure just brought to light after an obscurity of over a Century.

Profusely Illustrated with Steel and Wood Engravings made Expressly for this Work.
Complete in One Volume.
MINNEAPOLIS, MINNESOTA:
HALL & TRAVIS, PROPRIETORS AND PUBLISHERS.
1886.

HISTORICAL SKETCHES BY EMINENT AUTHORS.

THE OUTGROWTH OF OUR COUNTRY;

FROM OFFICIAL RESOURCES.

COMPILED AND ARRANGED

BY

GEORGE BARNES HALL.

MINNEAPOLIS, MINN.
PROPRIETORS AND PUBLISHERS:
HALL & TRAVIS.
1886.

PRINTED AND BOUND BY
J. F. TRAVIS,
No. 18 Fourth Street North.

Copyright by
HALL & TRAVIS,
1886.
All rights reserved.

PREFACE.

In presenting to our readers the trials, tribulations, massacres and great sacrifices endured in the attempts, and in the final colonization of America, which was the outgrowth of our country, our motive was to fill an acknowledged want not yet fully supplied. Two things have been aimed at; first, to avoid burdening the reader with dry and uninteresting details, with long winded accounts; and on the other hand to not sacrifice completeness for brevity's sake. But within the compass of our "condensed volume" we offer a work which is neither too brief to be of service to the student of our early history, and the outgrowth of our country, nor is it too detailed to repel the average reader. But we feel sure that it is a combination of history, biography and general information, nowhere else to be found. In the work will be found prominent and interesting features of great value. And in order to enable the young of our land, and all those of our readers not familiar with the construction of our government, a description is given showing how the government is constituted and administered in each of its various departments. It is as fascinating as a story or novel, verifying the old adage that "truth is often stranger than fiction." It is a complete library of historical sketches, biography, chronological and statistical tables of our country, and a portrait gallery of the presidents, philanthropists, explorers and generals, of our dictionary of great Americans. And in fact, to enable all to become more familiar with the causes and effects which led to the discovery of America by Christopher Columbus, and the final colonization of America and the outgrowth of the United States, in a condensed, attractive, illustrated and readable form, has been the inducement and incentive for the publication of this work.   G. B. H.

LIST OF ILLUSTRATIONS.

1	LANDING OF COLUMBUS,	Frontispiece.
2	COLUMBUS,	2
3	QUEEN ISABELLA,	8
4	LANDING OF PONCE DE LEON,	13
5	GATE TO ST. AUGUSTINE,	17
6	SIR WALTER RALEIGH,	24
7	POCAHONTAS SAVING CAPT. JOHN SMITH,	26
8	POCAHONTAS,	30
9	LO, THE GOOD INDIAN,	34
10	LANDING OF THE PILGRIMS,	42
11	PEQUOD INDIANS ATTACKING COLONISTS,	50
12	PETER STUYVESANT,	64
13	ROBERT LIVINGSTON,	68
14	LANDING OF ROGER WILLIAMS,	70
15	WILLIAM PENN,	88
16	FATHER RECCOLLECT HENNEPIN,	92
17	JOHN HANCOCK,	113
18	FRAMERS OF THE DECLARATION OF INDEPENDENCE,	114
19	FIRST CONTINENTAL CONGRESS,	115
20	WASHINGTON'S HEADQUARTERS, NEWBURG,	121
21	ROBERT MORRIS,	122
22	CAPTURE OF MAJOR ANDRE,	132
23	GEN. NATHANIEL GREENE,	134
24	BENEDICT ARNOLD,	136
25	GEN. PHILIP SCHUYLER,	140
26	SCHUYLER MANSION,	142
27	VAN RANSSELAER HOMESTEAD,	144
28	INAUGURATION OF WASHINGTON,	146
29	PRESIDENTS' AUTOGRAPHS,	148, 149
30	CAPITOL AT WASHINGTON,	150
31	GEORGE WASHINGTON AND ALL THE OTHER PRESIDENTS,	152-194
32	DISTRICT OF COLUMBIA,	194
33	JOHN A. LOGAN,	196
34	ROBERT FULTON,	198
35	BOISE CITY, CAPITAL OF IDAHO,	200
36	SITKA, CAPITAL OF ALASKA,	209
37	BISMARCK, CAPITAL OF DAKOTA,	212
38	HELENA, CAPITAL OF MONTANA,	213
39	SEATTLE, PUGET SOUND,	214
40	PORTLAND, OREGON,	215

WASHIGNTON.

No monument can tell the fame
    Which clusters round that honored name;
Its grandeur with the nation grows,
And is as fragrance to the rose.

What name in any clime or age,
Is so adored on History's page?
His virtues and his works have won
The hearts which bless our Washington!

When called as our chief with loud acclaim,
We hope each one as fair a fame;
Washington the name of "Father" won,
So may all prove a worthy son;

Profit by all the deeds he wrought,
Be guided by all the truths he taught,
And guide the ship of state with zeal,
And so promote the public weal.

CONTENTS OF SKETCHES.

INTRODUCTORY.

PART I.—Page 3.

Christopher Columbus. Home in Genoa. His first voyages. Idea of crossing the Atlantic. Genoa, Venice and Portugal. He leaves for Spain. Queen Isabella. To visit her at Cardova. His arrival at Cardova. He waits seven years. The King and Queen. Columbus disappointed, left the court. He starts for France. He meets Juan Parez. Became acquainted with Martin Alonzo Pinzon, a wealthy navigator. Columbus remains at Palos. Juan Parez sees the Queen in his behalf. Columbus invited to appear at court. His arrival at court. Another long wait. Columbus at last arouses Isabella. She gives him aid. The King and Queen sign the agreement. Columbus sails August 3, 1492. October 12 land was discovered. Columbus effected a landing.

PART II. Page 12.

Name of America. How it originated. Amerigo Vespucci, a distinguished navigator. Martin Waldsumuller and Rene. Henry VII. of England after prizes in the New World. John Cabot and his three sons. Vasco Nunez de Balboa. Landing of Ponce de Leon, 1512. Juan Verrozzani, all explorers. Disaster to Narvaez Ferdinand de Soto, a famous navigator. The Mississippi discovered. 1562, Admiral de Coligny, a French Protestant, under command of Jean Ribault. Sir John Hawkins. Pedro Melendez, a fierce soldier. Death to the Hugenots. Ribault and his command.

PART III.—Page 19.

Retaliation of the French. Dominie de Gourgues. A born Gascon. In 1603 Samuel Champlain denominated New France. The city of Quebec. Bay of Fundy. First settlement in America. Lake Champlain. Port Royal. Annapolis. River St. Johns. Preceding races.

Colonization by the English. Sebastain Cabot and Sir Hugh Willoughby. North Cape, Lapland and Moscow. Queen Elizabeth's patronage. Sir Humphrey Gilbert. His second voyage. Philip Amidaz and Arthur Barlow. Sir Walter Raleigh. The shores of Carolina. The name of Virginia. Sir Richard Grenville and Ralph Lane. Anchored at Wacocon. Help by Sir Francis Drake. A sudden storm. Abandonment of Roanoke. John White. The city of Raleigh. The Indians' vengeance. First child born. Gains of privateering. Raleigh a bankrupt. Exploration of Bartholomew Gosnold.

PART IV.—PAGE 26.

1603. Peace between England and Spain. Gosnold and companions. Lord Arundel and Capt. Weymouth. Petition to the King. Divided North America. The associates of Sir Thomas Gates and Sir George Somers. The Plymouth Company. What the charter granted. Liberty of trade with other nations. Historians of America. King James issues instructions for the government of Virginia. The first settlement in America. Other colonists sent to Virginia. The London Company. Wingfield and Sir Thomas Smith. Gosnold, Hunt and the famous Capt. John Smith. Put in confinement on the voyage. Site of the old colony. Name of Jamestown adopted. Smith honorably acquitted. Newport and Smith ascend the James. Newport returns with his ships to England. Smith taken prisoner by the Indians. Brought before Powhatan. Condemned to death. Saved by Pocahontas. Smith returns to England. Pocahontas meets him. She is another man's wife. Smith never revisited Virginia. Death of Pocahontas.

PART V.—PAGE 33.

The stability of the colony. Sir Thomas Dale exercises martial law. The colony from 1611 to 1616. At times under different leaders. Bad colonists. First slavery in Virginia. The Dutch vessel.

PART VI.—PAGE 36.

Settlement of New Netherland. A famous navigator, Henry Hudson. The Hudson river. He explores to Albany and Waterford. Hudson sails for home. He sails again and meets his fate in the bay that bears his name. Manhattan Island settled by the Dutch in 1613. The great city of New York. Adrian Block. Discovers East river, Hellgate and Long Island. The first Englishman to visit Manhattan, 1615. The first fort at Albany. Capt. C. J. May's exploits. The first to settle Long Island. Purchase of Manhattan Island. The restrictions on the colonists. The Patroons. Rensselaerwick, Swansdale and Pavonia. The purchase of the Pequods. Claim of the English to New Netherland. Swedes colonize Pennsylvania.

CONTENTS. vii

PART VII. Page 40.

Foundation of New England. Landing of the Puritans. The causes of the Puritans. Their hardships and trials. Their settlement in Holland of twelve years. They leave for America. The Mayflower and its hardships. Signs of insubordination. John Carver. The oath of allegiance. Foundation of the colony. The name of New Plymouth. Shawmut the site of Boston. Massachusetts Bay. Robert Gorges and his expedition. The expected colonists. Their new settlement. The four vessels. The colony of Winthrop that settled Boston. Death of Lady Johnson and husband.

PART VIII.—Page 46.

Progress of the New England colonies. The son of Winthrop and John Eliot. The arrivals in 1633. Six vessels arrive in 1634. The name of Boston. Roger Williams. His banishment. The subject of religion. Williams fled to the wilderness. Taken care of by the Narragansetts. Providence. Rhode Island. Friends join him. The fate of Mrs. Hutchinson and her followers. Saybrook. The Pequod war. The murder of Stone and Oldham. Canonicus, the sachem of the Narragansetts. Mason's slaughter. New London Indians sold into slavery. Sir Ferdinando Gorges and his charter. The scheme to govern Maine. Sir William Alexander. Trade increases towns and villages. The cost of colonization.

PART IX.— Page 53.

Progress of Virginia colonies. 1627. War with the Indians. Dr. John Potts. Horse stealing. Demand for powder and ball. Point Comfort. Revision of the laws. Election of officers. Harvey superceeded. Sir Francis Wyatt's administration. The aged chief. The freedom of Virginians. Vessels trading with the colony. Berkeley and Matthews. The house of Burgesses. The supremacy of the people.

PART X.— Page 56.

Origin and progress of Maryland colonies. Maryland in 1632. Lord Baltimore. George Calvert. First statutes of Maryland. Queen Henrietta Marie. The boundary of Maryland. Claybourn's appeal. Leonard Calvert. The Ark and Dove. Cool reception. New England people. The rebellion of Clayborne. Clayborne demanded by Calvert. The Parliamentarian. William Stone. Josiah Feudal, governor. Philip Calvert sustained by the Assembly.

PART XI.— Page 61.

Progress of New Netherland, New York and New Jersey. New Netherland, 1638. New Amsterdam. William Kieft. The Dutch coat of arms. Stratford, Stamford and Greenwich settled. New England's secretary. Massacre of the Indians. Retaliation. Stockade of New Amsterdam. Appeal to Holland Kieft unpopular. Peter Stuyvesant, director general. God's poor people. Beaverswick, now Albany. Wooden huts and rum shops. United colonies of New England. Stuyvesant siezes a ship. Fort Casimi. The Swedes take Fort Casimi. Friendly relations with Virginia. New Netherland and New York. The commission arrive. Stuyvesant surrenders the city. The Dutch reduced to submission. The Duke of York. New York retaken by the Dutch and ceded back to England. William Penn. East and West Jersey. First assembly in state of New York. The Charter of Liberties. Duke of York and throne of England. James II. Dongon governor of New York. Albany gets a charter. The Livingston manor.

PART XII.—Page 69.

United colonies of New England. New Hampshire settled. Deprived of their charter. The Narragansett chief, Miantonimoh. Colonial commission. Roger Williams in England. He obtains a charter. Providence Plantations. Hung for witchcraft. Mary Fisher and Ann Austin. The sect of Quakers. Robinson, Stephenson and Mary Dyer's fate. John Eliot. John Harvard and Cambridge. The first printing press in America.

PART XIII.—Page 73.

New England under Charles II. and James II. The regicide judges. King Charles' promises. Hugh Peters. Sir Henry Vane. Clarke and Winthrop. The royal commissioners. Billingham ordered to England. Number of inhabitants. The Indian war. Philip and Cononchet. Massacre of the Indians. Bloody Brook. Number of killed. Witamo, a female chief. New Hampshire a separate colony. Edward Randolph returns to England. Sir Edmund Andras governor. A writ of *quo warranto*. Andras demands Connecticut's charter. The charter disappears in the dark. The Charter Oak. Captain Wadsworth. Disthronement of James II. English Revolution, 1688.

PART XIV.—Page 79.

Progress of Virginia and Maryland colonies. Sir William Berkeley. Rights of freemen curtailed. Aristocratic cavaliers. Negro slavery. The plantations. Education discouraged. Lord Culpepper and Arlington. Commissioners dispatched to England. Indian war. Nathaniel Bacon. John Washington. Bacon's army. He burns Jamestown. Bacon demands a commission. Bacon dies suddenly. Berkeley returns to England.

PART XV.—Page 84.

Origin of the Carolinas. Charles First. Sir Robert Heath's patent. Earl of Clarendon. Eight Proprietaries. Freeman of the colony. Civil judges. Freedom of religion. Planters from Barbadoes. Lord Shaftesburg. Ashley and Cooper. Foundation of Charlestown. Sir John Yeamans. Captain William Sayle. Sothel banished. Afterward outsailed governor.

PART XVI.—Page 87.

Settlement of Pennsylvania by Penn. William Penn. His father the admiral. Penn's convertion by the Quakers. Expelled from Oxford. Penn makes a trade. Location of Philadelphia. Penn returns to England. English emigrants. Civil and religious freedom. Third printing press in America.

PART XVII.—Page 90.

The French colonial enterprise. Franciscan missionaries. The Five Nations. Dablon and Marquette. Mission of St. Mary. Fox and Wisconsin rivers. Exploring the Mississippi. Robert Cavalier de La Salle. Chevalier Tonti. Recollect Hennepin. Lakes Erie, Huron and Michigan. Greenbay. Fort of the Miamis. Falls St. Anthony. Name of Louisiana. The murderers. La Salle's untimely end. Population up to date, 1687.

PART XVIII.—Page 95.

The founding and progress of Georgia. The colony of Georgia. James Edward Oglethorpe. Bibles, prayer books and catechisms. The official seal. Savannah. Yamacrow Bluff. German Lutherans. The settlement of Ebenezer. Moravians and Jews. John and Charles Wesley. Town of Frederica. The Spaniards' demands. Oglethorpe's reply. The vindication. Military commandant of Georgia and Carolina. Oglethorpe returns to England. William Stevens governor, 1743. John Reynolds governor, 1754.

PART XIX.—Page 99.

Colonization of Louisiana and its progress. Lower Mississippi. Lamoine d'Iberville's exploits. Mouth of the Mississippi. Pascagoula and tribes of Biloxi. England wakeful. The English turn. Searching for gold. Tonti turns up. State of Alabama. Anthony Crozat. Perier appointed governor. Difficulties with the Natchez Indians. War against the Chickasaws.

PART XX. PAGE 103.

1700 to 1750. The progress and general condition of the colonies condensed. Population of Virginia in 1750. Capital at Williamsburg. First newspaper. Products of Virginia. Progress and population of Connecticut. Also Rhode Island. Negro slavery. The homes in Boston. Pewter, iron and copper. Provoking dissentions in the colonies. Friendship with the Indians. North Carolina in 1710. South Carolina in 1700 and 1730. Population of New York in 1750. First newspaper in New York. Population of New Jersey in 1738. Pennsylvania and Delaware. Population of Philadelphia in 1731. Value of exports and imports. Celeron de Bineville. The hour of collision near at hand.

PART XXI.— PAGE 113.

The framers of and the Declaration of Independence, illustrated.

PART XXII.— PAGE 120.

Washington's headquarters at Newburg. Robert Morris, Continental receiver.

PART XXIII.— PAGE 125.

West Point. General Arnold's treason. The capture and execution of Andre. Arnold's address to the American people. A brief sketch of General Philip Schuyler and his family and their historical mansions, and the Van Rensselaer manor house.

PART XXIV.— PAGE 146.

The inauguration of Washington Illustrated. The table of elections. Politics and majorities of all our Presidents and their autographs.

PART XXV.— PAGE 151.

The Constitution. The form of our national government and how each branch is administered. The portraits, autographs and biographical sketch of the Presidents. The first steam navigation and first steam used on railroads in America or the world.

PART XXVI.— PAGE 175

Prefatory. A historical and statistical table of the United States. A chronological discussion of our population and area from 1790 to 1880. The Territories and their capitals, the date of the organization of each Territory and the admission of each State, and electoral vote by States. Portraits, Autographs and Biographical Sketch of the Presidents continued. Sketch of John A. Logan. Financial history, growth of the U. S.

CHRISTOPHER COLUMBUS

Was born in 1435 in the city of Genoa, Italy, and followed the life of a mariner. Discovered America October 12, 1492. Died at Valladolid May 20, 1506, at the age of 71 years.

PART I.

EARLY LIFE OF COLUMBUS.

His Voyages—His Scheme of Crossing the Atlantic Ocean—Portugal Refuses Him Aid—He Starts for Spain.

1435.

The birthplace of Christopher Columbus (Genoa) was one of the great commercial republics of Italy, a city of long historic fame. His family were genteel—not above honest toil, but people of culture. His father (Dominie) possessed some small property at Genoa and places near it. He was by occupation a comber and weaver of wool. His father was, therefore, very comfortably well off. Christopher was born in a house belonging to his father outside the city walls, where the road winds off to the little town of Bassagno. Tradition, which recent proof sustains, shows that the future glory of Genoa was baptized in the hillside church of Santo Stefanodi Arco, by the Benedictines who preside there.

Christopher was the eldest son of three and the great hope of the house. His father sought to give him an opportunity to acquire knowledge greater than his own home afforded him. The commencement of his education was at Genoa, but at the age of ten years his parents sent him to the University of Pavia, for instruction in the Latin language, geometry, casmography, astronomy and drawing. His progress was rapid and successful. Strongly bent upon becoming a sailor, at the early age of fourteen, he made his first voyage in company with a hardy old sea captain of the same name of his father. After many years of adventure and various fortunes Columbus, in 1470, removed to Lisbon, which city at that time, owing to the ability and sagacity of Prince Henry of Portugal, was the busy port in Europe for commercial enterprise. He shortly after was married to the daughter of a celebrated navigator. Columbus was deeply stirred by reflection and study respecting the possibility of reaching the rich and attractive East Indies by sailing directly across the Western Ocean. Columbus was sure that, as the earth was spherical, if one sailed directly west he must, in due time, reach the lands of the East. The more he thought of the matter the more sure he became, and when once he had reached a conclusion it was a fixed and unalterable conclusion. Henceforth his only aim was how to get the money to prove the truth of his convictions. "It is singular," as Mr. Irving remarks in this connection, "how much the success of this great undertaking depended upon two happy errors: the imaginary extent of Asia to the east, and the supposed smallness of the earth. Both errors of the most learned and profound philosophers, but without which Columbus would hardly have ventured upon his enterprise." He first offered his services to John II., King of Portugal; but having been deceived and badly treated by the King and his advisers, and also having some time before lost his wife, he took his son, Diego, and in 1484 bade adieu to Portugal.

Columbus next repaired to Spain and made his suit at the court of Ferdinand and Isabella. The weary years of waiting upon the court of the impassive, calculating Ferdinand; the coldness, the repulses, the neglect, the sneers of contempt, the absurd prejudice and conceited ignorance which he encountered might well have worn out a man less resolute and determined than Columbus; but he never gave up his plan and purpose, and his constancy and courage finally obtained their just reward. Remember, that eighteen years elapsed after the time Columbus conceived his enterprise before he was enabled to carry it into effect. At last, through the generous impulses of the noble-hearted Isabella and the substantial family of the Pinzons, Columbus was enabled, on Friday, August 3, 1492, to embark on his voyage.

Herewith annexed is a condensed narrative of his expedition and his vessels, Santa Maria, Pinta and Nina.

One thing, in all probability, is certain: that if it had not been for the defeat of the Moors by the Spaniards in 1491, Columbus would not have received aid from the noble-hearted Isabella, and his expedition would not have taken place at the time it did, if ever at all, and Columbus might not have been known as the first to discover America.

It was the zeal, born of earnest and unswerving purpose, which reflected Columbus' true character and greatness. Imbued with the belief that he was God's chosen instrument to prove the sphericity of the earth, he constantly importuned the Governments of his day for needed assistance, until wearying from repeated rebuff, he visited Spain, and was informed by the Duke of Medina Celi that Isabella, Queen of Spain, had requested him to visit her at Cordova.

On his arrival at Cordova he found the Queen, surrounded by prelates and officers of the army, so engaged that she could not give him an audience and he became the guest of Alonzo de Quintanilla.

Columbus, after waiting seven years and suffering great disappointments, succeeded in having his theory discussed at a meeting of prelates and learned men at the convent of St. Stephens, at Salamanca, but his theory of the world's being a sphere was condemned. They also argued that the earth was a flat surface, bordered by the waters of the sea, on the yielding support of which rested the crystalline dome of the sky, and the sun, moon and planets were a subordinate nature, their use being to give light to man, who was elevated to supreme importance. The Patristic geography had governed the Christian church for twelve centuries, and was its authority for rejecting the theory of the sphericity of the earth.

Columbus defended his theory nobly and with religious fervor, but the decision was unfavorable to him.

The ancient philosophers and astronomers introduced various theories regarding the sphericity of the earth and the manner of its revolution. The Heliocentric theory, taught by Pythagoras about five hundred and fifty years, B. C., placed the sun as the center round which, with the other planets, the earth revolved, in circular orbits, each supposed to rotate on its axis as it revolved round the sun.

This theory was accepted by Aristarchus of Samos about three hundred and fifty years B. C., and was superceded by the Geocentric system of Ptolemy, about one hundred and fifty years, A. D., which system placed the earth in the center, fixed in space, the sun and other planets revolving round it, thus giving the earth the position of superiority. This theory was accepted by a large portion of the inhabitants of the earth for fourteen centuries.

No advancement was made toward establishing the theories of the ancients, or the geography of the earth, or the science of astronomy, until the advent of Columbus and his discovery of America in 1492, and the circumnavigation of the earth by Magellen in 1521, which proved its sphericity, and whose circumference is about twenty-five thousand miles.

The chains which bound physical science and astronomy for thousands of years were, through his fearless spirit and intrepid action, not only rent asunder, through the discovery of America, which proved the sphericity of the earth, but it opened the way for the introduction of the Heliocentric system. This system was awakened into life by Copernicus in the sixteenth century, and was adopted by Kepler, who introduced the principle of gravity without discovering its practical application.

Copernicus and Kepler labored under the same difficulty as the ancient astronomers, they having no telescope to assist them in proving the truths of their theories. Thus the theory of revolution and attraction of gravitation was left for Galileo and Sir Isaac Newton to demonstrate their truths.

In the year 1609, Lippershey, a Dutchman, made a small telescope. Galileo, hearing of it and realizing the importance it would be to him in discovering the solar system, made one of a magnifying power of three, and finally succeeded in making one that magnified thirty times, with which, in 1610, he discovered the four satelites of Jupiter revolving in orbits round that planet, and also that Venus, in her motion round the sun, showed phases like the moon. Further observation showed him that the earth and each of the planets rotated on its axis as it revolved in an eliptical orbit round the sun, which was the center and attractive force of the system.

Such important discoveries, made by Galileo and those that followed soon after, fully supported the system of Copernicus.

Sir Isaac Newton is crowned with the honor of demonstrating the theory of the attraction of gravitation, and his name became immortalized by the production of his great work, "Principia," in the year 1686.

We will now return to Columbus and his efforts to obtain aid for the purpose of carrying out his theories and convictions.

The King and Queen, despite the decision of the learned men at Salamanca, saw the advantage to be derived from the discovery of a new and direct route to the Indies, and if successful the gain would be incalculable, as the Kingdom of the Grand Khan of Tartary was supposed to abound in gold, silver and precious stones, and to contain inexhaustible wealth, which would inure to the benefit of Spain.

They also saw that such a discovery would add to the glory of their reign, and their country, and aid in the extension of their Christian faith, and fearing that Columbus might seek the assistance of some other government, they promised him that his project should receive attention as soon as the Moors were conquered and expelled from Granada.

Columbus, disappointed, left the Court of Spain, with the intention of laying his project before the King of France. On his way thence, arriving at the gate of the Convent of Santa Maria de Rabida, he asked for bread and water for himself and his child, he there met the prior, Juan Parez, to whom he stated his project. The prior became interested in his theory and introduced him to Martin Alonzo Pinzon, a wealthy navigator, who, upon hearing Columbus' explanation, became convinced of his ability to accomplish the voyage, and offered to bear one-eighth of the expense of such an expedition.

Columbus was urged to remain at Palos, whilst the prior, who at one time had been the Queen's confessor, should see her.

The prior's representations to the Queen induced her to invite Columbus to appear at court, and she sent him twenty thousand maravedus, a sum equivalent to about $60, to renovate his wardrobe and to defray his traveling expenses.

Columbus arrived at the court at the time the surrender of Granada was being consummated.

The time had now arrived when the plans of Columbus, according to promise, must receive attention, but when the conditions under which he would undertake the expedition came to be discussed, his demands for titles and privileges were princely, and in the eyes of the Court, so extravagant that his terms and propositions were refused, and as Columbus would not waver and would not listen to any other terms, he left the Court with the intention of visiting the King of France.

St. Angel and Alonzo Quintanilla described to the Queen the great wealth that would flow to Spain through the discovery of India at the small outlay of 15,000 florins (Columbus having agreed to furnish one-eighth of the money), and would far exceed the discoveries made by other nations, and would open between Spain and India a commerce of great value to the church and to Spain, and if not successful the loss would be nominal.

They also plead the cause of Columbus with such zeal that the enthusiastic and generous spirit of Isabella was aroused. The King coldly attempted to dissuade her from the idea, which caused Isabella to exclaim, "I undertake the enterprise for my own crown of Castile, and will pledge my jewels to raise the necessary funds."

The funds, about fifteen thousand florins, were advanced by St. Angel, receiver of the ecclesiastical revenues of Aragon, and were afterwards repaid out of the first gold brought by Columbus from the new world.

Columbus had proceeded about six miles from Grenada, when he was overtaken by a messenger from the Queen request-

QUEEN ISABELLA OF SPAIN

Was Born about 1445, and was Married to Ferdinand, King of Spain, in 1481—This Consolidated the Factions of the Spanish Empire—She Died in the year 1504.

ing him to return. Upon his appearing again at Court, the kind reception he received from the Queen atoned for past neglect.

An agreement was then drawn up by the Royal Secretary, which the King and Queen signed on the 17th of April, 1492, whereby it was stipulated that Columbus should have the office of Admiral in all lands and countries which he might discover. That he and his descendants were to receive the title of "Don," and that he was to be Viceroy and Governor-General of such lands and countries and have one-tenth of the net profits arising from gold and silver, and all articles of merchandise in whatever manner obtained. He had the further privilege of furnishing one-eighth the cost of the expedition, and if he did so, he was to receive one-eighth of the profits. This latter condition Columbus fulfilled, through the assistance of Martin Alonzo Pinzon.

A royal order was given, directing the authorities of Palos to furnish and equip two caravels. This order was disobeyed. Horror and dismay filled the minds of the sailors as they felt it would be certain death to enter the mysteries of the sea, and they refused to embark on the expedition.

Martin Alonzo Pinzon and his brothers, seeing the difficulty attending the procuring of the vessels and crews, came forward and furnished one vessel and crew thoroughly equipped and ready for sea. This induced others to consent to go, and they then succeeded in obtaining the other two vessels, and all were ready for sea on the first day of August, 1492.

The Santa Maria was commanded by Columbus, the Pinta by Martin Alonzo Pinzon (with his brother, Francisco Martin, as pilot) and the Nina by Vincento Yanez Pinzon.

The fleet consisted of the three small vessels just named, two being without decks, of fifty tons each, and the other being of eighty tons burden. In all, there were one hundred and twenty men on the expedition, of whom ninety were sailors.

When the squadron was ready to sail, Columbus, his officers and crews confessed to Juan Parez and partook of the sacrament.

On Friday morning, August 3d, 1492, the expedition sailed from Palos.

Columbus and his companions proceeded on their voyage of discovery, meeting with many disappointments and hardships, and as they entered into unknown regions fear and trembling overcame all except Columbus. The strength given to him came from his great faith—he felt that he was under the protection and guidance of the Almighty.

Columbus was so sanguine that he should reach India, that he carried with him a letter from Ferdinand, King of Spain, to the Grand Khan of Tartary.

On the 13th of September he was startled to find that the needle of his compass varied between five and six degrees to the northwest and no longer pointed to the pole. This phenomenon of magnetic declination produced great alarm among the mariners, for without the guide of their compass what was to become of them in a vast and trackless ocean? Columbus invented a plausible theory about the attraction of the polar star, which quieted the pilot's fears.

Columbus suppressed the mutinous tendency of the crews with extraordinary tact, and afterwards upon great flights of birds hovering about their vessels, they became reconciled and felt they must be near land. On the night of the 11th of October, Columbus beheld a moving light, which was seen several times but at last disappeared. This light was probably upon Walting's Island.

On the morning of October 12th, 1492, land was discovered, and all hearts were filled with joy and gladness. Columbus fell upon his knees and thanked his Maker that He had given him the strength and fortitude which enabled him to overcome all obstacles, and that He had blessed him with success in discovering what he thought to be India, the Kingdom of the Grand Khan.

As they approached the land, the air was soft and balmy, and the breezes ladened with sweet fragrance, perfumed the transparent atmosphere.

The island on which they landed was one of the Bahama group and Columbus named it San Salvador. Its inhabitants were nude, finely and beautifully formed, graceful in their manners, and strange and interesting in their habits. They were apparently an amiable, innocent and happy people, who at first thought that Columbus' fleet of vessels were large birds, and that their sails were wings, and that Columbus and his crews had descended from the skies.

Thus the expedition of Columbus, which resulted in his discovery, on Friday, the 12th day of October, 1492, of what he supposed to be a portion of the continent of India (hence he denominated the natives "Indians"), when in reality his discovery was that of America.

Of the future and important voyages and discoveries of Columbus, and of the varied fortunes which it was his lot to meet with, it is not our present purpose to speak. Envy, detraction, injustice and cruelty imbittered his latter life. Deprived of the honor (which was only his just due) of giving his name to the newly-discovered world, and rendered hopeless of all redress by the death, in 1504, of his patron and fast friend, the good Queen Isabella, Columbus died at Valladolid May 20, 1506, at peace with the world, and sustained in his last hours by hope and consolation of the Christian religion. Ferdinand did, indeed, order a monument to his memory, with the motto taken from Columbus' coat-of-arms : "A Castilla y a Leon nuevo mundo dio Colon." To Castile and Leon Columbus gave a new world, but it could add nothing to the fame of Columbus. It simply serves to stamp the character and conduct of Ferdinand as one who was an unfeeling, ungenerous, ungrateful King

PART II.

THE NAME OF AMERICA.

How It Originated, Etc.

The name of America, which was applied to a portion of the Western Continent soon after its discovery, and which has now become its unalterable title, took its rise from a voyage made in 1499, by Amerigo Vespucci, a distinguished Florentine navigator. Vespucci wrote several letters in Latin to Lorenzo de Medici, one of which was printed in 1505, being the first of his narratives that was published. He also wrote a letter, dated Lisbon, September 4th, 1504, addressed to Rene, Duke of Lorraine, in which it is claimed that he discovered the main land in 1497. Now, as he was a man of superior learning and intelligence, and his name was thus publicly connected with the new world as the discoverer of the continent, although he was not the first to reach terra firma, Columbus, and Cabot and others having preceded him. It happened that a famous cosmographer, Martin Waldsumuller, of Fribourg, patronized by Rene, thought good, in 1507, to apply this name of America to the new world. The geographical works of Waldsumuller, title, "Hyla Comylas," went through repeated editions, and thus the name America became familiarized to the larger part of the civilized world. And so must it remain, though there can hardly be any one who can repress a sigh of regret at the injustice which has thus been done to Columbus.

THE FIRST COLONY LANDING IN FLORIDA UNDER JUAN PONCE DE LEON, 1512.

The marvellous discovery of a new world aroused the spirit of maritime enterprise in England, and to one of her sons indisputably belongs the glory of having first reached the continent of North America. Yet when the news of what Columbus had done reached England, Henry VII., a shrewd and thrifty monarch, was ready at once to enter into competition for the prizes which the New World might disclose. Accordingly, he availed himself with eagerness of the offer of John Cabot, a Venetian merchant residing in Bristol, England, to fit out several vessels for discovery which might be made any where north of the route originally taken by Columbus. In a patent obtained from the king and signed at Westminister March 5, 1496, Cabot was authorized with his three sons, Lewis, Sebastain and Sancius, " to saile to all parts of the east, of the west and of the north, under our banners and ensigns, with five ships," with mariners and men on their proper cost and charge, to discover in any land, clime or countries that might be inhabited by heathens or infidels soever, not conflicting with the Christian religion in any parts of the New World that they might discover. The expedition sailed under the command of Sebastian Cabot, who was born in Bristol, England, a youthful but sagacious mariner, and on June 24, 1497, they discovered land, which was a part of the coast of Labrador, and which they named Prima Vista; they saw also an island, which they called St. John's Island, from the day on which it was discovered. Disappointed in his expectation of finding a northwest passage to the land of Cathay, or the Indies, with its marvels and wonders, as old Marco Polo tells them, Cabot returned to England. He made a second voyage to America, the particulars of which have been but scantily preserved. On a voyage in 1517 Hudson's Bay was undoubtedly entered, but his crew, terrified by the fields of ice, in the month of July clamored for a return, and Cabot reluctantly sailed back to England. This eminent navigator, having lived to a good old age, died in the city of London. It is an instructive lesson of the uncertainty of human distinction, that although he gave a continent to England, neither the date of his death is known, nor does the humblest stone show his memory or where his remains lie interred.

OTHER EXPLORERS.

In 1498, Vasco de Gama, under the patronage of Emanuel, King of Portugal, an able and enterprising monarch, doubled the Cape of Good Hope and opened to Portugal a new and most important route to the Indies. The same King, in 1501, sent Caspar Carterial with two vessels to explore the North-Western Ocean. This navigator sailed some seven hundred miles along the shores of North America. His only exploit was the kidnapping a number of the natives and carrying them to Portugal as slaves.

Juan Ponce de Leon, a hardy old Spanish warrior, and one of the companions of Columbus, having conquered Porto Rico, greatly enriched himself by the compulsory labor of the unhappy natives. He actually set out, in 1512, to find this wonder of nature. In the course of his voyage, on Easter Sunday, March 27th—which the Spaniards call Pascua de Flores—he discovered that peninsula which separates the Gulf of Mexico from the Atlantic. It was the beautiful season of flowers, and from this, as well as the day on which he saw the land, he gave to the new region the name of Florida.

It was about 1513 that another famous Spanish Captain, Vasco Nunez de Balboa, discovered the Pacific Ocean. This memorable event took place on the 26th of September, 1513. It certainly was one of the most sublime discoveries that had yet been made in the new world.

English and French mariners (fishermen from Brittany) discovered and named Cape Breton in 1504. "This fishery," says Hildreth, "on the coast and bank of Newfoundland formed the first link between Europe and North America, and, for a century, almost the only one."

Francis I., of France, although occupied in his contests with Spain and Germany, gave due attention to discoveries and settlements in the new world. Accordingly, he engaged Juan Verrozzani, a Florentine, to explore on his behalf, in 1524, new regions in the unknown West. With a single vessel, the Dolphin, he left Maderia and discovered a new land never before seen of any, either ancient or modern. This was the low level coast of North Carolina. Verrozzani also entered the harbors of New York and Newport, and coasted northwardly to the fiftieth degree of north latitude. No settlement, however, resulted from this voyage of Verrazzoni to America.

The first attempt, in 1536, at colonization by the English was disastrous in the extreme. In 1534 and up to 1540 the French tried to colonize, but gave up for a long time all further attempts at founding colonies in North America. What had been done, however, served in later days as a basis for claims, on the part of France, to the northern portion of the American continent.

The disastrous attempt of Narvaez, in 1528, to conquer and obtain possession of Florida did not deter other bold spirits from efforts of a like character. Ferdinand de Soto, a distinguished companion of Pizarro in annexing to Spain the golden regions of Peru, was sent out by Charles V., and he was created Adelantado of Florida, combining the offices of Governor-General and Commander-in-Chief. In May, 1539, De Soto sailed from Havana with six hundred men in the bloom of life, a number of Priests, besides sailors, about two hundred horses and a herd of swine. Arriving on the 30th of May, at the Bay of Spiritu Santo, on the western coast of Florida, he landed three hundred men and pitched his camp; but about the break of day, the next morning, they were attacked by a numerous body of natives and obliged to retire. In marching several hundred miles he passed through several Indian towns to Mavilla, a village enclosed by wooden walls, standing near the mouth of the Mobile river. The Indians, disgusted with the strangers and provoked by an outrage committed on one of their chiefs, brought on a severe conflict, in which two thousand of the natives and about twenty Spaniards were slain. The village was burnt in the action. After this engagement De Soto retreated to Chicaca, a small town in the country of the

Chickasaws, where he remained till March, 1541. His army now resumed its march through the Indian country, and after many hardships, mishaps, and very grievous discouragements, in the latter part of April, 1541, De Soto first beheld the Mississippi; this was not far from the thirty-fifth parallel of latitude. The Mississippi River was crossed by De Soto, and still further attempts were made to discover the wealth and magnificence which they had set out to find in Florida. But it was all in vain. Chagrined by a conviction of a total failure, De Soto sank under his disappointment, and died May 25th, 1542. To conceal his death, his body was wrapped in a mantle, and, in the stillness of the night, was silently sunk into the middle of the river. The discoverer of the great Mississippi slept beneath its waters. Soto had crossed a large part of the continent in search of gold, and found nothing so remarkable as his burial place. The remainder part of this fruitless expedition with which they had embarked, floated down the Mississippi to its mouth, and in September, 1543 reached a Spanish settlement near the present site of Tampico. Florida was thenceforth abandoned. Not a settlement was made; not a single site occupied by the Spaniards, yet Spain, under the name of Florida, laid claim to the entire sea-coast of America, as far north even as Newfoundland.

In the year 1562, Admiral De Coligny, an able French Protestant leader, was desirous of finding a home in America for the persecuted Huguenots. Accordingly, an expedition was fitted out under the command of Jean Ribault, of Dieppe, an experienced mariner and Protestant. Ribault reached Florida in May, entered a spacious inlet which he named Port Royal, and built a fort called Carolina, a name which still remains to us, although the early colony perished. Twenty-six were left to found a settlement, while Ribault returned in 1563 to France for supplies. Those remaining behind, becoming disheartened, resolved to abandon the settlement; the commander was killed in a mutiny; and, well-nigh starved, they were picked up by an English vessel and landed, part in France, and the rest in England. In 1564, Coligny again renewed his efforts. Three ships were sent out, under command of Landonniere, a companion of Ribault. They landed in June at the River May (now the St. John's) and built a fort. Mutinies and piratical expeditions occurred. They took two Spanish vessels, thus becoming the first aggressors in the New World. In great distress for provisions they were about to abandon this settlement, when the notorious Sir John Hawkins, the slave merchant, relieved them. Ribault arrived again in August with abundant supplies of all kinds. But the colony was by no means as yet in security. Pedro Melendez, a fierce and unsparing soldier, obtained permission from Philip II. of Spain to conquer and occupy Florida, and also to drive out the French as both intruders and heretics. "Death to the Huguenots!" was the cry. In 1565 with some three hundred soldiers and over two thousand volunteers, the expedition left Spain in July. Melendez did not delay, as he

CITY GATE, ST. AUGUSTINE.

was anxious to make quick work of his enemies. He sailed to the coast of Florida. Land was seen on the 28th of August, and Melendez named the inlet and haven which he entered two days after, St. Augustine. The town here founded by this name still remains, and, though not a place of large size, is by more than forty years the oldest town in the United States.

THE END OF RIBAULT AND HIS COMMAND.

Melendez was not long in finding the French colony. Ribault's vessels cut their cables and put to sea. A violent storm arose, and the French vessels were scattered and cast on shore. Melendez marched overland from St. Augustine, through the forests and swamps, surprised the French forts, and indiscriminately butchered men, women, and children. But Ribault and his shipwrecked companions, half famished, reached the fort to find it in the hands of the Spaniards. Relying on the word of honor of the perfidious Melendez, they gave themselves up and were massacred, near St. Augustine, with shocking barbarity, with the following inscription: "Not because they are Frenchmen, but because they are heretics and enemies of God."

Part III

RETALIATION OF THE FRENCH

When intelligence of this horrible outrage reached France, it excited a desire for vengeance. Charles IX. was invoked in vain to require of the Spanish monarch that justice should be awarded against his murderous subjects. An avenger was speedily found—Dominic de Gourgues, a brave Gascon—in 1567. He was determined to devote himself, his fortune, and his whole being to the achievement of some signal and terrible retribution. He found means to equip three small vessels, and to put on board of them eighty sailors and one hundred and fifty troops. Having crossed the Atlantic, he sailed along the coast of Florida, and landed at a river about fifteen leagues distant from the River May. The Spaniards, to the number of four hundred, were well fortified, principally at the great fort, begun by the French and afterwards repaired by themselves. Two leagues lower, towards the river mouth, they had made two smaller forts, which were defended by a hundred and twenty soldiers, well supplied with artillery and ammunition. Gourgues, though informed of their strength, proceeded resolutely forward, and, with the assistance of the natives, made a vigorous and desperate assault. Of sixty Spaniards in the first fort, there escaped but fifteen, and all in the second fort were slain. After a company of Spaniards, sallying out from the third fort, had been intercepted and killed on the spot, this last fortress was easily taken. All the surviving Spaniards were led away prisoners with the fifteen who escaped the massacre of the first fort, and were hung on the boughs of the same trees on which the Frenchmen had been previously suspended. Gourgues, in retaliation for the label Melendez had attached to the bodies of the French, placed over the corpses of the Spaniards the following declaration: "I do not this as unto Spaniards or mariners, but as unto traitors, robbers, and murderers." Having razed the three forts, and not being strong enough to remain in the country, he returned to France in May, 1568. Such was the end of the efforts of the French Protestants to found settlements in Florida.

OTHER EXPLORERS TO AMERICA.

In 1603, a company of merchants was formed at Rouen, and Samuel Champlain, an able and scientific officer, was sent out in command of an expedition. This celebrated man, after careful exploration and examination, selected the site of Quebec for a fort. In 1604, another expedition, consisting of four ships, sailed for America, and landed at Port Royal, now Annapolis. Champlain explored the Bay of Fundy, discovered and named the River St. John's, and selected a site for a settlement on the Island St. Croix, in the river of the same name. But the spot was not well chosen, and in the spring of 1605, the following year, the colony removed to Port Royal. Here the first actual settlement on the American continent by the French was made. In 1608, Champlain not only laid the foundation of the City of Quebec, but also the next year explored and was the first white man to enter the beautiful lake which bears his name and perpetuates his memory. This persevering man lived through severe trials and afflictions to establish the authority of his countrymen on the St. Lawrence. He died in 1635. Consequent upon the explorations of

Champlain and others, the French laid claim to that vast tract of Interior America which, together with Canada and Acadia, was denominated "New France."

THE PRECEDING RACES.

Without entering into a discussion of the question, Whence came the people who first settled America? a question more curious than profitable—it is quite certain that the Indian tribes scattered over the face of the country were the successors of a race or races which had passed away entirely, ages before the discovery of the New World by Columbus.

ATTEMPTS AT COLONIZATION BY THE ENGLISH.

From 1553 to 1606 the enterprising spirit of Englishmen led them into the work of discovery, in attempts at settlements and colonization. During the reigns of Henry the VIII. and Edward the VI., Sebastian Cabot in 1553 formed a company of merchants, at the head of which Cabot was placed, and an expedition was fitted out. The expedition was under the command of Sir Hugh Willoughby, who was lost, together with his expedition, near the North Cape, in the obscure harbor of Lapland. The Chancellor, his companion, more fortunate, entered the White sea and found shelter in the harbor of Archangel, and finally repaired to Moscow, instead of arriving in America. In 1518, under Queen Elizabeth patronage, an attempt was made by Englishmen to plant a colony in America. It was mainly due to Sir Humphrey Gilbert, a gentleman of distinction and marked ability as a soldier and a writer on navigation. Without difficulty he obtained a patent from the Queen. Six years were allowed for the establishment of the colony. As this is the first charter to a colony granted by the crown of England, and this expedition was a total failure, it is not our purpose to give the articles contained in the patent. But it is enough to know that Elizabeth authorized Gilbert to discover and take possession of all remote and barbarous lands unoccupied by any Christian prince or people; and finally it prohibited all persons from attempting to settle within two hundred leagues of Sir Humphrey Gilbert's Colony. In June, 1583, Gilbert set sail on his second voyage with a fleet of five ships and barks and a large body of men. The step brother of Gilbert was the illustrious Sir Walter Raleigh, who readily came to the aid of Gilbert, and furnished one vessel which bore his name. Gilbert, on reaching Newfoundland, early in August, he took possession of it in the name of Elizabeth. However, the mutinous and disorderly conduct of many sailors, and the loss of the principle ship and one hundred men they now decided to return home, and in doing so on September 9th in a heavy sea Sir Humphrey and his frigate and all on board went down. The other vessels reached Falmouth in safety, bearing the sad tidings of loss and disaster. Again in April, 1584, Raleigh, having secured a patent from Elizabeth, endeavored to carry out his favorite plan of colonizotion in America. He was constituted bard proprietary with powers almost unlimited, on condition of reserving to the Crown a fifth part of all gold or silver ore which might be found. In April two ships set sail under the command of Philip Amidaz and Arthur Barlow, and early in July they reached the shores of Carolina. They landed, and took possession in the name of the Queen of the island of Wococon. Charmed with the beauty of everything they saw, Amidaz and Barlow, with very limited explorations and taking with them two of the natives, Wauchen and Manteo, they returned to England. Raleigh was in raptures with the prospects before him, and Elizabeth expressed her desire that the new region should be called Virginia in honor of the virgin Queen of England. Seven leagues from Wococon was Roanoke Island, where the colony for a time was formed, and in April, 1585, seven vessels, with one hundred and eight colonists, sailed from Plymouth under the command of Sir Richard Grenville, one of the bravest men of the age. Ralph Lane was appointed governor, and Hariat was included in the expedition. Proceeding by way of the West Indies on the 20th of June they came to Florida, and to anchor on the 26th at Wococon.

Ralph Lane, being more of a soldier than a mild and judicious colonist, became involved in a quarrel with the Indians, as did Grenville himself, which proved disastrous to the expedition; and without provisions and the colony reduced to almost starvation, was about to dissolve, when unexpectedly Sir Francis Drake appeared with his fleet on his return from the West Indies. He supplied the wants of Lane, gave him a bark of seventy tons and arranged everything for the prosperous continuance of the colony. A sudden storm, however, destroyed the vessel which Drake had provided, and not only the colonists themselves, but Lane also, in great despondency, begged to be permitted to return with Drake's ships to England. The privilege was freely given and in June, 1586, the settlement of Roanoke and the third of the same kind was abandoned. In 1587 other emigrants with their families were sent out to make their homes in the New World. Municipal regulations were established. Mr. John White was appointed governor, and a charter of incorporation was granted for the "City of Raleigh." Leaving Portsmouth on the 26th of April they anchored off the coast on the 22d of July. An immediate search was made for the men left the year before on the Island of Roanoke, but in vain. The Indians had easily wreaked their vengeance upon them; desolation and ruin brooded over the scene. Raleigh had Chesapeake Bay marked out for the new settlement; but dissentions arrising, White was unable to proceed farther, and the foundations of the proposed city were laid on the island of Roanoke. As little progress could be made under so many discouraging circumstances, the united voices of the colonists begged White to return with the ship to England to secure prompt and abundant supplies and reinforcements. Only a few days before sailing the daughter of the governor, Mrs. Eleanor Dare, August 8th, gave birth to a daughter, who was the first child born of English parentage on the soil of the United States. She was appropriately named Virginia Dare.

White, leaving his family and the colony, returned home. He was never privileged to look upon them again. Raleigh was not forgetful of his colony. In April, 1588, he sent two vessels with supplies, but the ship's company sought the gains of privateering; they were worsted in an engagement and were compelled to put back, and thus they abandoned the colony to ruin.

The delay proved fatal. Raleigh was bankrupt and could do no more, and it was not till 1590 that White was enabled to return and search for his family and the colony he had left. Roanoke was literally a desert; nothing left but ruin and desolate habitations; nothing ever transpired to point out what had been their lot. Hence, in 1603, after a period of more than a hundred years from the time that Cabot discovered the continent of North America, and twenty years from the time that Raleigh sent out his first colony, not a single Englishman remained in the New World.

SIR WALTER RALEIGH.

In the last year of the reign of Elizabeth, 1602, Bartholomew Gasnold set out in a small vessel to make a voyage more direct to Virginia than by way of the Canaries and West Indies. In seven weeks he reached the coast of Massachusetts near Nahant. Keeping south in search of a harbor, he discovered the promontory which he called Cape Cod. This was the first spot in New England ever trod by Englishmen. Doubling the cape and passing Nantucket they entered Buzzard's Bay, which they called Gasnold's Hope. On the westernmost of the islands in the bay they made a settlement and called it Elizabeth, after the Queen. They built a fort and store-house on a rocky islet in the center of a small lake of fresh water, traces of which was seen by Dr. Belknap in 1797. They were delighted with the luxuriant vegetation of the scented shrubs, wild grapes and strawberries, and their wish was to remain there. But the smallness of their number, surrounded by Indians, the want of provisions and the recollection of what had befallen the hopeless settlers of Virginia, with the dissensions that sprung up, they shortly after returned to England.

PART IV.

THE ACCESSION OF JAMES I., 1603.

Followed by Peace Between England and Spain.

Merchants and others became interested in the reports of Gasnold and his companions, consequently two vessels were fitted out by the merchants of Bristol, under command of Martin Pring, to examine the discoveries of Gasnold, and ascertain the correctness of his statements. They returned with ample confirmation of his veracity. In 1605 a similar expedition, commanded by Captain Weymouth, equipped and despatched by Lord Arundel, not only produced additional testimony to the same effect, that all doubts were removed; and a company sufficiently in wealth and numbers powerful to attempt a settlement being soon formed, a petition was presented to the King for his sanction of his authority to its being carried into effect. James listened with a favorable ear to the application. But to grant the whole of such a vast region to any one body of men appeared to him an act of impolitic and profuse liberality. For this reason (1606) he divided that portion of North America which stretches from the thirty-fourth to the forty-fifth degree of latitude, into two districts nearly equal—the one called the First or South Colony of Virginia, the other, the Second or North Colony. He authorized Sir

POCAHONTAS SAVING THE LIFE OF CAPT. JOHN SMITH.

Thomas Gates, Sir George Somers, Richard Hakluyt, and their associates in the London Company, to plant anywhere between thirty-four and forty-one degrees north latitude, or between Cape Fear and the east end of Long Island. The Plymouth Company, composed of residents in the west of England, to plant anywhere between the thirty-eighth and forty-fifth degrees of north latitude, or between Delaware Bay and Halifax. But neither company was to begin its settlement within a hundred miles of any spot previously occupied by the other. Each colony was to extend along the coast fifty miles either way from the point inland a hundred miles, embracing ten thousand miles of continental territory. The charter granted the emigrant the privilege of holding lands in America by the freest and least burdensome tenure. The King permitted all the sustenance or commerce of these colonies to be exported from England during the space of seven years free, without pay or duty; and further, he granted them liberty of trade with other nations, and appropriated the duty to be levied on foreign commodities, as a fund for the benefit of the colonies for the period of twenty-one years. He also granted them liberty of coining money, of repelling enemies and detaining ships trading there without their leave. "In this singular charter," says Dr. Robertson, "the contents of which have been little attended to by historians of America, as some articles are as unfavorable to the rights of the colonists as others are to the interests of the parent state." In 1606, not long after the grant of this charter, James issued "Instructions for the Government of Virginia." He appointed a council as provided for in the charter, the King to increase or alter the council at his will, the president to have a double vote; the true Word of God, according to the Church of England, only to be preached. Under the auspices of this nature was the first permanent settlement effected by Englishmen in the New World, now "America."

OTHER COLONIES SENT TO VIRGINIA.

The London Company, consisting of Gates, Somers, Hakluyt, Wingfield and others, especially Sir Thomas Smith, one of the assignees of Raleigh's patent, fitted out three vessels, under command of Christopher Newport, and together with Wingfield, Gasnold, Hunt, the chaplain, and the famous John Smith, a hundred and five men embarked, on the 19th of December, 1606. The evident superiority of Smith excited envy and jealousy, and on a frivolous charge he was put in confinement on the voyage. Newport took the old route by the Canaries, so that he did not reach the coast of Virginia till April, 1607. By what might be termed a fortunate gale, he was driven quite past the site of the old colony, into the mouth of the noble Chesapeake Bay. The headlands were called Cape Henry and Cape Charles, and the deep water for anchorage led to the name Point Comfort. They explored the James River for fifty miles and then fixed upon a site for the colony. The name Jamestown was adopted, and it is the oldest town founded by the English in America. Smith was honorably acquitted and restored to his seat in the council. But for him the whole colony would soon have shared the like fate with that at Roanoke.

In company with Newport, Smith ascended the James river and visited Powhatan, who received them with ceremony, but with little cordiality. In June, Newport with his ships returned to England. The colonists, weak in number, sickness, without provisions, suffering from the summer heats, exposed to the hostilities of the Indians, their condition was truly deplorable. Half died before autumn, one of whom was Gasnold. The president of the council, Wingfield, was deposed for avarice and trying to desert the colony in its trouble; Ratcliffe, his successor, was incompetent, so that, in fact, the whole care and management of affairs fell into the hands of John Smith, and well was it for the colony that it was so. The fortifications were repaired, conspiracies of Wingfield and others crushed, and the approach of winter furnished plenty of wild game and fowl. Smith now set out to explore the Chickahominy, a tributary which entered the James river a little above Jamestown. Surprised by the Indians while on this expedition, Smith was taken prisoner; his presence of mind did not forsake him; he so astonished the Indians with his pocket compass and accounts of its marvellous powers that he was conducted by them with mingled triumph and fear from tribe to tribe as a remarkable being, whose character and designs they were unable to penetrate, in spite of all the incantations of their seers. At length he was brought into the presence of the aged Powhatan. The politic chief, seated in the midst of his women, received him with a display of barbaric ceremony. Whilst he was feasting they proceeded to deliberate upon his fate. Their fears dictated the policy of his destruction: his head was placed upon a large stone and the club already uplifted to dash out his brains, when Pocahontas, "the King's most dear and beloved daughter, a child ten or twelve years of age," after unavailing and passionate entreaties for the life of the white man, so noble a being to her youthful imagination, ran forward and clung to him with her arms, and laying her head upon his own, disarmed the savage fury of his executioners. The life of the wondrous stranger was preserved, and his open and generous character won the heart of the youthful Pocahontas.

By the promise of "life, liberty, land and women," they sought to engage Smith in an attack upon the colonists, but his address and influence turned them from the project, and he was after seven weeks' captivity dismissed with promises of support and amity. Like a tutelary genius, the loving Indian girl, after saving the life of their chief, "revived the dead spirits" of the colonists by her attention to their wants, bringing every day baskets of provisions; so the enmity of the savages was disarmed and food obtained. On his return in 1608 to Jamestown Smith found the colony on the brink of ruin, and only at the risk of his life succeeded in preventing the desertion of the forty persons yet remaining. Newport soon after arrived with supplies and a hundred and twenty emigrants. Soon after, Smith undertook in an open barge of three tons burden, the exploration of the vast bay of the Chesapeake. During three months he visited all the countries on the eastern and western shores, explored the Patapsco, the Potomac, and other tributaries that swell the basin of the Chesapeake on his return back to Jamestown. He had a map bordering on the Chesapeake, that long served as a basis of subsequent delineations. A few days after his return Smith was made president of the council, and speedily infused vigor and activity into the whole administration of the colony. The London Company, chagrined at its failure of acquiring sudden wealth, readily agreed to a change in its constitution. The limits of the colony were extended and many of the nobility and gentry, as well as tradesmen of London, became associated in the company. The first act of the new council was to appoint Lord Delaware governor and captain-general of the colony. Under such auspices an expedition consisting of nine vessels under the command of Newport, containing more than five hundred emigrants, were soon on their way out. The prosperity of Virginia seemed now assured; but an unforeseen and violent storm arose; the vessels on board of which were Gates, Somers and Newport, were separated from the rest, and after a narrow escape from foundering, was stranded on the coast of Burmudas without the loss of life. The rest of the ships, except one, reached Jamestown.

Smith meanwhile had been zealously occupied in maintaining order and security among the little band of colonists. The sudden arrival of so considerable a reinforcement disconcerted his arrangements. The new emigrants were "unruly gallants, packed off to escape ill destinies at home," and everything tended to a speedy dissolution of their little society. Jealousy of the Indians of their encroachments was steadily gaining ground. Powhatan, checked at times by the ascendency of Smith, at others formed plans for cutting them off. In these distresses and perils Pocahontas still proved herself the guardian angel of the unruly colonists; and "under God," as Smith declared in a letter to the Queen of James I., "the instrument for preserving them from death, famine and utter confusion." Although his authority had been superseded, Smith still continued to hold the helm until his successor arrived. But at this critical period, when everything seemed to be rapidly tending to anarchy and ruin, an accidental explosion of powder inflicted upon him a dangerous wound, which the surgical skill of Virginia could not relieve. Delegating his authority to Percy, he embarked for England. He received for his suffering, sacrifices and his perilous exertions not one foot of land, not the house he himself had built, not the field his own hands had planted, nor any reward

POCAHONTAS, ALIAS REBECCA.

Was born in the year 1595 in Virginia, near Jamestown, and was the daughter of Powhatan, chief of the Indians. In 1613 she was married to an Englishman named John Rolfe. In company with her husband they went to England. She died when only twenty-two years of age, leaving an infant son. This occurred at Gravesend, 1617.

but the applause of his conscience and the world. He was the Father of Virginia, the true leader who first planted the Saxon race within the borders of the United States. This illustrious man never revisited Virginia, although he was several times in New England in the service of the Plymouth Company. His death occurred in 1631, at London, in the fifty-second year of his age. The debt of gratitude due him is national and American, and so should his glory be. Wherever upon this continent the English language is spoken his deeds should be recounted and his memory hallowed. His services should not be forgotten but should be freshly remembered. Poetry has imagined nothing more stirring and romantic; and History, upon her ample pages, has recorded few more honorable and spotless names. The colony, having received on June 10th, 1610, a large acquisition of emigrants on the arrival of ord Delaware, and in May, 1611, by Sir Thomas Dale, and in August, by Sir Thomas Gates.

The colony now began to extend up James River, where a town was built called Henrica, and continued to increase in prosperity, a firm alliance having been effected between the English and Powhatan and the Indians, in consequence of the marriage of the gentle and affectionate Pocahontas. A foraging party, headed by Argall, had succeeded in carrying off this noble maiden, and when her father indignantly demanded her return it was refused. Hostilities were about to break out, when a worthy young Englishman (1613) named John Rolfe, winning the favor of Pocahontas, asked her hand in marriage. Powhatan was delighted. His daughter received baptism at the hands of that good man and minister of Christ, the Rev. Alexander Whitaker. The marriage was solemnized by the same clergyman, according to the usages of the Episcopal Church. About three years after her marriage she accompanied her husband to England, where she was much caressed for her great services to the colony. Here she fell in again with the gallant Smith, whom, from report, she supposed to be long dead; and who has left an interesting account of his interview, with her untimely death: "Being about this time preparing to set sail for New England, I could not stay to do her that service I deisred, and she well deserved; but hearing she was at Branford, with my friends I went to see her. After a modest salutation without any word she turned about, obscured her face, as not seeming well contented, and in that humor, her husband with divers others, we all left her two or three hours, repenting myself to have writ she could speak English; but not long after she began to talk, and remembered me well, what courtesies she had done, saying: 'You did promise Powhatan what was yours should be his, and he the like to you. You called him father, being in his land a stranger, and by the same reason so must I do you; which though I would have excused, I durst not allow of that title, because she was a king's daughter.' With a well set countenance, she said: 'Were you not afraid to come into my father's country and cause fear in him and all his people but me, and fear you here I should call you father? I tell you, then, I will, and you shall call me child, and so I will be for ever and ever your countryman. They did tell us always you were dead, and I knew no other till I came to Plymouth; yet Powhatan did command Uttamatomakkin to seek you and know the truth, because your countrymen will lie much.' The treasurer, council and company having well furnished Captain Samuel Argall, the Lady Pocahontas, alias Rebecca, with her husband and others, in the good ship called the George, it pleased God at Gravesend to take this young lady to his mercy." This sad event occurred in 1617, when Pocahontas was but twenty-two years of age. She left an infant son, who was educated in England, and through whom several families in Virginia claim direct descent from the daughter of Powhatan.

PART V.

THE STABILITY OF THE COLONY.

Sir Thomas Dale, though empowered to exercise martial law, was yet so discreet and just that no oppression was felt during the five years that he remained in the colony from 1611 to 1616.

The colony continued to flourish under the management of Yeardley, Dale and Wyatt, and during the year 1617 over twelve hundred emigrants were sent to Virginia. The King did the colony great injustice to send out a hundred dissolute vagabonds, picked out of the jails and sold to be servants for a term of years, a practice long continued, though protested against by the colonists. About this date a Dutch trading vessel brought into Jamestown a cargo of twenty negroes, who were sold to the planters as slaves. At intervals others were brought for the same purpose. This was the commencement of slavery in Virginia.

Sir Edwin Sandys, whose integrity and energy were of the highest value, had succeeded Sir Thomas Smith as treasurer. During the year that he held office he sent out to Virginia twelve hundred emigrants, among whom were ninety young women who became wives of the planters on the payment to the company of a hundred pounds of tobacco, equal to about $75. The Earl of Southampton succeeded Sandys as treasurer, and during the two years following twenty-three hundred emigrants were sent to Virginia. New plantations were established on James and York rivers; ten thousand acres was assigned for a college, where the Indians as well as the colonists were to be educated. The cultivation of tobacco and the new attempts were made to manufacture flax, silk, wine, glass, pitch tar and potash; some Italians and Dutch were sent out to instruct the colonists in these operations. The colony, thus far, on the whole, had not the promise of great results in the future. (1621) Sir Francis Wyatt superseded Yeardly as governor, and was instructed besides restricting the amount of tobacco each planter might raise to cultivate the good will of the Indians. But unhappily it was too late, and a fearful visitation fell upon the colony. The aged Powhatan was dead. Opechancanaugh, his successor, a bold and cunning chief, had bided his time, and in profound secrecy he arranged and matured a plan for an universal massacre of the whites. The Indians had been treated with contempt, as enemies of no moment; military exercises had gone into desuetude, and the Indians had generally become as dexterous as the colonists in the use of firearms. On the 22d of March, 1622, at a given signal in the midst of apparent security, they fell upon every settlement. Men, women and children were slaughtered without mercy, and had not a converted Indian, named Chanco, given warning the night before, the extent of the slaughter must have been nearly universal. As it was, three hundred and fifty perished, including six of the council. A savage war of retaliation and extermination ensued. Sickness and famine came upon them and in a short time the colonists were reduced from four thousand

I.O. THE GOOD INDIAN.

to twenty-five hundred. But the white men soon regained their superiorty over the red race, and the Indians were entrapped and slain without mercy. This state of warfare continued about fourteen years. In 1624, King James, without legal right, by the exercise of his prerogative alone, he ordered the records of the company in London to be taken at once, and appointed a commission to sit in judgment upon its proceedings, while another body was sent to Virginia to inquire into the condition and management of the colony. Paralyzed by the suddenness of this attack upon their privileges, they begged that they might be allowed time for consideration. An answer in three days' time was peremptorily insisted on. Upon their decided refusal, a writ of *Quo Warranto* was issued by the King against the company, in order that the validity of the charter might be tried in the court of King's Bench. At length the commissioners returned from Virginia, and made an earnest recommendation to the King to abrogate the democratic element which, it was asserted, had occasioned so much dissension and misrule. "This afforded additional ground," says Robertson, "for a decision perfectly consonant to the wishes of the monarch. The charter was forfeited, the company was dissolved and all the rights and privileges conferred on it returned to the King, from whom they flowed." Thus fell the Virginia Company in 1625, after spending nearly $700,000 in their efforts to establish the colony. The King had further plans in view, but his death on the 27th of March, 1625, finally closed his career, with all its good and all its evil.

PART VI.

SETTLEMENT OF NEW NETHERLAND.

About two years after the settlement of Jamestown, and nearly at the same time that Champlain was making explorations in Northern New York (1609) a famous navigator named Henry Hudson entered the service of the Dutch East India Company. He was by birth an Englishman, and an intimate friend of the illustrious Capt. John Smith. He had already made two voyages, and in April, 1609, was placed in command of a small vessel of eighty tons burden called the Half Moon for a third voyage. Impeded by the ice in the north seas, he ran along the coast of Acadia, entered Penobscot bay, made the land of Cape Cod, entered the Chesapeake and Delaware bays, and on the 2d of September discovered and entered Sandy Hook bay. On the 11th he passed through the Narrows, and on the 12th began his voyage up that noble river which now justly perpetuates his fame, pronouncing the country along the river's banks "as beautiful a land as one can tread upon." Hudson ascended the river with his ship as far as where the present city of Albany now stands, and thence sent a boat, which went somewhat beyond Waterford.

Mr. Hildreth stigmatizes Hudson's conduct towards the Indians on several occasions as marked by "reckless cruelty," which is hardly borne out by the facts. Decending the river,

Hudson, on the 4th of October, set sail for home and in a little more than a month arrived safely at Dartmouth, in England. Hudson was detained by a royal order, and soon after fitted out for a fourth voyage. From that voyage he never returned; but set adrift in an open boat with his young son and eight others, he perished in the frozen regions of that bay which still bears his name and reminds us of his fearful fate. The Dutch East India Company claimed a right to the new lands discovered by their agent, and immediately dispatched vessels to open trade with the natives. (1613) A few fortified trading houses were erected on the island of Manhattan, the nucleus of the future great city of New York. The state general had meanwhile granted a four years' monopoly to any enterprising trader, and soon after an Amsterdam company sent out five ships. One of these adventurers, Adrian Block, extended the sphere of discovery by way of the East river, ran through the formidable "Hellgate," and traced the shores of Long Island and the coast of Connecticut as far as Cape Cod. A few years later Capt. Thomas Dermes was the first Englishman who visited the Dutch at Manhattan, and sailed through Long Island sound. (1615) A fort was erected on Manhattan Island and another a few miles below Albany, as centers of traffic with the Indians. (1623) Two vessels were sent out under command of Capt. Cornlis Jocobsen May, the companion of Block, who became the first director of New Netherland. During his brief administration of one year a fort was built on the Delaware called Nassau. There was also one built on the Hudson where Albany now stands, named Fort Orange. A number of Walloons, who had been denied the privilege of settlement within the territory of the Virginia Company, came out in the vessel under command of May. These were properly the first colonists who settled on the northwest corner of Long Island at Walloon's bay, now Wallabout. In May, 1626, Peter Minuit arrived at Manhattan, as director-general of New Netherland, Manhattan was purchased of the Indians for sixty gilders—about $24—and a block house surrounded by a palisade was built at the southernmost point; this was called Fort Amsterdam. Staten Island was also purchased of the Indians. In 1629 a plan of colonization was drawn up by the assembly of nineteen. Any members of the company who might establish in any part of New Netherland within four years after the notice of his intention, a colony of fifty persons upwards of fifteen years of age was to be entitled, by the name of Patroon, to a grant of territory so occupied, sixteen miles in extent along the sea shore, on the bank of some navigable river, or eight miles where both banks were occupied, with an indefinite extent inland. The island of Manhattan and the fur trade with the indians was expressly reserved to the company and upon all trade carried on by the Patroons five per cent. was to be paid; these Patroons were to extinguish the Indian title and settle their lands with tenants, farmers, etc. Free settlers, who emigrated at their own expense, were allowed as much land as they could cultivate, and settlers of more to be free of taxes for ten years. The colonists were forbidden to make any woolen, linen or cotton cloth, or to weave any other stuffs on pain of being banished, or punished "as purjurers." This was done to keep them dependent on the mother country for all necessary manufactures. The scheme met with favor; several members of the company selected and purchased the most desirable locations on the Delaware bay, and on the west bank of the Hudson opposite Manhattan Island. The former was called Swansdale, and the latter to which Staten Island and others were added was entitled Pavonia. The agents of Patroon Van Rensselaer, who is well known to the inhabitants of Albany county, New York, their predecessors, purchased the lands in the vicinity of Fort Orange. The name Rensselaerwyck was given to this tract, twenty-four miles long and forty-eight broad. De Vries went to Swansdale and settled there with a small colony, where the town of Lewiston now stands. (1630) Large beginnings were made to colonize Rensselaerwyck and Pavonia. (1632) Minuit, on his return to Holland with a cargo of furs, he was compelled by stress of weather to put into Plymouth harbor, where he was detained and treated as an interloper. The Dutch title to New Netherland was discussed between the governments of England and Holland, the former insisting upon her right to the territory. In December of this year De Vries brought supplies to the little colony at Swansdale, but sad to relate, not a living being was to be found there. The Indians had completely destroyed everything. De Vries subsequently settled on Staten Island.

In 1633 the Dutch purchased of the Pequods a tract on the west bank of the Connecticut, near where the city of Hartford now stands, and built a trading house, which was fortified with two cannon, and named the house Good Hope. Soon after a small vessel came from Boston with a letter to Van Twiller, the director-general, from Winthrop, the governor, asserting anew the claims of England. (1634) New Amsterdam received marked improvement; a church, mills and barracks was erected, but the disputes with the Patroons was a serious hindrance to the progress of the colony, and Swansdale was sold back to the company for about $6,000. Van Twiller, (1635) with an eye to his own interests too much, complaints were made against him and soon after was recalled, (1637) and William Kieft was sent out as his successor in March of the next year. In 1637 the Swedes sent out an expedition under command of Minuit, who was previously director of New Netherland; two vessels with fifty men entered the Delaware. (1638) Lands were purchased of the natives near the head of the bay, and a fort was built called Christina in honor of the queen of Sweden. Kieft protested, but to no avail; it was unwise to attempt hostilities with the Swedes and he desisted. Emigration continued to increase for several years, and Printz, the governor, established a residence and built a fort near Philadelphia; thus Pennsylvania was occupied by the Swedes long before Penn become proprietary, and the bank of the Delaware from the ocean to the falls near Princeton were known as New Sweden. At enmity with the Dutch in all things, the Swedes, nevertheless, joined with them in keeping out the English, (1640) who attempted to settle within their limits. All who came were either driven out by force or rigidly compelled to submit to Swedish authority.

PART VII.

FOUNDATION OF NEW ENGLAND.

Landing of the Puritans, Nov. 11th, 1620.

For a number of years the sect known as Puritans were anxious to form a colony by themselves, on account of not having free liberty of worship; and being oppressed by the government, they were compelled to fly to Holland for refuge. During the twelve years of their stay in Holland a constant stream of disaffected persons from England set towards that country, where all were permitted to worship God according to the dictates of their own conscience. Winslow and Captain Miles Standish were among those who joined the church of Robinson after it had left England.

The Puritans not being at ease in their position, exiles for conscience sake, with an eye, too, to the temporal advantages that might accrue, they turned their attention towards the New World. "Well weaned from the delicate milk of our mother country and inured to the difficulties and privations of a strange land," as they express themselves in a letter to Sir Edwin Sandys, it did not require long to bring them to a fixed determination to embark for America. Having failed in an application to the Dutch government to join them at New Netherland the Puritans decided to emigrate to Virginia, favorable terms having been readily granted in 1619 by the Virginia Company. The next difficulty was to procure means, which only could be done by entering into an arrangement with some London merchants whose terms were not very favorable to the emigrants. The whole property in the colony was to belong to a joint stock company for seven years; the services of each emigrant were only to be equal to every ten pounds furnished by the capitalists. It was upon these hard terms they preferred to set sail for the New World. A small ship, the Speedwell, was purchased in Holland and was ready to convey the colony to Southampton. However, some were left behind with Robinson, being unable to find room in the vessel. On July 22d, the wind being fair, they got ready to go on board The parting with Robinson and their brethren was very affecting. In a few days they arrived at Southampton and were joined by the larger vessel, the Mayflower. The two vessels, well loaded with passengers, got under way, but the Speedwell proved to be unseaworthy in every respect; they were obliged to put into Dartmouth, then into Plymouth, leaving there a portion of their company, and crowding as many into the Mayflower as possible. Early in September they launched forth upon the reckless ocean. The voyage was tedious and full of danger, owing to the equinoctial storms whose fury the Mayflower encountered, and on the 9th of November they came in sight of the coast of New England, and no great distance from Cape Cod. As it was their object to settle near the Hudson river the course of the ship was turned south; getting entangled among the shoals they came to anchor in Cape Cod harbor. Weary of the hardships of the Mayflower they were eager to land. Being out of the limits of the Virginia Company, and signs of insubordination among a portion of the emigrants, it was judged best to enter into a voluntary compact as a basis of social polity, and to appoint a governor. John Carver was chosen to act as governor for the term of one year. The whole company, men, women and children, was one hundred and one souls, who affixed their signatures to the following document:

In the name of God, amen. We, whose names are underwritten, the loyal subjects of our dread sovereign lord, King James, by the grace of

God of Great Britian, France and Ireland, king, defender of the faith, etc., having undertaken for the glory of God and the advancement of the Christian faith and the honor of our king and country a voyage to plant the first colony in the northern part of Virginia, do, by these presents of God, and one of another, covenant and combine ourselves together into a civil body politic, for our better order and preservation and furtherance of the ends aforesaid; and by virtue hereof to enact, constitute and frame such just laws, ordinances, acts and constitutions, offices, from time to time as shall be thought most convenient for the general good of the colony; unto which we all promise all due submission and obedience. In witness whereof we have hereunder subscribed our names. Cape Cod, 11th November, in the reign of our sovereign lord, King James, of England, France and Ireland, 18, and of Scotland, 54, Anno Domini, 1620.

An exploring party was sent out at once. They found a country covered with pine forests and here and there a deserted wigwam, but did not get sight of the natives. A quantity of Indian corn was discovered buried in sand in baskets, which proved a very timely supply of seed for the following spring. Winter was now upon them in all its severity and it was absolutely necessary to fix upon some spot for a settlement, and lay foundations of the colony. Five weeks were spent and on Monday, December 21st, 1620, this band of pioneers first set foot on the far famed Plymouth Rock: remembering the kindness which they had received at Plymouth, England, the name of New Plymouth was bestowed upon the infant settlement. Here the whole colony was landed. On a bold hill commanding the bay they built a fort, which was garrisoned with a few small pieces of ordinance; at its foot two rows of huts were laid for the habitation of nineteen families. By privations and exposure to the rigor of the season already had the seeds of mortal disease been implanted; during the first winter they faded gradually away; one of the first to follow, January 29, 1621, was the wife of Capt. Standish; Bradford's wife had perished by drowning. But not to follow the bereavements, suffice it to say that during three dreary months one half their number were cut off. That winter they had to form seven times more graves for the dead than habitations for the living. During the following spring by means of Samoset and other friendly Indians, intercourse was opened, and finally a treaty of amity agreed upon

LANDING OF THE PILGRIMS ON CAPE COD, 1620.

with Massasoit, head chief of the Pokanokets or Wampanoags, who were immediate neighbors of the colonists. Carver was reelected governor, but died soon after; Bradford was chosen his successor. The Mayflower set sail for England April, 1621. The colonists, taking heart as the mild weather approached, sent out a party to explore Massachusetts bay. Some forty miles to the northward there for the first time they beheld the three crested peninsular of Shawmut, site of the present city of Boston. In November the Fortune arrived with thirty-five new colonists but no provisions; the result was a famine. No cattle had been yet imported. Mortality and distress had prevented them from tilling the soil. Hostilities among the Indians become apparent, and (1622) it was judged prudent by the colonists to build a stockade around their village, one mile in circuit with three gates. Weston, who had taken an active part in fitting out the Plymouth colony, was dissatisfied with the pecuniary results and resolved to send out a separate colony for a plantation of his own. He sent some sixty men, chiefly servants, to begin the settlement. They were fellows of hard characters and brought on hostilities with the Indians, greatly to the discomfort of the colony.

In 1623 Robert Gorges, son of Sir Ferdinand Gorges, obtained a grant of ten miles on the northern shore of Massachusetts bay; he was also appointed lieutenant-general of New England. Gorges brought with him a clergyman named Morrill. His mission was looked upon with no favor by the Puritans and he shortly returned to England. Lyford, who came in 1624, was expelled. Migrating to Nantasket, at the entrance of Boston harbor, the expelled colonists formed a new settlement at that point. The colony of New Plymouth, still feeble, gave encouraging signs of life and energy. Though there were no luxuries as yet, there was wholesome food and good pure water to drink. At the end of the fourth year the settlement of Plymouth had thirty-two dwelling houses and a hundred and eighty-four inhabitants; the general stock or whole amount of the investment, personal services included, amounted to £7,000, or $34,000. John Robinson died in Holland, and several years elapsed before his family and the rest could find means to transport themselves to New Plymouth. Those already the passengers by the Mayflower, the Fortune, Anne and Little James, were afterward distinguished as the "old comers, or forefathers." In 1627 the agreement between the Plymouth colonists and the London Company, came to an end. In 1630 the number of colonists at New Plymouth did not amount to three hundred, yet they considered themselves permanently established. The settlement at New Plymouth was soon after followed by another and more extensive one of the Puritans on the shores of Massachusetts bay. In 1628 John Endicott, a Puritan, first established himself at Naumkeag, now Salem, and soon after a strong party, chiefly from Boston, in Lincolnshire, followed. In 1630 a plan to transfer the charter to the company from England to the colony itself was next formed; this led to a very important increase in number and distinction of the emigrants. The principal of these were Sir Richard Saltonstall, Isaac Johnson, Thomas Dudley and John Winthrop. Winthrop was chosen governor, and by his admirable conduct, fully justified the general confidence. This expedition was by far the most important that had left England's shores for the wild and uncivilized America, consisting of fifteen vessels conveying about a thousand emigrants, among whom were four non-conformist ministers. The persons whom they sent out to America, as soon as they had landed there, considered themselves as individuals united together by voluntary association, possessing the natural right of men who form a society, to adopt what laws they deemed most conducive to the general felicity. Upon this principal they established their church in Salem, without regard to the institutions of the church of England of which the charter supposed them to be members, and bound, of consequence, to conformity with its ritual. Winthrop, Dudley, and others, embarked on board the Arabella, so named after the Lady Arabella Johnson, who with her husband was also a passenger. They arrived in the bay in June, and Endicott at Charlestown, where at first they contemplated a settlement. The opposite peninsula, however, was natural, and speedily attracted their attention. It was then in a state of nature and in the undisturbed possession of the solitary occupant, by name Blackstone.

Here Winthrop and his people determined to fix themselves and begin a settlement, which, after the English town of Lincolnshire they called Boston. Other parties of emigrants settled as they arrived in the vicinity of Boston, and gave names to the various towns and villages which they then and there founded. "Each settlement," says Mr. Hildreth, "at once assumed that township authority which has ever formed so marked a feature in the political organization of New England." Although the new settlers were not subjected to hardships so severe as the New Plymouth colony, yet owing to shortness of provision, debility, severity of the winter, etc., more than two hundred died before December, 1630, among them the Lady Arabella Johnson and her husband. Before winter was over the infant colony was threatened with famine, but the seasonable return of a vessel from England with provisions revived their deploring spirits and instead of the fast they observed a day of thanksgiving.

PART VIII.

PROGRESS OF THE NEW ENGLAND COLONIES.

The unfavorable reports carried back by those who returned from the first emigration operated greatly to discourage others. The number of new comers in 1632 was comparatively small. Among them, however, was the son of Winthrop, the governor, and John Eliot, afterwards the celebrated missionary to the Indians. In 1633 several hundred settlers arrived; among them were John Haynes and those ministers so distinguished in New England history—Cotton, Hooker and Stone. Cotton settled in Boston as colleague with Wilson, and Hooker and Stone settled at Newtown. There were already seven churches, eight principal plantations and some smaller ones; ferries had been established between Boston and Charlestown, a fort had been built, water and windmills had been brought into use; a flourishing trade with the Virginians and the Dutch had grown up, etc. While the court was (1634) in session six large vessels arrived with a large number of passengers and a goodly supply of cattle, and one month later fifteen more vessels entered the harbor. John Humphrey came out and brought a supply of ordinance, muskets, powder, and other things of value to the colony. By complaints in England against Massachusetts, a royal colonial commission was appointed over the American plantations, the church and charter. The news of this measure caused great alarm in Massachusetts, and steps were directly taken for the defence of Boston harbor. Dudley, Winthrop, Haynes, Humphrey and Endicott were appointed commissioners "to consult, direct, and give command for the managing and ordering of war that might befall for the space of one year next ensuing. The course persued by Roger Williams was not calculated to render matters more easy of adjustment. (1635) This active and energetic young Puritan appears to have grasped firmly one grand idea and to have held and acted upon it at all times with entire sincerity. This was called "soul liberty," meaning by the expression, the most perfect and complete right of every man to enjoy freedom of opinion on the subject of religion. The truth of these principles struck at the root of the theocracy which had become established in the colony. Alarmed by William's freedom of thought and its dangerous tendency, the court at Boston desired the removal of one whom they regarded as a troubler of the public peace, but his piety was so genuine and his character so noble and disinterested, that the people of Salem who knew and loved him reelected him for their pastor; for this act they were reprimanded and punished by withholding a certain portion of lands. Such harshness aroused Williams to retort by a spirited protest, and he engaged the Salem church to join him; he also made a general appeal to the other churches, against the injustice of which the magistrates had been guilty, a daring proceeding, for which the council suspended their franchise, and the church shrunk from their leader and he was thus left absolutely alone. Upon this he openly renounced allegiance to what he deemed a persecuting church. For his opinions and conduct the council pronounced against him a sentence of banishment, but decided shortly after to send him back to England. In the depth of a New England winter Williams fled into the wilderness and took refuge among the Narragansett Indians, with whom he had become acquainted at Plymouth. He wandered for fourteen weeks through the snow buried forests before he reached their wigwams, where he was received and sheltered with the utmost kindness. In the spring he departed in quest of a spot for those who like himself were persecuted for conscience sake. (1636) He first attempted a settlement at Seekonk, but afterwards, at the friendly suggestion of Winslow, the governor of Plymouth, he removed to Narragansett bay, where he received from the Indians a free grant of a large tract of country, and in June, 1636, fixed upon the site of a town, which he named Providence, as being a refuge from persecution and wanderings. "The city of Providence" still remains as the birthplace for universal freedom. Many of his friends from Salem joined him here, and he freely distributed his lands among them. This was the beginning of the state of Rhode Island, one of the most free and liberal in its institutions of any ever founded in America.

In 1636 Hugh Peters, chaplain to Oliver Cromwell, and Henry Vane, a young man of superior ability, came over to join the Massachusetts colony. The emigration of a man of Vane's distinction and family created considerable stir. Soon after, Vane was elected chief magistrate of the colony, and on the occasion of a new religious fermentation arising, he became a prominent actor in it. The whole colony were interested and agitated at the preachings of Mrs. Hutchinson. Vane, whose sagacity and acuteness seemed to forsake him whenever turned towards religion, espoused and defended her wildest tenets. "Like Williams, she spoke for soul liberty." Many conferences were held, days of fasting and humiliation were appointed, a general synod was called, and after dissentions which threatened the dissolution of the colony, Mrs. Hutchinson's opinions were condemned and she herself banished. Several of her disciples withdrew from the province of their own accord. Vane quited America in disgust, unlamented even by those who had lately admired him. The fate of Mrs. Hutchinson was as unhappy as her life was restless. After her retirement to Aquiday, or the Isle of Rhodes, where she participated in all the toils and privations of a new settlement, she continued to promulgate her doctrines with the utmost ardor. Her sons, openly arranging the justice of her banishment, were siezed and thrown into prison. To fly beyond the reach of persecution, the whole family passed over into the territory of the Dutch. At the time Kieft, the governor, had aroused by his rashness and cruelty, vindicative reprisals on the part of the Indians. The dwelling of Mrs. Hutchinson was set on fire and she either perished with her children—except a little granddaughter—amidst the flames or was murdered by the infuriated savages; this sad event occurred in October, 1643. In 1635 a permanent settlement had been formed in the valley of the Connecticut, and in 1636 the towns of Hartford, Windsor and Wethersfield were founded. The commissioners also sent a party by water to found a port at the mouth of the river which, since Lord Say-and-Sele and Lord Brooke were proprietaries, was called Saybrook. Exposed to trouble in consequence of the jealousy manifested by the Dutch towards the colony, it was besides placed in great peril from the hostility of the neighboring Indians. The Pequod war was, perhaps, the inevitable result of the suspicions and fears of the Indians, and the apprehensions of the colonists of sudden attack and massacre similar to that of which the settlers in Virginia had been subjected. The Pequods, at this date were the most powerful confederacy in the neighborhood of Narragansett bay and held authority over twenty-six petty tribes. (1636) A band of them had murdered one Stone, a drunken and dissolute master of a Virginia trading vessel; this caused some alarm in Massachusetts, and the Pequods sent to Boston offering to give up the murderers, and making an apology, which was accepted, but for some cause the murderers were not delivered up. Not long after, an old settler on Block Island named Oldham was murdered by a party of Indians, probably in revenge for his opening a trade with the Pequods. Canonicus, the sachem of the Narragansetts, offered ample apology for the crime, but the magistrates and ministers required something further at their hands. Accordingly, an expedition under command of Endicott, consisting of ninety men, was sent to punish the Block Islanders, and thence to go to the Pequods to demand the delivery of the murderers of Stone and a thousand fathoms of wampum for damages, equivalent to from three to five thousand dollars. After burning the wigwams and destroying the standing corn of the Indians on Block Island, Endicott sailed to Fort Saybrook and marched thence to the Pequod river. The Indians refusing his demands, he burned their villages, both there and on the Connecticut, and returned to Boston without the loss of a single man. The Pequods, enraged at what they deemed an unprovoked attack, retaliated in every way, killing during the winter about thirty in all, and endeavored to engage the Narragansetts in an alliance to cut off every white man from the soil. Happily, through the intervention of Roger Williams, who had sent timely information to the Massachusetts' magistrates, this dreadful coalition was prevented and the good will of the Narragansetts secured.

At a special session of the general court, held early in December, 1636, the militia were organized into three regiments and officers were appointed in the respective grades; watches were ordered to be kept and travelers were to be armed. No active measures were taken until the spring of 1637, in consequence mainly of the ferment and trouble arising out of Mrs. Hutchinson's case, of which we have already spoken of previously. Orthodoxy having triumphed, vigorous attention was directed to the Pequod war, and a considerable force was raised to send into the field. But the decisive battle had been fought before the arrival of the Massachusetts troops. In the battle seventy wigwams were burned and five or six hundred Indians perished either by the sword or in the flames. It had been previously concluded not to burn the fort, but the captain afterwards found it the only expedient to obtain the victory and save his men. Thus parents and children, sannap and squaw, the old man and the babe, perished in promiscuous ruin. At the close of this unrelenting massacre a new body of Pequods from other villages were fast approaching. Filled with rage at the sight of their ruined habitations and slaughtered companions, they rushed furiously upon the white men, but it was in vain. The destructive firearms soon checked them, and Mason and his party easily made good their retreat to Pequod harbor, now New London. The wounded were sent by water and Mason marched his troops to Saybrook, where he was received by the discharge of artillery. The work of extermination thus begun by the Connecticut soldiers was in conjunction with the Massachusetts forces carried forward in the summer of 1637 to final completion. The warriors were killed, the women and children were distributed as slaves among the colonists. Sassacus, their head

PEQUOD INDIANS ATTACKING COLONISTS.

sachem, having fled to the Mohawks, was murdered by them at the instigation of the Narragansetts, and the adult male prisoners were sold into slavery in the West Indies. It was reckoned that about nine hundred of the Pequods had been killed or taken and the few that had escaped were scattered among the Narragansetts and Mohegans, were forever forbidden to call themselves Pequods.

The Pequods, having been exterminated, the attention of the ministers and magistrates was next turned to the rooting out of heretical pravity, a species of work which they were constantly called upon to undertake, but which, however well done, seemed very frequently to have to be done over again. One beneficial effort resulted from the stringent regulations in Massachusetts, and that was the causing of emigration in different directions. Roger Williams laid the foundation of Rhode Island, and Davenport in 1638 established the colony of New Haven. Wheelwright, banished for his participation in the heresies of Mrs Hutchinson, planted Exeter. Captain Underhill, involved in the same quarrel, was expelled and retired to Dover. Others also departed as occasion demanded, and thus separate congregations and settlements were sprinkled over the face of the country. Among those was that of Rowley, in Massachusetts, formed by a company of Yorkshire clothiers under the pastoral care of Ezekiel Rogers. In the spring of 1638 eight ships which were in the Thames were preparing to embark for New England, the privy council interfered to prevent them from sailing. The ships were delayed only a few days when the king removed the restraint and the vessels arrived in safety in Massachusetts bay. The coast of Maine had also here and there a few settlements but their progress was for some time extremely slow. Sir Ferdinando Gorges, who during twenty years had persevered in his efforts at colonization, and had sunk in these efforts nearly $100,000, obtained a royal charter for his American provinces in 1639. On receipt of this charter Gorges drew up an elaborate scheme for the government of Maine, and sent out Thomas Gorges as deputy, with subordinates, to administer it. (1640) A Scotchman, Sir William Alexander, had obtained from James I. the territory of Acadia in 1627, and given to it the name of Nova Scotia. During the war between France and England he had taken forcible possession of the province. Under the treaty of peace, however Canada, Cape Breton and Acadia were restored again in 1632 to the French. The progress of the colony in spite of the internal dissensions and trouble was, on the whole, steady and rapid.

Trade continued to increase; vessels were built, mills were erected, and towns and villages began to assume a settled appearance. Intercourse was mostly carried on between the settlements by coasting, in consequence of the forests and uninhabited regions intervening. Probably no plantation in America had made as safe and substantial progress as this during the time that the energetic sons of England had been on the soil of the New World. (1640) The coast of New England colonization thus far, according to Mr. Hildreth, has been estimated at a million of dollars, which, being a great sum, is probably short of the truth. Therefore (1640) now east of the Hudson twelve independent communities, comprising fifty towns or settlements, soon after, however, by separate jurisdiction, were reduced to six. The colonists regarded their successes in this war of destruction of the "bloody heathen" as ample proof of divine approbation.

PART IX.

PROGRESS OF THE VIRGINIA COLONIES.

In 1627 war against the Indians was still existing. There was but little enterprise and capital, and in fact, the staple product was that "nauseous, unpalatable weed, tobacco, neither of necessity nor ornament to human life." Notwithstanding, however, in 1628, more than a thousand emigrants arrived from Europe. Dr. John Potts was elected by the council in 1629, which office he held for a short time, until the arrival of John Harvey, who had recently been appointed to the government of the colony. Potts fell into trouble under charge of no very creditable character, viz., that of horse stealing, but nothing of moment grew out of it. Harvey built a new fort at Point Comfort at the entrance of the James river, and demanded a fee, in powder and ball, of every ship that passed. Salt works were also established on the eastern shore of Chesapeake bay. In 1632 a revisal of the laws took place by which they were consolidated into a single statute. The regulations in regard to religion and morals were numerous, and evince the care to premate godliness among the people. These regulations covered such points as the publishing bans of marriage, catechising children, the number of times the ministers should preach during the year and administer the communion, the tithes for the support of of religion, punishments for drunkenness, profane swearing, adultery, slander, etc.

Attempts were made to limit the amount of tobacco produced and thus increase its price in the English market. The price then was only six pence per pound. The colonists were also required to cultivate a certain portion of the soil in corn, and plant and rear vines. Military exercises were to be kept up; no parley was allowed with the Indians; no emigration to New England was to be allowed without permit from the governor. This revised code was read at the beginning of every monthly court and a manuscript copy furnished open to public inspection. In 1634 the colony was divided into eight counties, the governor appointing the lieutenants for each county and the people choosing the sheriff. So after the many trials and hardships in way of growth Virginia, the new empire, was fast rising into prominence in the Western hemisphere. At this time a new colony had taken root in Maryland, but was looked upon with disfavor by the Virginians as an encroachment on their just rights. Harvey became unpopular by obnoxious measures and was suspended by the council. Harvey went to England to answer any charges that might be preferred against him. The charges were not even heard and the deposed Harvey returned in 1636 with a new commission, and with a spirit not in kindliness toward the colonists. According to some writers he exercised his powers with much severity and even tyranny, until at length he was superseded by Sir Francis Wyatt in 1639. His administration was quite acceptable to the people. However, in 1641, Sir William Berkeley was appointed governor, and the year following, 1642, he arrived in Virginia. He was a man of high and honorable character and proved himself well adapted to the station he had been elevated. Hostilities with the Indians became apparent and in 1644, a favorable opportunity having presented itself, arising out of the dissensions caused by the civil war in England, and its general effect upon the colony, a sudden furious assault was made under the aged chief Opechanough's directions, which resulted in the slaughter of some five hundred of the colonists. A general war ensued against the Indians and the aged chief was taken prisoner, and soon after of wounds inflicted by a brutal soldier, died. His successor was willing to make peace (1646) and all the lands between James and York rivers were ceded to the Virginians. Thus did it happen, to use the words of Mr. Bancroft, that the colony of Virginia acquired the management of all its concerns; war was levied, and peace concluded and territory acquired in conformity to acts of the representatives of the people. So at last the colonists enjoyed all the prosperity which a virgin soil, equal laws and general uniformity of condition and industry could bestow. Their number increased, the cottages were filled with children, as the ports were with ships and emigrants. At Christmas, 1648, there were trading in Virginia ten ships from London, two from Bristol, twelve from Holland and seven from New England; the number of the colonists was already twenty thousand; they were attached to the cause of Charles, not because they loved monarchy but because they cherished the liberties of which he had left them in the undisturbed possession; and after his execution, 1649, some from ignorance, as the Royalists affirmed, favored Republicanism. The government recognized his son without dispute. Charles the Second, a fugitive from England, was still the sovereign of England. Virginia was whole for monarchy and the last country belonging to England that submitted to obedience of the commonwealth. In 1652 Berkeley's commission was revoked and Richard Bennet, one of the Parliamentary commissioners, was elected governor. Bennet retired in 1655, and Edward Diggs was appointed. He served till 1658, and Samuel Matthews followed him as chief magistrate. Matthews having fallen into a dispute with the house of Burgesses, a declaration of popular sovereignty was made, the former election declared void, and Matthews was reelected to the very office from which he had just been removed. The governor submitted and the spirit of popular liberty established its claims. Matthews died in 1660. The Burgesses convened, declared afresh their inherent powers of sovereignty and elected Sir William Berkeley governor. Thus steadily intent upon securing the liberty which they engaged, the Virginians established the supremacy of the popular branch, the freedom of trade, religious toleration, exemption from foreign taxation and the universal elective franchise.

PART X.

ORIGIN AND PROGRESS OF MARYLAND COLONIES.

The settlement of Maryland in 1632 was in several respects different from that of Virginia or Massachusetts. The former had many perilous and hard struggles before its existence and liberties were secured; the latter put forth many sincere but fruitless efforts to establish itself on a foundation of theocracy, where private judgment and religious toleration should obtain no resting place. Maryland, too, furnishes the first instance in which the local proprietary was exempt from the control of the crown and from the power of parliamentary taxation. In 1624, about the beginning of James the First's reign, George Calvert, a native of Yorkshire and a graduate of Oxford, was so popular in his own county, by far the largest in England, as to be chosen its representative in Parliament, and was so great a favorite at court as to have become one of the secretaries of state. (1619) Calvert, however, had sometime previously become a convert to the Romish church. With honorable candor he avowed his opinions and tendered the resignation of his office. Far, however, from losing the influence he had obtained he was loaded with fresh favors and soon after created an Irish peer by the title of Lord Baltimore. He had been one of the original associates of the Virginia Company and had tried an experimental colony of his own (1622) at Avalon on the island of Newfoundland. After having twice visited it and expended in the attempt at colonization more than $100,000, he at length resolved to abandon it. He then turned his attention to Virginia, where he met with little encouragement, to engage in a settlement. The oath of allegiance was so framed that no Roman Catholic could conscientiously subscribe to it. He thus became desirous of obtaining a settlement to which those of like faith with himself might repair unmolested; and on his return to England he had little difficulty in obtaining from Charles I. a grant of a considerable tract on the Potomac river, which in compliment to the queen, Henrietta Maria, he denominated it Maryland. Lord Baltimore was a man of clear and comprehensive mind and of high and generous character. (1632) He appreciated the necessity of a popular government, as well as of its independence of the despotism of the crown, and thus the charter which gave to him and to his heirs the absolute proprietorship in the soil together with the power of making necessary laws, was coupled with the condition that nothing should be enacted without the advice and consent of the Freemen of the province. Nothing was enacted but what was in spirit, if not in letter, consonant with the laws of England. The boundary of his grant was the Potomac, with a line due east from its mouth across the Chesapeake bay and the peninsula called Eastern Shore; on the east it had the ocean and Delaware bay; on the north the fortieth degree of latitude, the southern boundary to the great New England Patent, and on the west, a line due north from the westernmost head of the Potomac. Before the patent had passed through all the formalities Lord Baltimore died, but the charter was issued and confirmed to his son, Cecilius Calvert, whose zealous energies were devoted to the carrying out of his father's purposes. Considerable opposition was excited against the charter and its privileges by William Clayborne, (1633) secretary of and one of the council of Virginia. Clayborne's appeal to the privy council was set aside, and orders were sent to Virginia insisting upon a good understanding being maintained, and forbidding that either should entertain fugitives from the other.

Leonard Calvert, a son of the first Lord Baltimore, was appointed by his brother Cecil to the command of the company destined to found the colony of Maryland. They embarked in the Ark and Dove in November, 1633, proceeded by way of the West Indies and early next year, 1634, arrived in the Chesapeake. The number of new settlers was about two hundred, mostly Roman Catholic, and many of them ranking among the gentry. They were courteously received by Governor Harvey, and had no difficulty in fixing upon a site for a settlement. Calvert entered the Potomac and upon a spot about to be abandoned by the Indians, and was ceded by them the next year in full to the emigrants, he built the little village of St. Mary's. In August of the present year (1634) Calvert sent the Dove to Massachusetts with a cargo of corn to exchange for fish, but notwithstanding the friendly advances of Calvert backed by Harvey of Virginia, the Puritans received them with anything but cordiality. Some sharp words passed between the ship's people and the inhabitants, and when the Dove was allowed to depart the master was charged "to bring no more such disorderly persons." Clayborne's hostility did not sleep. Besides trying to injure the colonists with the Indians, he even ventured to fit out a small vessel under color of his exclusive right to trade, and gave orders to capture all the water crafts of the colonists. Two armed boats from St. Mary's pursued the vessel, an engagement took place; several lives were lost and the officers made prisoners. Clayborne escaped to Virginia, and was demanded by Calvert as a fugitive from justice, (1635) but Harvey declined giving him up and he was sent to England. Colonization proceeded steadily, though not rapidly. During the first two years he expended (1636) nearly $200,000 on the colony. The first colonial assembly was held in 1635; they passed a body of laws that the proprietary rejected. Soon after he sent over a collection of statutes, which he had drawn up, to be laid (1638) before the second assembly. That body refused to admit the proprietary's claim or to adopt the laws prepared by him. Lord Baltimore, with great good sense, yielded the point, and a third assembly (1639) was held, at which the first statutes of Maryland were enacted. The assemblies of the three following years maintained the principle of toleration firmly and steadily and in 1639 "an act of toleration" was enacted by both houses of assembly. A profession of belief in the doctrine of the Trinity was required and blasphemy was punished, but with this limitation, the terms of the statute forbade any interference in, or even reproachful censure of, the private opinions or modes of worship already established among the citizens. In 1643, during the civil-war in England, Clayborne, urged by a desire for revenge, stirred up rebellion in the province. Repossessing himself of the Isle of Kent while Calvert was in England and Giles Bent in charge of the administration, early in 1645 the rebels were triumphant; but Calvert obtained assistance from Virginia, suppressed the rebellion, (1646) though not without bloodshed, and in a short space of time rightful authority resumed its sway. Calvert died in 1647; Thomas Green succeeded him, but Lord Baltimore deemed it advisable to displace him in 1648 and appoint William Stone, a zealous Protestant and Parliamentarian, as governor of Maryland. But after the execution of Charles First, and Charles Second ascending the throne, he appointed Sir William Davenant governor without regard to the chartered rights of Lord Baltimore. Maryland was now claimed by four separate aspirants. In 1652 Stone was deposed but reinstated on submission. Stone re-established Lord Baltimore's authority in full, which brought Clayborne again into the field. The government was taken away from Stone and retaliatory ordinances passed against the Papists. (1655) Stone next year himself, blamed by Lord Baltimore, engaged in an attempt to put down his opponents, but without any success, himself being taken prisoner and narrowly escaping death, to which his principal adherents were condemned. In 1656, Josiah Fendel was appointed by Lord Baltimore as governor, and for a time the colony was divided between two ruling factions, the Romanists at St. Mary's and the Puritans at St. Leonard's. In March, 1658, a compromise was effected, and Fendel acknowledged. Just before the restoration of Charles II. the assembly of Maryland, as in case of Virginia, (1660) took occasion to assert its ligitimate and paramount authority, and Philip Calvert was established firmly in the position of governor. The population of Maryland at this date is estimated at ten thousand, and despite the various trials and troubles which marked its earlier history, the colony gradually increased in wealth and numbers.

PART XI.

PROGRESS OF NEW NETHERLAND.

NEW YORK AND NEW JERSEY.

New Netherland in 1638 had fallen under the administration of William Kieft. He protested against Swedish colonization on the Delaware and to the encroachments of the New England people on the Connecticut, which was all unsuccessful. Valuable privileges were offered to settlers, the Patroonships were limited, the monopoly of the Indian trade was relinquished, the Dutch Reformed Church was declared to be the established religion which was publicly taught, etc. The English settlement at Red Hill, now New Haven, was considered by the Dutch an alarming encroachment on their territorial rights. Long Island was claimed by Lord Sterling's agents, and under that claim insult was offered by a party from Lynn, Massachusetts, (1640) who attempted to settle on the western end of the island. They pulled down the Dutch coat of arms, and put up an indecent caricature. The Dutch made prisoners of them and on their apologizing allowed them to retire to the eastern barren end of the island (1641) where they founded Southampton and put themselves under the jurisdiction of Connecticut. Other efforts made by New England colonists resulted in the founding of Stratford, Stamford and Greenwich. In fact, the inhabitants had increased so rapidly that an English secretary was found necessary, and George Baxter was appointed to fill the office. The people of New Haven wished to found a settlement on Delaware bay, and some fifty families set out for this purpose. On touching at New Amsterdam Kieft sent two sloops to break up the settlement. About the same date serious troubles began to arise with the Indians. (1642) Soon after a Dutchman was murdered by a Hackensack Indian who had been made drunk and robbed. Keift would have no redress but that of blood. While this dispute was yet unsettled the Tappan Indians fled to the Dutch on being attacked by the Mohawks, (1643) and it was while they were thus trusting to the hospitality of white men that the detestible plan was hastily and wickedly formed to cut them off. In spite of the remonstrances of the best men in the colony the cry for blood prevailed, and in February, 1643, the shrieks of the victims were heard even across the icy river. Warriors, old men, women and children were slain without mercy to the number of eighty or more; infants with their mothers perished in the river; the wounded were killed the next morning in cold blood, and about thirty prisoners were taken to New Amsterdam. Retaliation followed as a matter of course. Eleven tribes joined together to make war on the Dutch. The scattered boweries extended twenty and thirty miles to the north and east, were furiously attacked, houses were burned, men, women and children killed and carried into captivity; the colonists fled in terror to New Amsterdam. Kieft was bitterly reproached for what had happened, and a fast was proclaimed. The Indians, their revenge satiated for the time, soon made advances for peace and a treaty was arranged early in the spring of the same year, (1643) but war broke out again in the autumn. Great distress and a wretched condition was the result of the colony. It was at this date that " a good solid fence" or stockade was erected as a protection to New Amsterdam, where the far famed Wall street, New York, now stands.

Various expeditions against the Indians occurred during 1643 and 1644 and with ultimate success. The horrors of the Pequod massacre were to some extent acted over again. Kieft's conduct was warmly complained of by the "eight men" in an appeal to Holland respecting the war, and it was not till August, 1645, that a treaty of peace was agreed upon and a day of thanksgiving appointed. The settlements about New Amsterdam were almost ruined by the late war, and hardly a hundred men could be mustered; only five or six remained out of some thirty flourishing boweries, and it appeared on examination that New Netherland up to this time (1645) had cost the West India Company more than $200,000 over and above all receipts.

Kieft become more and more unpopular by his tyranny, exaction and arbitrary exercise of lawful authority. It was high time to supercede him and appoint a new director. Accordingly Petrus Stuyvesant, (1646) governor of Curacoa, a staunch old soldier, was appointed director-general of New Netherland, with New Amsterdam the sole port of entry. Poor Kieft, having freighted a vessel with a cargo of furs worth about $100,000 he set sail for home, was wrecked on the coast of Wales, and himself with some eighty others was lost. (1647) The general opinion was, if Winthrop may be credited, that this calamity was a mark of divine displeasure against such as had opposed or injured God's poor people of New England, "so prone are men to pronounce harsh and uncharitable judgments respecting calamities which it pleases God to send upon individuals." On Stuyvesant's assuming the director-generalship of the government in May, 1647, the colony was far from being in a prosperous condition, as compared with Virginia, Maryland and New England. The former numbered some twenty thousand inhabitants and New England about as many, while New Netherland had hardly three thousand including the Swedes on the Delaware. Beverswick, the site of the present city of Albany, was a hamlet of ten houses; New Amsterdam was a village of wooden huts with roofs of straw and chimneys of mud and sticks, and a large proportion of rum shops and shops for the sale of tobacco and beer. The united colonies of New England sent Stuyvesant a congratulatory letter on his arrival, (1647) but wound up with numerous complaints. In September, 1650, an award was effected by the arbitrators appointed by the litigants in the case. "By this award all the eastern part of Long

Island, comprising the present county of Suffolk, was assigned to New England. The boundary between New Haven and New Netherland was to begin at Greenwich bay, to run northerly twenty miles into the country, and beyond, as it shall be agreed, but nowhere to approach the Hudson nearer than ten miles." Fugitives were to be mutually given up. Adventurers from New Haven undertook an expedition to the Delaware. Stuyvesant resisted the attempt and siezed the ship, (1651) detained the emigrants and built a fort—Fort Casimir—on the present site of New Castle.

In 1654 the Swedes by a stratagem got possession of Fort Casimir, but as Sweden no longer held rank of a formidable power, the company directed Stuyvesant to subdue the Swedes and take possession of the South bay and river. The year following, 1655, the director embarked for the Delaware with a force of six hundred men and without difficulty accomplished his object, so that New Sweden became again a part of New Netherland. The affairs of New Netherland seemed now to be decidedly on the improvement. Good friendly relations with Virginia, but with Maryland, however, there was some dispute. Further difficulties in 1659 occurred with the Indians. Murders on their part were followed by retaliatory steps on the part of the Dutch, and many lives were lost in consequence. A peace was made in 1660, but in 1663 the savages waiting for revenge on old Stuyvesant for sending away some Indians to the West Indies, attacked the settlers at Esopus with unpitying fury; late in the year the Indians were subdued and peace restored for a time. New England spirit seemed destined to be the plague of Stuyvesant's life. Connecticut was in pursuit of territory, and on obtaining a royal charter, (1662) began to press a claim to Long Island, West Chester, and in fact all land east of the Hudson. Unfortunately for Stuyvesant, the assembly could not yield him any assistance. The days of New Netherland were numbered. The Duke of York had bought up the claims of Lord Sterling, (1664) and in March, 1664, he had received from his brother, Charles II., a charter for a large and valuable tract between the Connecticut and the Delaware principally, and swallowing up entirely New Netherland, now New York.

PETER STUYVESANT.

Born in Friesland, Holland, 1602. First director of the Dutch West India Company in the province of New Netherland on the Hudson. Arrived at New Amsterdam May, 1647. Ruled until 1664, when he surrendered to the English, who named the town New York. He remained and died there August, 1682.

Prompt measures were adopted. Three ships, with six hundred soldiers, having on board Colonel Richard Nichols, Colonel George Cartwright, Sir Robert Carr and Samuel Maverick, were dispatched in August, 1664, to sieze upon New Netherland for the Duke of York. Rumors of their design had reached the city but no effectual defence had or could be made by the Dutch. Stuyvesant determined at least to put a bold front upon the matter; he sent in concert with the deputies to request of the English commander the reason of his appearance. Nichols replied by asserting the claims of England, and demanding an immediate surrender of New Amsterdam on conditions that lives, liberties and property of the inhabitants should be respected. Stuyvesant retorted by a spirited protest, detailing the manner in which the Dutch had obtained a lawful possession of the country, effecting to doubt whether " If his majesty of Great Britian were well informed of such passages, he would be too judicious to grant such an order as that by which he was summoned, especially in a time of profound peace." And reminding the commissioners that it was "a very considerable thing to affront so mighty a state as Holland, although it were not against an ally and confederate." Neither argument nor threats produced any effect upon the English commander, who refused to protract the negotiation and threatened an immediate attack upon the city. Mortifying as it was to an old soldier to surrender without a struggle, Stuyvesant was compelled to submit to the circumstances. The majority of the inhabitants were unwilling to run the risk of an assault to which they could not hope to offer any effectual opposition in defence of a government with which they were discontented, and against another which many among them were secretly disposed to welcome. A liberal capitulation was arranged, the rights and privileges of the inhabitants were guaranteed, and New Amsterdam quietly passed into the possession of the bold invaders—the English. A few days after Fort Orange, on the Hudson, capitulated, and the name of Albany bestowed upon it. A treaty was here concluded with five nations, whose hostilities had occasioned so much distress to the Dutch. Sir Robert Carr meanwhile entered the Delaware, and plundering and ill using the Dutch soon reduced them to submission. Thus it was that by a claim firmly persisted in and enforced without shedding a single drop of blood, New Netherland became an integral part of the growing and important colonial empire of England. The Dutch inhabitants readily acquiesced in the change of rulers, and even the sturdy Governor Stuyvesant, attached to the country, spent the remainder of his life in New York. It seems but fair in the history of New York to quote the words of Mr. Brodhead, who claims that the Dutch have hardly received justice at the hands of American historians.

New Netherland, while in the possession of the Dutch, had three governors, viz.: Van Twiller, Kieft and Stuyvesant. The latter surrendered to the English New Netherland, and thereby the Dutch lost all their claim to the New World.

The reduction of New Netherland was now accomplished. All that could be further done was to change the name; and, to glorify one of the most bigoted princes in English history, the royal province was ordered to be called New York. The flag of England was at length triumphantly displayed where for half a century that of Holland had rightfully waved; and from Virginia to Canada the king of Great Britian was sovereign. This treacherous and violent seizure of the territory and possesions of an unsuspecting ally was no less a breach of private justice than of public faith. New Jersey was established at this date. (1664) The country between the Hudson and the Delaware had been conveyed by the Duke of York to Lord Berkeley and Sir George Carteret. The latter had been governor of the island of Jersey, and thus was the name of the province New Jersey derived. The proprietaries offered the most favorable terms to settlers— absolute freedom of worship and a colonial assembly. Having the sole power of taxation many were attracted to New Jersey; it was considered almost a paradise on account of its liberal institutions and beauty of the climate. (1670) Philip Carteret was appointed governor and attempted to collect the quit-rents for the proprietaries in 1670 which caused much discontent and finally broke out into open insurrection. In 1673 war having been declared between England and Holland, through the artifices of Louis XIV., a Dutch fleet suddenly appeared before

New York; a general disaffection prevailed among the citizens, and Colonel Manning, who in the absence of Governor Lovelace held possession of the fort with a small body of English soldiers, surrendered without resistance. He was afterwards adjudged guilty of cowardice and treachery. For a while New York was in the hands of the Dutch and under a Dutch governor, but by the treaty of Westminister it was mutually agreed that all conquests should be restored. New York again passed into the hands of the English. Soon after (1672) the taking of the province from the Dutch, Berkeley, one of the proprietors, disposed of his share of New Jersey to John Fenwick, of whom William Penn became one of the assigns. A dispute between the proprietors was settled by arbitration of Penn. This was the first appearance of his name in American history.

In 1676, by the partition of the province into two parts, called East and West Jersey, the latter became a colony of Quakers; and together with liberty of conscience, democratic equality was established. Large numbers of Quakers emigrated and the colony gave evidence of growth and prosperity. In 1682 East Jersey was purchased from the heirs of Carteret by twelve Quakers under the auspices of Penn, and in 1683 the proprietors increased their number to twenty-four. They obtained a new patent from the Duke of York. During the two following years New Jersey afforded refuge to numbers of Scotch Presbyterians who escaped for their lives from home. Freedom of trade had been established in New Jersey. This was quite obnoxious to Andros, the new governor of New York, and he attempted to put a stop to it, but to no avail. These high handed measures roused the Quakers to remonstrances; Penn drew up a document, mild in tone, yet firm in asserting constitutional rights, but everything went unfavorable for the Duke of York, and by the advice of Penn was at length compelled to yield, and Dongan, a Roman Catholic, was sent as governor empowered to accede to the wishes of the colonists and to summon the freeholders to choose their representatives. Accordingly, on the 17th of October, 1683, a meeting was held, which was the first popular assembly in the state of New York, consisting of the governor and ten councilmen, with seventeen deputies elected by freeholders. A declaration of rights was passed, trial by jury confirmed, taxes levied only by the consent of the assembly. Every freeholder was entitled to a vote for the representatives, and religious liberty was declared. One of their acts was entitled "The Charter of Liberties and Privileges Granted by His Royal Highness to the Inhabitants of New York and its Dependencies." The following year (1684) the affairs of their flattering prospects was sadly interrupted by the accession of the Duke of York to the throne of England under the title of James II. Dongan had a new commission granted him in 1685 authorizing him to enact laws and impose additional taxes. As in the case of Effingham in Virginia, he was specially charged to allow no printing. The press was regarded a dangerous element among people situated as the colonists mostly were. Dongan in 1686 also gave a charter to the city of Albany and bestowed upon Robert R. Livingston a sort of feudal principality on the Hudson river near Albany known as Livingston Manor.

The present city of Albany is the capital of the state of New York, and is the second city in the state in point of population. It is situated on the western bank of the Hudson river, about one hundred and fifty miles north of New York. Albany was first settled in 1612 by the Dutch, and with the exception of Jamestown, in Virginia, which dates from 1607, and St. Augustine, Florida, is the oldest town in the Union. It was originally a Dutch fort called Fort Orange. Somewhat later it took the name of Beaverwick and also Williamstadt; the latter it retained till 1664, when the colony fell into the hands of the English. Its present name is derived from James II., to whom, when Duke of York and Duke of Albany, Charles II. granted the proprietorship of the colony.

ROBERT R. LIVINGSTON.

Born in New York City, 1747. Graduated at King's College, 1764. Studied law under Chief Justice Smith. Was Secretary of State from organization of the Federal Government until 1783, when he became Chancellor of the State of New York. Administered the oath to President Washington April 30, 1789. Minister to France, 1801. Died February 26, 1813.

PART XII.

UNITED COLONIES OF NEW ENGLAND.

New Hampshire, still in its infancy, sought and obtained annexation on favorable terms with her powerful neighbor, Massachusetts. Not long after, in 1643, the various colonies in New England feeling the need of mutual aid, formed a confederation under the name of "The United Colonies of New England." It consisted of the colonies of Massachusetts, New Plymouth, Connecticut and New Haven. These colonies entered into a firm and perpetual bond of friendship and amity, for offence and defence for their own mutual welfare. This confederacy, which was declared to be perpetual, continued until James II. deprived the New England colonies of their charters. Gorton, expelled from Plymouth, (1637) retired to the vicinity of Providence, became involved in a dispute with the inhabitants He was cited to appear before the magistrates of Boston, but he preferred to retire still farther from their reach. He purchased some land at Shawomet of Miantonimoh, the Narragansett chief, but the rightfulness of this grant was denied by two inferior sachems, and again Gorton was summoned to the Boston court. He replied with a denial of jurisdiction of Massachusetts' courts and he was clearly in the right. He offered to submit the case to the arbitration of the other colonists, but he was siezed, taken to Boston, tried, and with his adherents convicted on the charge of being a blasphemous subverter of true religion and civil government, and with many of his adherents sentenced to death. The sentence was commuted in 1644, and Gorton and his followers were imprisoned at hard labor during the winter, mercilessly deprived of their cattle and stores, were finally released and expelled. Gorton returned to England but failed to obtain redress. Miantonimoh, the Narragansett chief, was deadly hostile to Uncas, the sachem of the Mohegans. (1643) Having fallen into the hands of Uncas, he was by the advice of the colonial commissioners, savagely put to death. The war which had protracted sometime was finally brought to a close by the colonists. It was in March of 1643 that the venerated Roger Williams proceeded to England to solicit a charter. While in England he published his "Key to the Language of America," which contained interesting notices of the Indian manners.

He also attacked the principle of religious despotism in his "Bloody Tenet of Persecution for the Cause of Conscience," to which Cotton replied in a tract called the "Bloody Tenet Washed and made White in the Blood of the Lamb." Williams was successful in the object for which he had visited England. Vane favored his wishes and added his influence. The charter obtained included the shores and islands of Narragansett bay west of Plymouth and south of Massachusetts as far as the Pequod river and country. The name of Providence Plantations was adopted, and the inhabitants were empowered to rule themselves as they might choose. "The first legislator who fully recognized the rights of conscience was Roger Williams, a name less illustrious than it deserves to be. After some wanderings he pitched his tent at a place to which he gave the name of Providence, and there became the founder and legislator of the colony of Rhode Island. It deserves to be put on record that in 1648 Massachusetts set the first example of an execution for witchcraft. The unhappy victim was a woman named Margaret Jones, who was charged with having "a malignant touch." The Quakers were a sect which took its rise in England about 1644 under the preaching of George Fox. Their belief was peculiar and was denounced as anti-Christian and intolerable.

While Cromwell had declared that "he that prays best and preaches best will fight best," the Quakers denied the right to defensive warfare and refused to bear arms. Their "yea was yea, and their nay was nay." They believed every man and woman at liberty to preach if he or she was moved to do so and regarded a settled ministry as hirelings and wolves amid the flock. Accordingly in July, 1656, two women came from Barbadoes, Mary Fisher and Ann Austin, looked upon as possessed by the devil; they were speedily arrested, imprisoned for five weeks and their books burned; they were sent out of the colony. The Quakers—Robinson, Stephenson and Mary Dyer persisting in proving the penalty denounced against them, were tried and condemned. The younger Winthrop sought to prevent their execution. Many thought it would be foolish and cruel to proceed to extremities, but the will of the majority prevailed and Stephenson and Robinson were brought to the scaffold. "I die for Christ," said Robinson. "We suffer not as evil doers but for conscience sake," said Stephenson. (1659) Mary Dyer, with crape around her neck, after witnessing the execution of her two companions, exclaimed: "Let me suffer as my brethren, unless you will annul your wicked laws." At the intercession of her son she was almost forced from the scaffold, on condition of leaving the colony in eight and forty hours. After her trial she addressed from her prison an energetic remonstrance against the cruelty of the council: "Woe is me for you; ye are disobedient and decieved. You will not repent that you were kept from shedding blood, though it was a woman." She returned to defy the tyrants of the "Bloodytown" and to seal her testimony against them with her life. She was taken and hanged on Boston common in June, 1660.

The labors of John Eliot, the Indian missionary, deserves a passing notice. He was born in England in 1604, was educated at Cambridge, and emigrated to New England in 1631. Earnestly desiring the spiritual improvement of the Indians, Eliot, though discharging the duties of a minister over a church at Roxbury, added to his regular charge and toil of learning the dialect spoken in New England, so as to translate the Bible for the benefit of the natives. He began his efforts as far back as

1645, preaching his first sermon to the Indians on the 28th of October, 1646. Eliot died in 1690, full in years, charity and honors.

The founders of New England, to their credit be it said, were anxious to promote sound learning. Free schools and grammar schools were provided, a sort of training college had been established at Newtown, a suburb of Boston, which Mr. John Harvard at his death in 1638 endowed with his library and half his estate. The college was styled after the name of its generous benefactor, and the place was called Cambridge after the famous university in England. By annual grants, donations, etc., the new college was enabled to lay a foundation of its future strength and influence. It was at Cambridge about 1640 that the first printing press in America was set up. Who could then have dreamed what less than two hundred and fifty years has brought forth, or have predicted the mighty power of the press in the nineteenth century.

PART XIII

NEW ENGLAND UNDER CHARLES II. AND JAMES II.

It was with no little anxiety that the New England colonists watched the rapid progress of that revolution in the mother country which led to the restoration of Charles II. to the throne of England; and it was on the same vessel which brought the news to Boston in July, 1660, that brought also two of the regicide judges—Whalley and Goffe—who had fled to the New World to escape the vengeance of the son of Charles I. Soon after, however, in 1661, an order arrived for the arrest of Whalley and Goffe, but they had retired to New Haven. In the struggle which it was evident was approaching, the leaders in New England felt that they must trust, under providence, mainly to their own determined energies. At length after more than a year's delay Charles II. was formally proclaimed, but all demonstration was strictly forbidden. Besides the enemies of the colonists in England there were many active opponents of the ruling party at home. Even among the theocratic freemen themselves there was a diversion of opinion, but the majority sternly resolved to maintain their independence of English supremacy whatever might be the issue, to avert, however, if possible, the necessity of a recourse to an armed resistance. Weary of the unsettled state of things in the last days of the commonwealth all classes had welcomed the restoration. Charles promised everything, but his promises were very soon forgotten. The Royalist party had to the utmost gratified their thirst for revenge. Such of the regicides as could be taken were hung, drawn and quartered. Among them Hugh Peters, father-in-law to young Winthrop and minister to Salem. A more illustrious victim, Sir Henry Vane, was soon after conducted to the block. In 1662, on the 23d of April, Winthrop obtained a patent under the great seal, granting the most ample privileges and confirming to the Connecticut colony, and such as should be admitted freemen, on all the lands formally granted to the Earl of Warwick and by him transferred to Lord Say-and-Sele and his associates. A very large part of Providence Plantations having been included in the charter of Connecticut, Clarke and Winthrop entered into an agreement by which Poweatuck was fixed upon for the limit between the two colonies.

This agreement, as Mr. Hildreth says, was set forth in the (1663) charter of Rhode Island and Providence Plantations. While Connecticut and Rhode Island were rejoicing in the privileges of their charters Massachusetts was uneasy and unwilling to any submission. The commissioners, Nichols, Carr, Cartwright and Maverick, arrived in Boston in July prepared to enter upon the work, but they met coolness, and stedfast and determined opposition. The commissioners were recalled in 1666. Under the influence of mortified feelings they had made such a report that the king issued an order that Bellingham, the governor, and some others, should proceed to England to answer for their defiance of his majesty's authority.

At the end of fifty years from the arrival of the emigrants at Plymouth, the New England colonies are supposed to contain one hundred and twenty towns and probably sixty or seventy thousand inhabitants. The habits and industry and economy that had been formed in less happy times continued to prevail and give a competency to those who had nothing, and wealth to those who had competency. The wilderness receded before adventurous and hardy laborers, and its savage inhabitants found their game dispersed and their favorite haunts invaded. The Indians again became aroused to seek revenge. A leader was all that was wanted to direct their exertions, and Philip of Pokanoket, sachem of the Wompanoags, a tribe living within the boundary lines of Plymouth and Rhode Island, assumed that honorable but dangerous station. He exerted all the arts, intrigue, powers and persuasion of which he was master to the Indians in all parts of New England, to unite for the destruction of the whites. He succeeded in forming a confederacy able to send into action of three or four thousand warriors. In 1675 the bloody struggle commenced sooner than Philip intended. A hasty act of revenge placed him in open defiance of the colonists, and he had no other alternative but yield or to carry out his plans. Philip plundered the houses nearest Mount Hope, his residence. Soon after he attacked Swanzey and killed a number of the inhabitants; this was in June, 1675; the Indians fled and marked their course by burning houses, murdering and scalping the whites. The troops persued, but unable to overtake them, returned to Swanzey. The whole country was alarmed and the number of the troops augmented: panic prevailed throughout the colony. But the settlers fled for security to the towns, where they spread fearful accounts of the atrocities of the Indians. Meanwhile the war spread along the whole frontier of Connecticut, Massachusetts and New Hampshire; the villages were isolated; many were shot dead as they opened their doors; murder and savage barbarity was carried on to the disadvantage of the whites; provisions sent to their assistance were waylaid and seized and their escort cut off in ambush. Such was the fate of the brave Lothrop, at the spot which still retains the name of Bloody Brook. During the summer, the Indians being concealed in the woods and forests, were able to carry on a very harrassing and destructive warfare, but when winter came, the colonists by a vigorous effort raised a force of a thousand men and determined to strike a decided blow. Josiah Winslow, of Plymouth, was appointed commander-in-chief. On the 18th of December the troops formed a junction in the territory of the Narragansetts after a long march through the snow and a night spent in the woods, they approached the stronghold of the tribe. This was about one o'clock. The Indians had entrenched themselves on a rising ground in the midst of a swamp surrounded by a palisade. The leaders were all shot down as they made the charge, but this only excited the colonists on, who, after having once forced an entrance, had been repulsed after a fierce struggle for two hours, they burst infuriated into the Indian fort. Revenge for the blood of their murdered brethren was alone thought of. Mercy was implored in vain. The fort was fired, and hundreds of Indians' wives and children perished in the midst of the conflagration, while their provisions, gathered for a long winter, being consumed, and their wigwams burned, those who escaped from fire and sword wandered through the forests to perish with cold and hunger.

This was the most desperate battle recorded in the early annals of the country, but the victory was decisive. One thousand Indian warriors were killed; three hundred more and as many women and children taken prisoners, yet the price of the victory was dear indeed. Six captains and eighty men were killed and one hundred and fifty men were wounded. The Inddians were desperate; they vented their fury upon all who came within their reach. But their power (1677) was broken, and ere long began to fade out of sight. The leaders alone, Philip and Canonchet, sachem of the Narragansetts, refused to yield. The latter died rather than attempt to make peace with the whites. The unhappy Philip, the author of the war, wandered from tribe to tribe, assailed by reproaches for the misery he had brought upon his people and with a heart full of the bitterest anguish. Compelled, he returned to his old haunts, where he was sustained by Witamo, a female chief and relative, he was presently attacked by the English, who carried off his wife and child as captives; shortly after he was treachously shot by one of his own adherents who deserted to the English. Thus perished Philip of Pokanoket, who in many respects was worthy of a better fate. His child was sent to Bermuda and sold into slavery. Peace was welcome indeed.

In 1680, New Hampshire at the solicitiation of John Mason, to whose ancestor a part of the territory had been granted, was constituted a separate colony. Massachusetts, apprehending the loss of Maine, also purchased of the heirs of Gorges their claim to the soil and jurisdiction for about $6,000. Edward Randolph was sent over in July, 1680, as collector of the royal customs. The magistrates ignored his commission, and refused to allow him to act, so that he was compelled to go back to England. He speedily returned in February, 1682, with a royal letter demanding that agents be sent at once fully empowered to act for the colonies. In 1683 a *scire-facias* was issued in England, and in 1684 the charter was declared to be forfeited. Thus the rights and liberties for sixty years of Massachusetts, so long and so dearly cherished, lay at the mercy of Charles II. who was known to meditate the most serious and fundamental innovations, but who died before any of them could be carried into effect. A temporary government was established by the appointment of Joseph Dudley, son of the former governor. Soon after, however, in 1686, James II. placed Sir Edmund Andros over the colonists. He came fully prepared to forward his arbitrary and tyrannical designs; he brought with him in the royal frigate two companies of troops to enforce his authority, if need be. Dudley was made chief justice and Randolph, the old antagonist, was made colonial secretary. The press, previously placed under his control, had been gagged; now it was entirely suppressed. Connecticut and Rhode Island suffered from the same arbitrary exercise of power. A writ of *quo warranto* had been issued and Andros repaired to Hartford and demanded the charter of the assembly then in session. "That body," says Trumbull, "was extremely reluctant and slow with respect (1667) to any resolve to surrender the charter, or with respect to any motion to bring it forth." The tradition is, Governor Treat strongly opposed to surrender the patent and privileges so dearly bought and so long enjoyed. The important affair was debated and kept in suspense until evening, when the charter was brought and laid upon the table where the assembly were sitting. By this time great numbers of people were assembled, and men sufficiently bold to enterprise whatever might be necessary or expedient. The lights were instantly extinguished and Capt. Wadsworth of Hartford, in the most silent and secret manner carried off the charter and secreted it in a large hollow tree fronting the house of the Honorable Samuel Wyllys, then one of the magistrates of the colony. The people appeared all peaceable and orderly. The candles were officiously relighted, but the charter was gone, and no discovery could be made of it, or of the person who had conveyed it away. Andros, however, declared the charter forfeited, and at the end of the records inscribed the expressive word, "Finis." The arbitrary proceedings of Andros were not continued for any great length of time. The infatuated James II was rapidly bringing on that crisis in England which resulted in his dethronement, and the revolution of 1688 effected a complete change in affairs not only at home but also in the colonial dependencies of England. The fate of Andros was wrapped up in that of the weak tyrant, his master, and his fall, so far as Massachusetts was concerned, was sudden and complete. Capt. Wadsworth was the originator of the "charter oak," so long known to our country.

PART XIV.

PROGRESS OF VIRGINIA AND MARYLAND COLONIES.

Sir William Berkeley, a staunch Royalist, had been elected governor by the Burgesses in 1660. At that date popular liberty and privileges were well established, as before noted. Important changes took place, by which the powers of the governors and councillors was increased in the exact proportions that those of the assembly and freemen were curtailed. A brief glance at them is all our space will admit. Originally settled by offshoots or adherents of English nobility, Virginia had received a more decidedly aristocratic influx of cavaliers who carried with them to the New World prejudices conferred by birth and a contemptuous disregard of rights and pretensions. Underlying this class was another of free descendants of the first settlers of inferior rank, and also indented servants who were bound to labor for a certain number of years, and were virtually in a state of serfdom. Negro slaves had also been introduced into the colony, and from the general work on the plantations negroes had largely increased in Virginia.

In 1661 Berkeley was sent to England to get relief, but without success, though he did succeed in getting for himself a share of the newly made province of North Carolina. Meanwhile the proceedings of the Virginia assembly were very much like those of the government of England. Intolerance obtained the ascendency, old edicts were revised and fresh ones enacted against Puritans, Baptists and Quakers, who were visited with fines and banishment, although it is but fair to say, Virginia did not like Massachusetts, hang and put to death the followers of George Fox. Education, too, was discouraged. "I thank God," are the words of Berkeley in 1671, "that there are no free schools, nor printing." "God keep us from both," he piously concluded. Such was the aim of the party in power to maintain the domination of a body of wealthy aristocratic planters over a submissive and ignorant commonalty and a still lower class of indented white servants and negro slaves.

The popular discontent was not allayed by the news that the prodigal, Charles II., had granted away the colony to Lord Culpepper and Lord Arlington, two courtiers whom it was necessary to satisfy. Measures were taken to see if these two claimants could be bought off. In 1673 Colonel Moryson, Secretary Ludwell and General Smith, were dispatched to England on this business, and the governor and assembly took the opportunity to solicit a royal charter. Their petition was granted, (1675) but was cut short by means of a rebellion in Virginia. The occasion of this popular outbreak was an Indian war; the man who presented himself as the leader was Nathaniel Bacon. Virginia had suffered too deeply from the treacherous Indians not to be predisposed, even after an interval of thirty years' peace. Certain outrages of the Indians had been resented by the planters, among others by John Washington, who had emigrated from the north of England and who became the founder of that family from which a century later sprung the illustrious father of his country. In 1676 Bacon was among the most earnest complainants. The people were greatly excited when the news came that the Indians had killed some of Bacon's servants. He instantly flew to arms, and being joined by some five or six hundred men, set off in pursuit of the enemy. The governor, looking upon this proceeding as an insult to his authority, proclaimed Bacon a rebel, deprived him of his seat in the council and called upon all those who respected his authority to disperse immediately. Governor Berkeley gathered a body of troops and proceeded to march after Bacon and his men, but his progress was arrested by an outbreak in the lower counties. His own authority at the capital passed out of his hands; the old assembly was dissolved and Bacon was among the newly elected Burgesses. Bacon having gotten together some four hundred men his demands had to be listened to, although the old fiery governor, it is said, tore open his dress, and exposing his naked breast, exclaimed, "Here, shoot me! 'Fore God! Fair mark! Shoot!" But Bacon not giving way to excitement, replied: "No, may it please your honor, we will not hurt a hair of your head nor of any other man's. We are come for a commission to save our lives from the Indians, which you have often promised, and now will have it before we go."

The insurgents also made the same demand, accompanied by menaces in case of refusal, against the assembly itself. The warm partisans of Bacon were content enough to give way before the popular movement and to compel the governor, though sorely against his will, to yield, and also to appoint Bacon to the command of the forces sent against the Indians. This point being settled the assembly proceeded to enact many salutary reforms popularly known as "Bacon's Laws," all tending to abate the exhorbitant pretention of the aristocratic party, and to restore to the mass of the people the privileges of which they had been deprived. But there was yet a further struggle between the contending parties. Hardly had Bacon set out on his work of subduing the Indians before Berkeley issued a proclamation denouncing Bacon as a rebel, setting a price on his head and commanding his followers to disperse. Indignant at this treatment Bacon immediately retraced his steps, and the governor fled in dismay from the capital. Steps were taken directly to reorganize the government, and elect new burgesses in October. Bacon set out again to carry on the war against the Indians. This led Berkely to contrive by promises of pay and plunder to recover his lost authority. Quite unexpectedly, he succeeded, but it was only a passing triumph. Bacon made a rapid descent from the upper country with an army that had just gained the victory at the Bloody Run. Jamestown was invested and speedily retaken; and further, to prevent its again being occupied by Berkeley, it was by Bacon's orders burned to the ground. Bacon was now completely victorious and at liberty to carry out his designs to their fullest extent. Precisely what he proposed, however, can never be known, for just at this juncture he was suddenly stricken down by the hand of death. This was in January, 1677. Bacon's supporters were mostly taken and Berkeley again restored to power, pursued a course of malignant revenge utterly disgraceful to his name and position. No less than twenty-five persons were executed during the few succeeding months. Horsford was hanged, and Drummond, formerly governor of South Carolina, shared the same fate. So furious had Berkeley become that the assembly protested. His conduct excited indignation in England. King Charles exclaimed, " The old fool has taken away more lives in that naked country than I did here in England for the murder of my father!" Berkley not long after returned to the mother country and in a brief space ended his days there.

The issue of Bacon's rebellion was injurious to the colony. The whole of " Bacon's Laws " enacted by the popular assembly was annulled. Oppressed with the still stricter navigation laws, reduced the price of their staple tobacco, supporting a body of English soldiers, forbidden even to set up a printing press, the Virginians had to bear their trials as best they might, in hope that a day of redress would sooner or later arrive. The grant of the colony to Arlington and Culpepper has been already mentioned. The latter nobleman had obtained the cession of his partner's share in 1680 and had been invested with the office of governor for life as the successor of Berkeley. Culpepper's administration was one of greediness, by means of perquisites and peculation. After thus conducting his admistration for three years he was glad to surrender his patent and take in its place a pension of about $2,400. In 1684 Lord Howard Effingham succeeded Culpepper as governor. He was of the same stripe and quite surpassed his predecessor in extorting money. At this period Maryland was in a prosperous condition. Lord Baltimore's wise and prudent measures had rendered Maryland more successful to the proprietary than any other of the American colonies. In his old age he obtained a handsome return for s heavy outlays. At his death the province had ten counties, ith about sixteen thousand inhabitants, the largest part of hom were Protestants. (1676)

PART XV.

ORIGIN OF THE CAROLINAS.

Charles the First granted a patent to Sir Robert Heath, his attorney general, in 1630, for a tract southward of Virginia, to be called Carolina, but does not appear to have led to a settlement. Heath's patent was declared void, the conditions not being fulfilled. Different points, however, in this fertile region, during the fifteen or twenty years following was occupied by emigrants. Certain persons suffering from religious difficulties in Virginia fled to the banks of the Chowan, north of Albemarle sound. A small party of New Englanders settled near the mouth of Cape Fear river about 1660, but as the land was not productive and the Indians not well disposed, the greater part of the emigrants returned home. Contributions were forwarded by Massachusetts in 1667 to the relief of those who remained and were in great distress. Soon after the restoration a body of noblemen of the highest rank—the Earl of Clarendon, Monk Duke of Albemarle, Lords Berkeley, Craven and Ashley, Sir George Carteret, Sir John Colleton and Sir William Berkeley (1663) begged for a certain country in the parts of America not yet cultivated and planted, and inhabited by barbarous people "who had no knowledge of God." Charles II. readily granted their petition and erected out of the territory south of the Chesapeake the new province of Carolina, embracing the region from Albemarle sound southward to the river St. Johns and westward to the Atlantic. The charter empowered the eight joint proprietaries named above to enact and publish any laws which they should judge necessary with the assent, advice, approbation of the freemen of the colony; to erect courts of judication and appoint civil judges, magistrates and officers; to erect forts, castles, cities and towns; to make war, and in case of necessity to exercise martial law; to build harbors, make ports and enjoy the customs and subsidies imposed with the consent of the freemen on goods loaded and unloaded. One of the provisions of this charter deserves special notice. The king authorized the proprietaries to allow the inhabitants of the province such dispensations in religious affairs as they in their discretion should think proper and reasonable; and no person to whom such liberty should be granted was to be molested, punished, or called in question for any differences in speculative opinions with respect to religion, provided he did not disturb the civil order and peace of the community.

Some planters from Barbadoes after examining the coast of Carolina entered into an agreement with the proprietaries to remove to Cape Fear river, near the neglected settlement of the New Englanders. Sir John Yeamans, one of their number, (1665) was appointed governor of the new district, which received the name of Clarendon. He made things easy for the New Englanders, from which the greatest emigration were expected. He also opened a profitable trade and arranged the general affairs of the colony with great prudence and success. The proprietaries of Carolina were desirous of making still larger additions to their territory. Accordingly, in June, 1665, they obtained a second charter which extended the limits of Carolina both northwardly and southwardly, and by an additional grant in 1667 the Bahama islands were also conveyed to the same proprietaries. Every freeman of Carolina was declared to possess absolute power and authority over his negro slaves, of what opinion or religion soever. After a long delay three vessels were sent out with a body of emigrants under the command of Captain William Sayle. An expense of £12,000 was incurred in providing necessaries for the plantation of the colony. Touching at Port Royal, they found traces of the fort erected by the Huguenots.

They finally settled at a spot between two rivers, which they called the Ashley and the Cooper, the family names of Lord Shaftesbury, and where they laid the original foundation of Charlestown: whence they removed some years after to the commodious situation occupied by the present city. Before this removal took place, Sayle died, and was succeeded by Sir John Yeamans. (1672) Slave labor soon became established in Carolina to the soil and climate of which it was peculiarly adapted. Yeamans introduced a body of negroes from Barbadoes, who afterward recruited so largely that they were twice as numerous as the whites. Sothel, lately banished from Albemarle, appeared on the field. (1690) He put himself at the head of the opposition: a new assembly was called. Colleton was deposed and banished and Sothel was installed in his place. Notwithstanding these difficulties the progress of the Carolinas both the northern and southern settlements, were securely planted, with the reasonable prospect of a prosperous future.

PART XVI.

WILLIAM PENN AND PENNSYLVANIA.

The name of William Penn is one of the most eminent in American colonial history, and well deserves the esteem and respect with which it has been and is regarded by philanthropists and patriots. This remarkable man was the only son of Admiral Penn, distinguished during the protectorate of Cromwell by the conquest of the island of Jamaica, and afterwards by his conduct and courage during the war with Holland, in the reign of Charles II., with whom and his brother, the Duke of York, he was a great favorite. (1661) Young Penn was entered at Oxford at the period when the Quakers persisted in their offensive tenets. Through the earnestness of one of their preachers, the son of the admiral became converted to the doctrines of the new sect, and entering upon an enthusiastic advocacy of his views, he was fined and expelled from the university. The exasperated old admiral, his father, at first beat him and turned him out of doors, but afterwards sent him on a tour of Europe. On his return to London for the purpose of studying the law at Lincoln's Inn he was considered quite a "modish fine gentleman." "The glory of the world," he says, "overtook me, and I was ever ready to give up myself unto it." At once he entered upon the career of preaching his beloved doctrines. For this he was imprisoned in Ireland, and on his return home his father for the second time expelled him from home. But the spirit of Penn was too high and calm to be intimidated or exasperated. "Tell my father," he said, after having been sent to the Tower, "that my prison shall be my grave before I will budge a jot, for I owe my conscience to no mortal man; I have no need of fear; God will make amends for all." He was at length released through the influence of the Duke of York, the friend of his father as well of himself. The high spirited old admiral on his death bed, became fully reconciled to his son. His father had bequeathed to him a claim against the government for £16,000. As it was almost hopeless to expect the liquidation of this debt from a king like Charles II., Penn became desirous of obtaining in lieu of it a grant of American territory, a wish that the Duke of York and the leading courtiers at length enabled him to realize. "This day," he observes in a letter dated January 5, 1681, "after many waitings, watchings, solicitings and disputes, my country was confirmed to me under the great seal of England, with large powers and privileges. By the name of Pennsylvania, a name the king gave it in honor of my father, I chose New Wales, being a hilly country; and when the secretary, a Welshman, refused to call it New Wales, I proposed Sylvania, and they added Penn to it, though I much opposed him and went to the king to have it stricken out. He said 'twas past, and he would take it upon him. Thou mayst communicate my grant," he adds, "to my friends and expect shortly my proposals. 'Tis a dear and just thing and my God that given it me through many difficulties will, I believe, bless and make it the seed of a good nation. I shall have a tender care to the government that it be well laid at first." The charter differed but little from that of Maryland. It created Penn "true and absolute lord" of Pennsylvania, with ample powers of government, but "the advice and consent of the freemen of the province" were necessary to the enactment of laws. A vote was reserved to the Crown and to Parliament the right of levying duties and taxes. In England (May, 1681) a company was formed, and three vessels set sail in July with a body of emigrants for the shores of the Delaware. Early in 1682 Penn issued his "Frame of Government." In order to prevent all future pretence of

WILLIAM PENN.

Born in London, October, 1644. Educated at Oxford. Became a Quaker while a student and was driven from home and imprisoned by his father. Returned to the Quakers and was chosen preacher. Procured a grant of present Pennsylvania, 1681. Founded Philadelphia. Died July 30, 1718.

claim on the part of the Duke of York, or his heirs. Penn obtained of the Duke his deed of release for it. Penn set sail, accompanied by a hundred emigrants, and during the year was followed by twenty ships, all of which arrived in safety. At length, toward the end of October, the ship entered the broad and majestic Delaware and came to an anchor at New Castle.

As soon as the news of Penn's arrival spread abroad, the magistrates and settlers flocked together to greet him at the court house. His title deeds were produced and he conciliated the assembled multitude with promises of civil and religious freedom. The tract at the confluence of the Schuylkill and the Delaware having appeared to Penn very desirable for the location of his capital city, that locality was fixed upon early in 1683. It was entitled Philadelphia, meaning "brotherly love." In August, 1684, Penn set sail for home, having firmly planted and organized his province, and leaving judicial affairs in the hands of five judges chosen from the council, with Nicholas Moore for chief justice, Lloyd president of the council and Markham, secretary.

Pennsylvania, when Penn returned to England, contained already twenty settlements and seven thousand inhabitants. (1685.) It may be worth noting that the charter of Pennsylvania was the only one in America against which a *quo warranto* was not issued. In 1689 the third printing press in America was set up in Philadelphia. Penn also in the same year gave a charter to a public high school. The downfall of James was fatal to Penn's favor at court and subjected him to severe trials. Penn himself, however, was very soon deprived, by order of the privy council, of the administration of colonial affairs in both Delaware counties and also in Pennsylvania.

Part XVII.

THE FRENCH COLONIAL ENTERPRISE.

In 1626 the Mohawks having prevented the French from occupying the upper waters of the Hudson and cut off all progress towards the south, Franciscan missionaries who had accompanied Champlain to Canada, were led to penetrate along the northern shore of Lake Ontario till they reached the rivers flowing into Lake Huron. When Canada was restored to the French in 1632 Jesuits obtained the vast missionary ground which New France laid open to their efforts. In 1635 a Jesuit college was established at Quebec. The French missionaries were not favored with any success among the Iroquois, or Five Nations or allied communities comprising the Senecas, the Cayugas, the Onondagas, Oneidas and the Mohawks. These occupied the country between the banks of the St. Lawrence and the Hudson.

Some Frenchmen had ventured to establish a colony at Oswego. Collisions took place with the Indians and a third time war again burst forth. The distress was now so extreme that the company of New France, reduced to a mere handfull, resigned in 1662 to the king. The protection implored by the Jesuits was afforded, and a French regiment commanded by Tracy, (1665) a measure which at length effectually restrained the persevering hostility of the Five Nations. Under this favorable change of affairs Allouez coasted Lake Superior, and two years later in company with Dablon and Marquette, established the mission of St. Mary, the first white settlement within the limits of our northwestern states. Various missions were established and explorations made. Fired by the rumors of a great river in the west, Marquette was presently sent by the Intendant Talon to search it out. Accompanied by Joliet, a merchant of Quebec, with five Frenchmen and two Algonquin guides, they ascended on the 10th of June, 1673, to the head of Fox river. Carrying their canoes across the intervening ground which separates the eastern from the western streams they launched their canoes again upon the waters of the Wisconsin river. For seven days they floated down the stream, when at length to their great joy they emerged (1673) upon the " mighty father of waters," the Mississippi, that "great river"—for so its name imports—rolling through vast verdant prairies dotted with herds of buffalo and its banks overhung with primitive forests. With the feelings of men who have discovered a new world they passed the mouths of the Des Moines, the Illinois, the Missouri and Ohio. Keeping on as far as the Arkansas, they landed to visit the astonished Indians upon the shores, who received them with hospitality and invited them to form a permanent settlement. As they floated on day after day, they were greeted by richer scenery and by a different climate. Joliet, satisfied that the river must empty into the Gulf of Mexico, and fearful of falling into the hands of the Spaniards, reluctantly turned his steps back again towards Canada. Leaving Marquette at Green Bay at his missionary work, Joliet carried the news to Quebec. Marquette's health soon after gave way, and while engaged in missionary efforts among the Illinois, he died, May 18, 1675, at the age of thirty-eight.

Robert Corelier de La Salle, an energetic young French adventurer who met with great success in his explorations on Lakes Ontario and Erie, was aroused by the news of the discovery of the "great river." La Salle hurried to France and received from Calbert a commission to proceed with further discoveries on the Mississippi. (1678) Accompanied by the Chevalier Tonti, a veteran Italian, as his lieutenant, he returned to Frontinac, built a small bark with which he ascended the Niagara river to the foot of the rapids below the great fall, and above them near the shore of Lake Erie began the construction of the first rigged vessel that ever sailed upon the western waters. In this little bark of sixty tons, called the "Griffin," accompanied by Tonti and some missionaries, La Salle traversed Lake Erie and passed through Detroit, or "the strait" named St. Clair, (1679) and sailing across Lake Huron and by the Straits of Mackinaw into Lake Michigan, and came to anchor in Green Bay.

From this point, after sending back the vessel for supplies, La Salle and his associates proceeded in canoes across Lake Michigan to the mouth of St. Joseph's river, where Allouez had established a station and a trading post called the "Fort of the Miamis." Awaiting the arrival of the Griffin, which had been wrecked on the way back, La Salle and Tonti and their followers crossed over to the Illinois river some distance below Peoria; here he erected another fort. There were no tidings of the missing vessel and to proceed without supplies was impossible. Detaching Tonti and the Recollect Hennepin to continue their explorations, La Salle set out (1680) with only three followers, making his way back across the vast wilderness to Frontinac, where though reported dead, he gathered fresh materials for his enterprise. His agents, meanwhile were engaged in carrying out his instructions. Hennepin explored the Mississippi to the Falls of St. Anthony, the present site of the city of Minneapolis, having in the last thirty-five years become a city of one hundred and fifty thousand inhabitants. Hennepin, returning afterwards to France, published there an account of his travels. Tonti, less fortunate, who had been directed to establish himself among the Illinois, was driven by the hostility of the Iroquois, and was obliged to take refuge at Green Bay. La Salle at length returned with provisions and reinforcements, collected his scattered men and constructed a capacious barge in which he descended the Mississippi to the Gulf of Mexico. Formal possession of the mouth of the river was taken for France April 9, 1682, and the name Louisiana was conferred upon the newly acquired territory. La Salle returned to France with an ardent desire to colonize the fertile region which he had discovered.

FATHER RECCOLLECT HENNEPIN.

Hennepin was born in France about 1645. Came to America with La Salle. Explored Lakes Erie, Huron, Michigan, and Illinois river. Ascended the Mississippi in 1680 and discovered the Falls of St. Anthony, the present site of the City of Minneapolis. Shortly after he returned to France, where he died.

(1683) He got together an expedition consisting of a frigate and three ships and two hundred and eighty persons in all, (1684) soldiers, mechanics and emigrants, and speedily got under way to plant a colony at the mouth of the Mississippi but no success attended the enterprise. La Salle falling into disputes and even quarrels with Beaujeu, commander of the fleet under him, missed the entrance of the river, and in February, 1685, was compelled to land his dispirited and dispairing company at some point on the coast of Texas.

In April, 1686, he set out with twenty men to find the Illinois, where Tonti was awaiting him, but without avail. Yet as his only hope lay in extricating himself and his followers—less than forty—by an overland passage early in January, 1687, he set out again with seventeen men on his forlorn enterprise. Three of the company conspired to commit murder. They slaughtered Moragnet, Nika and Saget, and when La Salle came to inquire after the missing men Duhaut discharged his musket from ambush and shot the unhappy La Salle through the head. This was on the 19th of March, 1687. Good Father Anastase dug his grave, buried him, and erected a cross over his remains. "La Salle died somewhere about the spot where now stands the town of Washington," says Mr. Gayarre. The murderers of La Salle, quarrelling over the spoils of their leader, met with the same retributive fate at the hands of some of their associates. Joutel, the narrator of these dismal events, with no more than five others, made their way to the banks of the Mississippi where they fell in with two Frenchmen left there by Tonti on his return from a vain search after his old commander. The twenty men left behind at the fort by La Salle also perished, and thus, after the most brilliant prospects of success, the colony of La Salle came to an untimely end, a sad termination to a gallant leader.

At this date, according to Mr. Bancroft, the twelve oldest states of our Union "contained not very many beyond two hundred thousand inhabitants, of whom Massachusetts, with Plymouth and Maine, may have had forty-four thousand; New Hampshire and Rhode Island, with Providence, each six thousand; Connecticut from seventeen to twenty thousand; that is, in all New England, seventy-five thousand souls; New York, not less than twenty thousand; New Jersey, ten thousand; Pennsylvania and Delaware, twelve thousand; Maryland, twenty-five thousand; Virginia, fifty thousand or more; and the two Carolinas, which then included Georgia, probably not less than eight thousand souls. Such was the condition and state of the early affairs of the colonies when William III. mounted the English throne, and the American colonies were involved in the war that soon raged between France and England.

PART XVIII

FOUNDING AND PROGRESS OF GEORGIA.

1732 to 1754.

In 1732 the colony of Georgia was planted in that waste and unproductive portion of Carolina between the Savannah and the Alatamaha rivers. Its origin was due to kindly and benevolent motives and desires, notwithstanding the errors of judgment into which the founders fell; and the name of James Edward Oglethorpe will always be held in deserved honor and esteem. This philanthropic man was intent upon mitigating evils, and hoped also to provide seasonable relief for the struggling poor of England who might desire to live soberly and industriously and reap the fruits of their efforts. In conjunction with Lord Percival and other noblemen and gentlemen, Oglethorpe obtained a charter from Parliament of a part of Carolina south of the Savannah river to be settled for the purposes just named. The official seal had on one of its faces a group of silkworms with the motto, "*Non sibi, sed aliis,*"— Not for themselves, but for others. Oglethorpe offered to endure the fatigue of planting the colony himself. Accordingly, with thirty-five families— about a hundred and thirty-five persons— a clergyman with bibles, prayer-books and catechisms; a person to instruct in the cultivation of silk, and several officers of justice. Oglethorpe set sail from Deptford November 17th, 1732, reached Charleston early in 1733, where he and his company were hospitably entertained and soon after landed on the shore of the new province. On ascending the Savannah river, a pine covered hill somewhat elevated above its level shores, the Yamacrow Bluff, was fixed upon as the seat of the capital, which was laid out in broad avenues and open squares, and named Savannah, after the Indian name of the river. Immediate steps were taken for setting forward the work of colonization and settlement. A battery commanded the river, a palisade was erected, and an experimental garden was laid out for vines, mulberry trees, etc., and a storehouse was built. Soon after a body of German Lutherans from the valley of the Alps obtained assistance from the English Parliament enabling them to emigrate. Headed by their ministers they left the home of their fathers and walked to Rotterdam on foot; here they embarked. They touched at Dover where they had an interview with their English patrons, and on reaching Georgia in March, 1734, formed a short distance above Savannah a settlement piously called Ebenezer, where they were shortly after joined by others of the community. In 1735 were added several Moravians, the deciples of Count Zinzindorf. A company of forty Jews, destitute, were furnished with means by their wealthy brethren to emigrate also to Georgia.

Oglethorpe returned to England in April, 1734, and by means of a Parliamentary grant of £26,000 steps were taken for occupying the region lying near to Florida. Early in 1736 a body of Scotch highlanders founded New Inverness on the Alatamaha. Oglethorpe returned to Georgia with these settlers, having in his company John and Charles Wesley, the celebrated Methodist divines. John was involved in difficulties afterwards concerning a marriage. Wesley, charged with a number of other abuses of authority, and finding the public feeling decidedly against him, "shook off the dust of his feet," as he phrases it, and left Georgia in disgust. He never afterwards revisited it.

The Germans and Scotch were tolerably well contented with their position but soon became clamorous for the privilege of having rum to use and the keeping of slaves, both of which had been expressly forbidden by the trustees. By constant agitation during ten years or so that followed their wishes were yielded to and slavery was introduced into Georgia. Oglethorpe, aware of the importance of strengthening his position, took measures to fortify the colony against the neighboring Spaniards. A fort was built on an island near the mouth of the Alatamaha river where a town called Frederica was laid out and built; and ten miles nearer the sea, on Cumberland island, was raised a battery commanding the entrance into Jekyl sound. The Spaniards took umbrage at these proceedings and sent a commission from Havana to demand an evacuation of all the territory south of St. Helena sound, as belonging to the King of Spain. Oglethorpe, of course, resisted such a demand. "He nobly devoted all his powers to serve the poor and rescue them from their wretchedness." And though he himself possessed no share of territory in Georgia, he determined to shelter it if needful with his life. "To me," he said to Charles Wesley, his secretary, "death is nothing." Having proceeded to England, he raised and disciplined a regiment and returned to Savannah in September, 1738, with the appointment of military commandant of Georgia and the Carolinas, with directions to "repel force by force." In 1739 Oglethorpe travelled three hundred miles through the forests and met the Creeks near the site of the present city of Columbus, S. C., who promised to maintain amity and concord with the English and to exclude all others. In 1742 the Spaniards determined to attack Georgia and Carolina with a force of three thousand men. Oglethorpe was able, however, to repel an attack upon Frederica without serious difficulty. Notwithstanding, however, his devotion to the interest of Georgia, Oglethorpe experienced much the same trials as other men placed in like positions and was exposed to a large share of petty meanness and ingratitude. The discarded colonists sent over Thomas Stevens as their agent to England laden with complaints. Having been duly examined by the House of Commons, were pronounced to be "false, scandalous and malicious," Oglethorpe, in 1743, himself went to England to answer to charges against his character, which he so effectually succeeded in vindicating that his accuser, Cook, who was his lieutenant-colonel, was deprived of his commission. Marrying presently and accepting a home position, the founder of Georgia never afterwards revisited America; but he lived long enough to see the establishment of the independence of the United States. Oglethorpe died July 1, 1785, at the great age of ninety-five years. Upon Oglethorpe's return to England, (1743) William Stevens was appointed governor, and notwithstanding his advanced age he discharged effectively the duties of his office. In 1752 Georgia contained only three small towns and some scattered plantations, with seventeen hundred white inhabitants and four hundred negroes. Two years later the board of trade having recommended a form of government, in 1754 John Reynolds was sent over as governor. The legislature was similar in its construction to that of other colonies under the Crown of England.

PART XIX.

COLONIZATION OF LOUISIANA AND ITS PROGRESS.

1698 to 1753.

For some years after La Salle's untimely death (1687) the whole region of the lower Mississippi remained undisturbed. The French wishing to carry out their favorite project of establishing a line of communication between Canada and the Gulf of Mexico, Lemaine d'Iberville was chosen as the leader in this important enterprise. He was well known as a brave and skillful naval officer and stood high in the esteem of his Canadian countrymen. On the 17th of October, 1698. he embarked with two frigates and some two hundred settlers, mostly disbanded soldiers, to plant a colony at the mouth of the Mississippi which as yet had not been entered from the sea. Early in February, 1699, the Spaniards having prevented his entering the harbor of Pensacola, d'Iberville landed on Dauphine island, near Mobile, and soon after discovered the river Pascagoula and the tribes of Biloxi. Leaving most of the colonists in huts on Ship island, d'Iberville in company with his brother Bineville and about fifty men, took two barges and set out to find the entrance to the Mississippi. Guided by the muddy waters, on the 2d of March they discovered the mouth of the great river, which they ascended as high as Red river, and received from some Indians the letter which Tonti had written to La Salle in 1684. Turning again down the river d'Iberville left the main stream and passed through the lakes Maurepas and Pontchartrain, made his way back by a shorter passage to where the main body of the colonists were waiting his movements. At the head of the bay of Biloxi a fort was erected in May. D'Iberville returned to France leaving his brothers Sauvalle and Bienville in command. Such was the beginning of the colony, and though it was plainly impossible to look for prosperity there, still it was an important movement in advancing the purpose of the French in America. The boundless southern region made a part of the French empire by lilies carved on forest trees, or crosses erected on bluffs, and occupied by French missionaries and forest ranges—was annexed to the command of the governor of Biloxi. England, ever wakeful in her jealously of France, determined to assert a claim to the region thus occupied, and an expedition under Coxe, a London physician who had purchased the old patent of Carolina, set out for the mouth of the Mississippi. In September, 1699, as Bineville was exploring the forks below New Orleans he met an English ship of sixteen guns; with ready wit of genius he persuaded the English commander that the region where he then was, was already occupied and settled by the French, and thus got rid of a very troublesome visitor. The point where this occurred in the river is still known to this day as the English Turn. D'Iberville returned early in December, 1699, and various important prospects were entrusted to him to carry out, but especially was he to seek for and find gold. D'Iberville and his brother ascended the Mississippi and visited various tribes of Indians, but all enquiring and search for gold was in vain.

The aged Tonti with a few companions from the banks of the Illinois river, (1700) joined d'Iberville in this expedition, and ascended the Mississippi some three or four hundred miles. Billious fevers carried off numbers, the amiable Sauvolle among the earliest, and when d'Iberville again returned from France to which he had gone for provisions and soldiers, he found only a hundred and fifty alive.

In 1702 d'Iberville was taken with yellow fever and his health was broken down by its effects upon his constitution. He died in Havana in 1706. Louisiana at his death was a little more than a wilderness; in the whole of its borders there was not more than thirty families. The major part of the settlers found it necessary to abandon Biloxi, and removed to Mobile, near the head of the bay of that name. This was the first European settlement within the limits of what is now the state of Alabama. Hardly sustaining itself the colony became a burden to Louis XIV., and in 1712 he granted to Anthony Crozat the exclusive privilege for fifteen years of trading in all that immense country, which with its undefined limits, France claimed as her own under the name of Louisiana. Crozat, being unable to get his share of the trade with the Indians which was monopolized by the English, begged the government in 1717 to take the colony off his hands. At this date the population was only about seven hundred. In March, 1718, three vessels reached Louisiana with three companies of infantry and sixty-nine colonists; and in June of the same year eight hundred persons—colonists— also arrived. These were the first installments of the six thousand whites and three thousand negroes which the Mississippi Company agreed to introduce. Bineville was appointed governor, and soon after sent a party of convicts to clear up a swamp, the present site of the city of New Orleans, so named after the regent of France, where a few years later Bineville removed the seat of the government. Rice was the principle crop, the main resources for feeding the population, to this was added tobacco and indigo. The fig had been introduced from Province and the orange from St. Domingo. In 1727 the population amounted to something more than five thousand; half of this number were negroes. Perier, in 1726, was appointed governor in place of Bineville, soon after difficulties began to arise with the Indians. The Natchez tribe, who had at first amicably received the French, and in whose territory Fort Rosalie had been erected, became jealous of their growing demands for territory, urged on by the Chickasaws, and falling suddenly upon the fort in 1729 they massacred all the male inhabitants and carried away the women and children into slavery. But a year or so afterwards the French nearly exterminated the whole tribe and sent several hundred of them to be sold as slaves in Hispaniola.

The Mississippi Company in 1732 resigned Louisiana into the hands of the King, and Bineville was again appointed governor, and directed to make war against the Chickasaws. With a fleet of sixty boats and canoes and about twelve hundred Choctaws as allies, Bineville ascended the Tombigbee river to the head of navigation and attacked the Chickasaws near that point; but the French were repulsed and compelled to retreat. (1735) Three years later (1739) the whole force of the French was put forth to overcome this powerful tribe. Sickness, scarcity of provisions, and dissensions among the officers, in 1740 they were glad to withdraw their forces and leave the Chickasaws unsubdued. Bineville's ill success in this undertaking, and other failures shortly after, in 1743, the Marquis de Vaudreuil was sent out as his successor. Bineville at the age of sixty-five left Louisiana never to return to the colony he loved and served so long and well. From this date onward for many years Louisiana, under the administration of the Marquis de Vaudreuil, enjoyed comparative tranquility, and gradually advanced in prosperity. In 1753 De Vaudreuil was transferred to Canada, and Kerlerec, a captain in the royal navy, succeeded him as governor of Louisiana.

PART XX.

THE PROGRESS AND GENERAL CONDITION OF THE COLONIES CONDENSED.

1700 to 1750.

At this stage of the progress of our narrative it will be profitable as well as interesting to stop and pause for a while, and take a glance at the position and general condition of the American colonies from the beginning of Columbus to 1750, and see what the outgrowth of the discovery of America has done for civilization up to the present time. We have already here and there called attention to the trials, tribulations, sickness, famines, massacres, wealth and improvement and developments, and the energy of all the colonies. It will conduce, to additional clearness of ideas as well as better understanding of the actual—though not yet understood or appreciated—strength of the colonies, if we devote a few pages more particularly to this subject and endeavor by this condensed condition, progress and foundation of the colonies during the first half of the eighteenth century clearly understood, so that the reader may see at a glance our intention. In doing this we shall rely mainly upon Mr. Grahame, whose resume of this topic, as far as it goes, we look upon as worthy of entire confidence.

At the beginning of the eighteenth century the population of Virginia amounted to sixty thousand, of whom about one half were slaves. The militia were then in numbers less than ten thousand. In 1722 they numbered eighteen thousand, from which it is fair to infer a proportionable great increase in the general population. In 1750 Virginia numbered at least one hundred and sixty thousand inhabitants more than half of whom were slaves. At Williamsburg, the seat of government, there were three public buildings in 1727, which were considered the finest specimens of architecture in the country—the capital, the college and the state house. Hospitality to a profuse extent and card playing among the upper classes were quite common, and hunting and cock fighting were amusements in which all were interested. There was also in this town a theatre, the first that arose in the British colonies. (1729) Printing was first established in Virginia and the first newspaper in this colony was published at Williamsburg in 1736; from Virginia and Maryland there were now annually exported about one hundred thousand hogsheads of tobacco, (valued at £8 per hogshead) and two hundred ships were commonly freighted with the tobacco produce of these two provinces. The annual gain to England from this trade was about £500,000. The articles of iron and copper ore, beeswax, hemp and raw silk, were first exported from Virginia to England in 1730. The inhabitants consider that this province is of far greater advantage to her majesty, Queen Anne, than all the rest of her provinces besides on the main land, and therefore they conclude that they ought to have greater privileges than the rest of her majesty's subjects. The assembly think themselves entitled to all the rights and privileges of an English Parliament, and begin to search into the records of that honorable house for precedents to govern themselves by. The council imagine that they stand upon equal terms with the British House of Lords." The Virginians, no doubt, justly complained of the insolence of the commanders of ships of war sent to cruise off the coast for the protection of trade, insolence which at no late day became utterly insufferable and added not a little to the readiness of the provincials to measure arms with the haughty and overbearing regulars, who prided themselves so much on their superiority in all respects.

Virginia was warm in its attachment to the parent country,

but they, too, had begun generally to question the right to impose restrictions on commerce, a right constantly claimed and almost as constantly resisted or evaded; and the Virginia assembly had no disposition to keep in repair forts and such like, which might be turned to their hurt in case of contest. Massachusetts not less than Virginia had advanced in population during this period. At the beginning of the eighteenth century there were about eighty thousand inhabitants; in 1731 the number is estimated at one hundred and twenty thousand freemen and two thousand six hundred slaves; and in 1750 it had reached not less than two hundred thousand. Six hundred ships and sloops were engaged in trade amounting to at least thirty-eight thousand tons; one half of these vessels traded in Europe; about six thousand persons were engaged in its fisheries.

Connecticut appears to have made steady progress, and in 1750 is computed to have had one hundred thousand inhabitants. Rhode Island, which at the beginning of the eighteenth century had about ten thousand inhabitants, in 1730 possessed a population of eighteen thousand, of whom nine hundred and eighty-five were Indians and one thousand six hundred and forty-eight negro slaves; in 1750 there were thirty thousand inhabitants in this colony. Newport, which was the metropolis, contained a population of something less than five thousand, including negroes and Indians. The first newspaper was published in this colony in 1732. In the year 1738 Newport contained seven places of worship. There was a large society of Quakers at Portsmouth, and in the other eleven townships of the colony there were twenty-five assemblages for Christian worship. In regard to New Hampshire, we find in "Holm's Annals" that its population in 1750 is computed to have been twenty-four thousand. The militia of New England as a whole is computed to have amounted to fifty thousand. Iron was the only metalic ore which the colonists had undertaken to improve, and there were now six furnaces for hollow ware, and nineteen forges, in New England. In 1730 fifty hundred weight of hemp, produced in New England and Carolina, were exported to Britian. In early days the stearn old Puritans had endeavored to restrain extravagance and luxury by sumptuary regulations, but their power was no longer felt, at least to any great extent, in such matters, and as wealth increased, display and even luxurious indulgence obtained place in New England. A picture like the following is decidedly instructive as well as suggestive. "In the principle houses in Boston," says the writer, "there was a great hall ornamented with pictures and a great lantern and a velvet cushion in the window seat that looked into the garden. A large bowl of punch was often placed in the hall from which visitors might help themselves as they entered. The chambers were well supplied with feather beds, warming pans and every other article that would now be thought unnecessary for comfort or display. The pantry was well filled with substantial fare and dainties, prunes, marmalade and Maderia wine. Silver tankards, wine cups and other articles of plate were not uncommon, and the kitchen was completely stocked with pewter, iron and copper utensils. Very many families employed servants; among the property of one we see a Scotch boy invoiced at £14. Negro slaves also often formed part of a New England household of that day. Even before this period, in the matter of dress certain of the ladies were eager to copy the London and Paris fashions. As a matter of interest it may be noted here that the first portrait painter in America was John Smibert, a Scotch artist, who came over with Berkeley, and painted that picture of the bishop and his family which is preserved at Yale College. An art so pleasing was not long in making its way over the colonies, and has preserved to posterity the youthful appearance of our beloved Washington. But though art and literature were making their way, public amusements were still frowned upon by the New England magistrates. Otway's play of "The Orphan" was enacted in 1750 at a coffee house in Boston; but such exhibitions were forthwith prohibited, as tending to discourage industry and frugality, and greatly to increase impiety and contempt of religion. A London company of actors contrived however, shortly afterwards to gain a footing in New York Philadelphia, and other towns further south. The probable designs of the New Englanders at this date in regard to the question of bye and bye throwing off the yoke of the mother country afforded matter for considerable discussion in England

Some members of the board of trade entertained and expressed apprehension of such a determination on the part of the colonists. They even went so far as to give it as their opinion that nothing but the effective interposition of Parliament could arrest the manifest tendency to independence.

The folly of provoking such discussion in the colonies, we need not enlarge upon. The youthful giant would throw off all parental control soon enough without provoking him to measure his strength prematurely with his sire. In 1734 the population of Maryland appears to have been thirty-six thousand taxable inhabitants, by which is meant the white men above sixteen years of age, and negroes, male and female, from sixteen to sixty. The state of society and manners in Maryland was naturally very much the same as in Virginia. A printing press was established in Maryland in 1726, three years before Virginia enjoyed that privilege. The people of this colony are said to have derived much advantage from their knowledge of the medicinal uses of certain herbs and plants, from the fact that long peace and friendship with the Indians had induced great freedom of intercourse between the white and the red men. The salaries of public officers were very low. In 1732 the assembly made tobacco a legal tender for the payment of all debts at a penny per pound, and Indian corn at twenty pence per bushel. Probably the Roman Catholics were still in the majority in the colony. Many Protestants, however settled on the frontier counties of Virginia and Maryland. The population in North Carolina in 1710 was six thousand; probably it had considerably increased some years later. It must be confessed, however, as we have in substance noted, that in the early part of this century the people of North Carolina formed one of the most turbulent, irreligious and illiterate communities in America. In South Carolina the population in 1700 was less than six thousand; in 1723 it amounted to thirty-two thousand, of whom eighteen thousand were slaves. Besides the commercial intercourse with England, an extensive trade carried on almost entirely in British ships, was kept up between Carolina and the West Indies, New England, Pennsylvania and New York. Between 1720 and 1730 rice to the amount of over forty-four thousand tons was exported from South Carolina. In the year 1730 the negroes amounted to twenty-eight thousand, and large accessions to this class of population continued to be made from year to year. In respect to social life the habits of the planters were generally frugal, and luxury had not yet obtained much influence. Printing was introduced in 1730, and a newspaper established in 1734. The majority of the inhabitants were attached to the Church of England, but the Presbyterian denomination also flourished.

During the summer of 1728 the weather in South Carolina proved uncommonly hot, the surface of the earth was parched, the pools of water dried up and the beasts of the field reduced to the greatest distress. In the same year that fearful scourge, yellow fever, broke out to an alarming extent and with a malignity that swept off large numbers. Subsequently to this the increase of wealth among the Carolinians led to a corresponding increase in expenses of living and its usual concomitants of display and luxurious indulgence. At the beginning of the century New York numbered thirty thousand persons; in 1732 this number had more than doubled, of whom about seven thousand were slaves; and in 1750 there were nearly one hundred thousand inhabitants in the province.

The annual imports of this colony were reckoned at £100,000, and in 1736 two hundred and eleven vessels with cargoes entered, and two hundred and twenty-two vessels with cargoes departed from the port of New York. A taste for tea was gradually making progress; this led to considerable contraband trade on the part of the colonists, so that they might obtain tea at a less rate than that charged by the English East India Company; in fact they did get it by this means some thirty per cent. lower. A public school was founded in New York city by the legislature in 1732 wherein Latin, Greek, and the mathematics were to be taught. A newspaper was first published in New York in 1725. Some remaining influence of the Dutch manners and habits still prevailed in New York, although it was evident that English and French tastes were predominant. The citizens were lively and sociable in manners. There were weekly evening clubs, and in the winter balls and concerts. Living was on a less expensive scale than at Boston, and the New Yorkers were at that day, as well as now, devoted to business and the gains of trade. The city of Albany at this date on the outskirts of civilization retained much more of the flavor of its Dutch origin. The architecture was like that of Delft or Leyden; all the houses stood with their angular zigzag gables turned to the street, with long projecting gutter pipes, which like those of the towns of continental Europe at the present day, discharge their unsavory current of dirty water or melted snows upon the heads of the unwary passengers. The stoops or porches were furnished with side seats, well filled in the evening with the inmates, old and young, of both sexes, who met to gossip or to court, while the cattle wandered almost at will about the streets of the half rustic city. In the interior of the Dutch dwellings Dutch cleanliness and economy were established; the women, as at the present day in Holland, were considered over nice in scrubbing their floors and burnishing their brass and pewter vessels into an intensity of luster; from the dawn of day until late at night they were engaged in the work of purifaction; they lived, too, with exemplary sobriety, breakfasting on tea without milk and sweetened by a small bit of sugar passed round from one to the other: they dined on buttermilk and bread, and if to that they added sugar it was esteemed delicious, though sometimes they indulged in broiled and roasted meats. The use of stoves was unknown, and the huge fireplaces, through which one might have driven a wagon, furnished with ample logs, were grand and cozy nestling places during the long winter evenings, which the wail of the snow storm and the roar of the forest trees rendered more deliciously secure. Under the English the same simplicity of manners long prevailed.

The population of New Jersey in 1738 had increased to forty-seven thousand three hundred and sixty-seven, of whom about four thousand were slaves. In 1736 a college was founded at Princeton named Nassau Hall. The general prosperity of this colony was due, doubtless, to the virtuous and industrious character and habits of the people. In 1750 the population of New Jersey was about seventy thousand.

In regard to Pennsylvania and Delaware, no entirely reliable computation can be made of the population of these colonies. Probably it was considerably less than Virginia at the same date. The colonists traded with England, Portugal and Spain, with the Canaries, Maderia and the Azores, with the West India Islands, with New England, Virginia and Carolina. In 1731 Philadelphia is said to have numbered about twelve thousand inhabitants, being probably somewhat in advance of New York. In 1736 the vessels arriving and departing were considerably less than we have noted in the case of New York. The importations into Pennsylvania are reckoned at the annual value of £150,000, being much more than those of New York. The value of the exports from Great Britian to North America, according to Mr. Hildreth, for the ten years from 1738 to 1748, was on an average annually about $3,500,000. The imports from the colonies were somewhat less. The balance against the colonies was paid in specie, the produce of their West India and African trade.

From this brief outlined sketch of the general condition of the American colonies, it will be evident that there existed among them the undoubted elements of strength, decision of character, and firm resolves to maintain their just rights and privileges. In the preceeding pages we call attention to the colonization of Georgia and Louisiana. Prosperity had fallen to their lot in a large degree, and with prosperity the natural restlessness of the Anglo-Saxon race urged them on to greater and more far-reaching designs. The neighbors, the French, they had never liked; already had there been many a contest between them, and now the day was fast approaching when the final struggle was to take place and the mastery be attained by one or the other. It was not possible much longer to put off the contest. "France, thus far secure in the west," to use the language of Mr. Parkham, "next essayed to gain a foothold upon the sources of the Ohio, and about the year the sagacious Count Galissoniere proposed to bring over ten thousand peasants from France and plant them in the valley of that beautiful river and on the borders of the lakes. But while at Quebec, in the bastue of St. Louis, soldiers and statesmen were revolving schemes like this, the slowly moving powers of England bore on with silent progress from the east. Already the British settlements were creeping along the valley of the Mohawk and ascending the eastern slope of the Alleganies. Forests crashing to the axe, dark spires of smoke ascending from autumnal fires, were heralds of the advancing host; and while on the other side of the Alleganies Celeron de Bineville was burying plates of lead, engraved with the arms of France, the ploughs and axes of Virginia backwoodsmen were enforcing a surer title on the other." The adverse powers were drawing near. "The hour of collision was at hand." To the history of this last measuring of arms between the ancient rivals and its bearing on the position of the colonies in their disputes with the mother country we shall leave at this time, hoping that the reader will readily see that our aim has been accomplished by the contents of this book.

PART XXI.

THE OUTGROWTH OF OUR COUNTRY

THE
OUTGROWTH OF OUR COUNTRY,

CONTAINING THE

DECLARATION OF INDEPENDENCE,

THE CONSTITUTION,

THE FORM OF OUR NATIONAL GOVERNMENT

A Historical Statistical Table ; A Chronological Discussion of the Population and Area of the U. S.; the Growth and Distribution of the Population ; the Electoral Vote.

The Territories and their Capitals; The Date of Organization and Admission of each Territory and State.

A BIOGRAPHICAL PORTRAIT GALLERY;

AUTOGRAPHS, ELECTION, POLITICS, AND MAJORITY OF ALL THE PESIDENTS.
Biography of Gen. Logan, And Financial History of the U. S.
A COMPLETE POLITICAL COMPENDIUM.

Washington's Headquarters; Arnold's Treason; Capture and Execution of Andre: Arnold's Address to the American People; The Historical Mansions of Schuyler and Van Rensselaer.

FIRST STEAM NAVIGATION AND FIRST RAILROAD TRAIN.

JOHN HANCOCK.

Born in Braintree, Mass., 1737. Graduate at Harvard College, 1754. Became counting-room clerk for his uncle. Entered public life, 1766. An abettor of the tea-riot in Boston Harbor, 1773. President Provincial Congress of Massachusetts. President of the Continental Congress when the Declaration of Independence was signed. Governor of Massachusetts several years. Died October 8, 1793.

DRAFTING THE DECLARATION OF INDEPENDENCE.

Franklin.   Jefferson.   Sherman.   Adams.   Livingston.

FIRST CONTINENTAL CONGRESS

The House Committee appointed to draft the Declaration of Independence consisted of the following: Mr. Jefferson, John Adams, Dr. Franklin, Mr. Sherman and Philip Livingston; and was reported to Congress just as Thomas Jefferson had written it. After being discussed and amended in several respects, it received the vote of every colony on the 4th of July, 1776, and was published to the world.

THE COMMITTEE PRESENTING TO CONGRESS THE DECLARATION OF INDEPENDENCE, JULY 1, 1776.

"Proclaim liberty throughout all the land, unto all the inhabitants thereof," is the significant text of scripture inscribed on the bell in the steeple of the time honored state house, Philadelphia. That bell rung out a joyous peal on the 4th of July, 1776. It has continued to do the same year after year, and by God's blessing it will continue to do the same unto the latest ages.

THE DECLARATION OF INDEPENDENCE.

Mr. Jefferson had preserved a copy of the original draft as reported by the committee—Franklin, Jefferson, Adams, Livingston and Sherman—with the amendments made to it by Congress, which has been published in his correspondence. The following is as amended by the Continental Congress of the thirteen original states:

A declaration by the representatives of the United States of America in Congress assembled.

When in the course of human events it becomes necessary for one people to dissolve the political bands which have connected them with another, and to assume among the powers of the earth the separate and equal station to which the laws of nature and of nature's God entitled them, a decent respect to the opinions of mankind requires that they should declare the causes which impel them to the separation. We hold these truths to be self-evident: That all men are created equal; that they are endowed by their creator with certain inalienable rights; that among these are life, liberty and the pursuit of happiness; that to secure these rights governments are instituted among men deriving their just powers from the consent of the governed; that whenever any form of government becomes destructive of these ends it is the right of the people to alter or abolish it and to institute new government, laying its foundation on such principles and organizing its powers in such form as to them shall seem most likely to effect their safety and happiness. Prudence, indeed, will dictate that governments long established should not be changed for light and transient causes; and accordingly, all experience hath shown that mankind are more disposed to suffer while evils are sufferable, than to right themselves by abolishing the forms to which they are accustomed. But when a long train of abuses and usurpations pursuing invariably the same object evinces a design to reduce them under absolute despotism, it is their right, it is their duty, to throw off such government and to provide new guards for their future security. Such has been the patient sufferance of these colonies and such is now the necessity which constrains them to alter their former systems of government. The history of the present King of Great Britian is a history of repeated injuries and usurpations, all having in direct object the establishment of an absolute tyranny over these states. To prove this let facts be submitted to a candid world. He has refused his assent to laws, the most wholesome and necessary for the public good; he has forbidden his governors to pass laws of immediate and pressing importance, unless suspended in their operation till his assent should be obtained, and when so suspended he has utterly neglected to attend to them; he has refused to pass other laws for the accommodation of large districts of people, unless those people would relinquish the rights of representation in the legislature, a right inestimable to them and formidable to tyrants only.

He has called together legislative bodies at places unusual, uncomfortable and distant from the depository of their public records, for the sole purpose of fatiguing them into compliance with his measures.

He has dissolved representative houses repeatedly for oposing with manly firmness his invasions on the rights of the people; he has refused for a long time after such dissolutions to cause others to be elected, whereby the legislative powers, incapable of annihilation, have returned to the people at large for their exercise, the state remaining in the meantime exposed to all the dangers of invasion from without and convulsions within.

He has endeavored to prevent the population of these states; for that purpose obstructing the laws for the naturalization of foreigners, refusing to pass others to encourage their migrations hither, and raising the conditions of new appropriations of lands.

He has obstructed the administrations of justice by refusing his assent to laws for establishing judiciary powers; he has made judges dependent on his will alone for the tenure of their office and the amount and payment of their salaries.

He has erected a multitude of new offices, and sent hither swarms of officers to harass our people and eat out their substance.

He has kept among us in times of peace standing armies, without the consent of our legislatures; he has affected to render the military independent of and superior to the civil power.

He has combined with others to subject us to a jurisdiction foreign to our constitutions and unacknowledged by our laws, giving his assent to their acts of pretended legislation; for quartering large bodies of armed troops among us; for protecting them by mock trial from punishment for any murders which they should commit on the inhabitants of these states; for cutting off our trade with all parts of the world; for imposing taxes on us without our consent; for depriving us, in many cases, of the benefits of trial by jury; for transporting us beyond seas to be tried for pretended offences; for abolishing the free system of English laws in a neighboring province, establishing therein an arbitrary government, and enlarging its boundaries, so as to render it at once an example and fit instrument for introducing the same absolute rule into these colonies; for taking away our charters, abolishing our most valuable laws, and altering fundamentally the forms of our governments; for suspending our own legislatures and declaring themselves invested with power to legislate for us in all cases whatsoever.

He has abdicated government here by declaring us out of his protection and waging war against us.

He has plundered our seas, ravaged our coasts, burned our towns and destroyed the lives of our people. He is at this time transporting large armies of foreign mercenaries to complete the works of death, desolation and tyranny already begun, with circumstances of cruelty and perfidy scarcely paralelled in the most barbarous ages, and totally unworthy of the head of a civilized nation. He has constrained our fellow citizens, taken captive on the high seas, to bear arms against their country, to become the executioners of their friends and brethren, or to fall themselves by their hands.

He has excited domestic insurrections among us, and has endeavored to bring on the inhabitants of our frontiers the merciless Indian savages, whose known rule of warfare is an undistinguished destruction of all ages, sexes and conditions. In every stage of these oppressions we have petitioned for redress in the most humble terms; our repeated petitions have been answered only by repeated injuries. A prince whose character is thus marked by every act which may define a tyrant, is unfit to be the ruler of a free people. Nor have we been waiting in attention to our British brethren. We have warned them from time to time of attempts by their legislature to extend an unwarrantable jurisdiction over us, we have reminded them of the circumstances of our emigration and settlement here. We have appealed to their native justice and magnanimity, and we have conjured them by the ties of our common kindred to disavow these usurpations which would inevitably interrupt our connection and correspondence. They, too, have been deaf to the voice of justice and of consanguinity. We must, therefore, acquiesce in the necessity which denounces our separation, and hold them as we hold the rest of mankind — enemies in war: in peace, friends.

We, therefore, the representatives of the United States of America in general Congress assembled, appealing to the Supreme Judge of the world for the rectitude of our intentions, do in the name and by authority of the good people of these colonies, solemnly publish and declare that these united colonies are, and of right ought to be, free and independent states; that they are absolved from all allegiance to the British crown, and that all political connection between them and the state of Great Britian is, and ought to be, totally dissolved; and that as free and independent states, they have power to levy war, conclude peace, contract alliances, establish commerce, and do all other acts and things which independent states may of right do. And for the support of this declaration with a firm reliance on the protection of Divine Providence, we mutually pledge to each other our lives, our fortunes and our sacred honor.

The names of the members who subscribed to the Declaration of Independence were as follows, viz.:

JOHN HANCOCK — President.

New Hampshire —
Josiah Bartlett,
William Whipple,
Matthew Thornton.

Massachusetts Bay —
Samuel Adams,
John Adams,
Robert Treat Paine,
Elbridge Gerry.

Rhode Island —
Stephen Hopkins,
William Ellery.

Connecticut —
Roger Sherman,
Samuel Huntington,
William Wiliams,
Oliver Walcott,
George Taylor,
James Wilson,
George Ross.

Delaware —
Cæsar Rodney,
Thomas McKean,
George Reed.

Maryland —
Samuel Chase,
William Paca,
Thomas Stone,
Charles Carroll, of Carrollton.

Virginia —
George Wythe,
Richard Henry Lee,
Thomas Jefferson,
Benjamin Harrison.

New York —
William Floyd,
Philip Livingston,
Francis Lewis,
Lewis Morris.

New Jersey —
Richard Stockton,
John Witherspoon,
Francis Hopkinson,
John Hart,
Abram Clark.

Pennsylvania —
Robert Morris,
Benjamin Rush,
Benjamin Franklin,
John Morton,
George Clymer,
James Smith,
Thomas Nelson, Jun.,
Francis Lightfoot Lee,
Carter Braxton.

North Carolina —
William Hooper,
Joseph Hughes,
John Penn.

South Carolina —
Edward Rutledge,
Thomas Hayward, Jun.,
Thomas Lynch, Jun.,
Arthur Middleton.

Georgia —
Button Gwinnett,
George Walton,
Lyman Hall.

PART XXII.

HEADQUARTERS OF WASHINGTON, NEWBURG, N. Y., APRIL, 1782.

While Washington had his headquarters at Newburg in 1781-2, one of the first measures of the English administration was to appoint Sir Guy Carleton commander-in-chief in America, in the room of Sir Henry Clinton, and to authorize Admiral Digby and himself to negotiate respecting peace. One object of conferring this power was to pursuade, if possible, Congress to agree to a peace separate from their allies.

Carleton arrived at New York early in May and informed Washington of the fact, and that he and Admiral Digby were charged with a mission respecting terms of accommodation. He requested a passport for his secretary as bearer of dispatches to Congress on the subject. The commander-in-chief immediately forwarded the communications to Congress, but as the bill to enable the King to conclude peace with America had not then passed into a law, as there was no assurances that the present commissioners were empowered to offer any other terms than those which had already been rejected, as Congress and Washington also was suspicious that the offer was merely intended to put them off their guard that they might be successfully attacked when reposing in security, and as they were resolved to enter into no separate treaty, the passport was refused. Washington, fearing that delusive hopes were entertained in consequence of the splendid success of American arms in Virginia, urgently recommended vigorous preparations for another campaign. "Whatever may be the policy of European courts during this winter," were his words, "their negotiations will prove a precarious dependence for us to trust to. Our wisdom should dictate a serious preparation for war, and in that state we shall find ourselves in a situation, secure against every event." Congress, availing itself of Washington's presence and his council while he was in Philadelphia, voted with promptness and unanimity new requisitions of money and supplies. They re-

WASHINGTON'S HEADQUARTERS,
NEWBURG, N. Y., 1782.

solved to keep up the military establishment of the preceding year, called upon the states to furnish their quota of troops at an early day, and prevailed upon the commander-in-chief to write two circular letters to the governors of all the states; these letters were sent out at the close of January, and contained arguments and exhortations most forcibly expressed, and well calculated to arouse the states to active exertion. As on many previous occasions, Washington was sadly disappointed at the result. The state legislatures declared the inability of their constituents to pay taxes. Instead of filling the Continental treasury, some were devising means to draw money from it; and some of those who passed bills, imposing heavy taxes, directed that the demands of the state should be first satisfied, and that the residue only should be paid to the Continental receiver. Although by the judicious arrangements of Morris the public expenses were much diminished, yet they were necessarily great and must so continue, although the means of meeting them thus unexpectedly failed. At the commencement of 1782 not a dollar remained in the treasury. "Yet to the financiers," says Marshall, "every eye was turned; to him the empty hand of every public creditor was stretched forth, and against him, instead of the state governments, the complaints and imprecations of every unsatisfied claimant, were directed." Morris, feeling deeply the ingratitude of his countrymen, resolved, nevertheless, not to abandon the cause of the people. Writing to Washington the unpleasant news, that the taxes, due in July, would not be paid in till December, he added: "With such gloomy prospects as this letter affords I am tied here to be baited by Continental clamorous demands; and for the forfeiture of all that is valuable in life, and which I hope at this moment to enjoy, I am to be paid by invective. Scarcely a day passes in which I am not tempted to give back into the hands of Congress the power they have delegated, and to lay down a burden which presses me to the earth. Nothing prevents me but a knowledge of the difficulties which I am obliged to struggle under. What may be the success of my efforts God only knows; but to leave my post at present would, I know, be ruinous. This candid state of my situation and feelings I give to your bosom, because you who have already felt and suffered so much, will be able to sympathize with me."

About the middle of April, 1782, Washington returned from Philadelphia and joined his army at Newburg. He was directly informed of a very shameful proceeding on the part of some refugees from New York and felt compelled to give the matter his serious attention. The circumstances were these: Captain Huddy, who commanded a body of troops in Monmouth county, New Jersey, was attacked by a party of refugees, was made

ROBERT MORRIS.

Born in Lancashire, England, January, 1733. Came to America, 1774. Became heavy importer in Philadelphia. Member Continental Congress, 1775. Signer of the Declaration of Independence. Established the first National Bank, 1781. Declined Secretaryship of the Treasury under Washington. Died May 8, 1806.

prisoner, and closely confined in New York. A few days after they led him out and hanged him with a label on his breast declaring that he was put to death in retaliation for some of their number who they said had suffered a similar fate. Washington took up the matter promptly, submitted it to his officers, laid it before Congress, and wrote to Carleton demanding that Captain Lippincott, the perpetrator of the horrid deed, should be given up. The demand not being complied with, Washington, in accordance with the opinion of the council of officers, determined upon retaliation. A British officer of equal rank with Captain Huddy was chosen by lot. Captain Asgill, a young man just nineteen years old and the only son of his parents, was the one upon whom the lot fell. The whole affair was in suspense for a number of months. Both Clinton and Carleton, his successor, reprobated the act of Lippincott with great severity. Yet he was not given up, it being considered by a court martial that he had only obeyed the orders of the board of loyalists in New York. Great interest was made to save Asgill's life; his mother begged the interference of Count de Vergennes, who wrote to Washington in her behalf. Early in November Washington performed the grateful task of setting Captain Asgill at liberty.

The quota of troops expected from the different states were not filled up, as the commander-in-chief hoped they would be, promptly and fully. With an army of not more than ten thousand men Washington, even if disposed, was unable to undertake offensive operations, consequently the summer passed away in inactivity at the north. Sir Guy Carleton, on his part, was quiet in New York, and the contest seemed to have ceased. Early in August Carleton and Digby informed the commander-in-chief that negotiations for a general peace were begun at Paris; that the independence of the thirteen United States, would be acknowleged; that Mr. Laurens was at liberty, and that passports were preparing for such Americans as had been hitherto detained prisoners in England. We may properly mention in this place that on the capture of Henry Laurens, John Adams was sent to Holland as minister plenipotentiary, and empowered to negotiate a loan. After considerable delay he was officially recognized, and the United Provinces on the 19th of April, 1782, acknowledged the independence of the United States of America. This was the second European power that made that acknowledgement. Mr. Adams concluded a treaty of amity and commerce early in October, and was also successful in effecting the desired loan in behalf of his country in Holland. Thus the Dutch was finally one of the vital sparks by which the United States became a free nation.

PART XXIII

ARNOLD'S TREASON—WEST POINT: N. Y., SEPTEMBER 21, 1780.

GENERAL BENEDICT ARNOLD IN COMMAND OF ALL THE FORCES IN THIS DEPARTMENT—WAS WHERE ARNOLD, THE ARCH-TRAITOR CONNIVED WITH CLINTON, THROUGH THE SPY ANDRE, TO PUT THE ENGLISH IN POSSESSION OF WEST POINT AND DESTROY THE AMERICAN ARMY UNDER ARNOLD'S COMMAND—ANNEXED IS THE PLOT AND THE CONSEQUENCES IN

While Washington and our patriot fathers were struggling amid these many difficulties and trials, the whole country was startled and astounded by the providential discovery of a deeply laid plan of treachery, which, if it had been successful, might have proved fatal to the cause of liberty. Benedict Arnold was the man who sold himself to the enemy, and the name of Benedict Arnold must forever be consigned to infamy.

Arnold had a large share in the esteem and confidence of the country for daring and impetuous valor; he was renowned among American officers; his romantic expedition to Canada, his naval battle on Lake Champlain, and especially his desperate bravery at Behmus's Heights, had covered him with military glory. Disabled from active service by a wound received on this last occasion, he had been appointed to the command of the troops in Philadelphia. Here, as one of the leading men of the city, he had established himself in the house of Penn, and had furnished it in the most sumptuous manner. Enticed by the display of wealth which he made and dazzled by the eclat of his position, Miss Shippen, a young lady not yet eighteen, and the daughter of Mr. Edward Shippen, of Philadelphia, listened to Arnold's addresses, and after a very short acquaintance they were married. Arnold's play, his table, his balls, his concerts, his banquets, would have exhausted even a very large fortune. His own, and the emoluments of his employment, being far from sufficient to defray such extravagance, he had betaken himself to commerce and privateering. His speculations proved unfortunate, his debts accumulated, his creditors tormented him. His boundless arrogance revolted at so many embarrassments, yet he would diminish nothing of his princely state, and he resorted to practices discreditable to him in the highest degree as an officer and a man. The president and council of Philadelphia, brought heavy accusations against him, which were referred to a court martial. The court sentenced him to be publicly reprimanded by the commander-in-chief, who with mingled firmness and delicacy discharged this unpleasant duty. "Our service,"—such were his words—" is the chastest of all. Even the shadow of a fault tarnishes the luster of our finest achievements. The least inadvertence may rob us of the public favor so hard to be acquired. I reprimand you for having forgotten that in proportion as you had rendered yourself formidable to our enemies, you should have been guarded and temperate in your deportment towards your fellow citizens. Exhibit anew those noble qualities which have placed you on the list of our most valued commanders. I will myself furnish you as far as it may be in my power, with opportunities of gaining the esteem of your country." Bronzed must be the cheek of Arnold, if it did not tingle with burning shame at the thought of what he even then was, in purpose at least, a traitor to the cause of his bleeding country.

To a man of violent passions like Arnold, disgraced in the eyes of his countrymen by well founded suspicions of his integrity, desperately in debt, and with no way in which to retrieve his affairs, and obtain means to riot still further in vicious extravagance, the temptation came at an opportune moment. Revenge was within his grasp and gold held out its lure to him. The coffers of England he knew might be open to him, and treason bore with him a high price. He gave form to his guilty intentions in a letter to Colonel Robinson, who immediately communicated them to Sir Henry Clinton. For more than a year before the consummation of his traitorous act he kept up a secret correspondence with Major Andre, adjutant-general of the British army under the assumed names respectively of Gustavus and Anderson. Besides a large sum of money Arnold was promised a rank in the British army equal to that which he then enjoyed. He, on his part, engaged to render to the British some signal service. None could equal in importance the placing of West Point in the enemy's power, and Arnold argreed to do that which, had it been successful, would have been a most deadly blow at the freedom of America. Pretending an aversion to longer residing in Philadelphia, and alleging his wish to resume active service in the army, he requested and obtained the command at West Point, and of all the forces stationed in that quarter. He arrived at West Point the first week in August, 1780, and thence forward watched a favorable opening for carrying out his treasonable designs, which contemplated not only the delivery of the fortress to the enemy, but the scattered troops in the vicinity, so that Clinton might easily fall upon them by surprise and cut them all off at one stroke. The absence of Washington on a visit to Hartford to meet the French officers was thought to afford a suitable opportunity of bringing the affair to a close. Accordingly the sloop-of-war Vulture, having ascended the Hudson and anchored in Haverstraw bay, some half dozen miles below King's Ferry. Major Andre landed from her for the purpose of meeting Arnold, and concerting the arrangements necessary to consumate his treachery. It was about midnight when he landed, and the whole night was spent in conference with Arnold. Andre, urged to accompany Arnold as far as the house of Joshua H. Smith, reluctantly complied with this request. Mounting a horse brought by a servant, he passed with Arnold the American lines at

Haverstraw, and having reached Smith's house, "probably an accomplice of Arnold's in his traitorous designs." The forenoon was spent in completing the details of his treachery. Arnold furnished him with an exact account of the force at West Point, gave him a pass in the name of Anderson to cross the lines, and then returned to his headquarters at Robinson's house, opposite West Point.

Meanwhile Andre became very uneasy at the position in which he was placed, and was anxious to return on board the Vulture. That vessel, however, was compelled to retire farther down the river in consequence of being fired upon from the shore, and hence Andre could not get the boatmen to undertake to put him again on board. There was no alternative but to attempt to return by land. Having exchanged his regimentals for a citizen's dress, over which he wore a dark, loose great coat, and accompanied by Smith, Andre set out a little before sunset, crossed the river at King's Ferry to Verplanck's Point, and it being now dark took the road towards New York. At the outposts they were challenged by a sentinel. Andre's pass was closely scrutinized by Captain Boyd, the officer on duty and numerous inquiries were addressed to him. At length, much to his satisfaction, he was released with an apology, and advised to remain all night on account of the marauders with which "the neutral ground" was infested. It was only after great persuation on the part of Smith that Andre consented to do so, and the former afterwards declared that Andre passed the night in great restlessness and uneasiness. At the dawn of day they were again in the saddle; and now considering himself beyond the reach of danger the spirits of the young officer which had hitherto been depressed by the sense of danger recovered their natural elasticity. After breakfasting on the road they parted, and Andre continued his journey towards New York alone. About ten o'clock on this morning of September 23, 1780, while Andre was riding over the neutral ground, a tract some thirty miles in extent along the Hudson river between the American and British lines, and when he was about half a mile north of Tarrytown, three armed militia men sprang out from the roadside, siezed his bridle and demanded where he was going. Andre supposing himself among friends, said, "I hope you belong to our party?" "What party?" was asked by one of the men. "The lower party." Being answered in the affirmative, Andre avowed himself a British officer on pressing business, but immediately after perceiving his blunder he had made, he showed Arnold's pass, and urged them not to detain him a moment. The men—John Paulding, David Williams and Isaac Van Wart —refused his request and causing him to dismount, they took him one side among the bushes and searched him. Having pulled off his boots and stockings, they found next to the soles of his feet the papers which Arnold had written out respecting West Point, its defences, the state of the force, etc. Andre offered the men large sums of money if they would release him, but providentially for the cause of our country they rejected the glittering bribe, and a few hours afterwards he was delivered up to Lieutenant-Colonel Jameson, who was in command at North Castle, the nearest military post. This officer, astounded at sight of the papers, seems to have lost possession of whatever sense or native sagacity he may at any time have possessed. With such plain, outspoken evidence of Arnold's base treason before his eyes, Jameson, nevertheless, wrote a short note, and resolved to send the prisoner on immediately to the traitor Arnold. At the same moment that he did this happily he deemed it best to dispatch an express with the papers to meet the commander-in-chief, supposed to be on the road returning from Hartford. Major Tallmage, the second in command, came in from White Plains in the evening. Filled with astonishment at the news he heard, he begged Jameson by all means to detain the prisoner. To this the colonel reluctantly acceeded, but still persisted in sending his letters to Arnold, giving him, the very information which enabled him to escape the punishment due to his detestable crime.

Andre, aware that the papers found on him had been sent to Washington and convinced that further attempts at concealment would be unavoidable, he wrote a letter on September 24th, addressed to Washington, revealing his name and rank. Less soliciatious about his safety than to prove that he was not an imposter or a spy, he endeavored to refute appearances which were against him. He affirmed that his object had been to confer with a person upon neutral ground, and that thence he had, without knowing it, been drawn within the American lines. Washington, meanwhile, arrived at Fishkill, eighteen miles from Arnold's headquarters, in the afternoon of September 24. He intended to reach West Point that evening, but M. De La Luzrene, urging him to do so, he remained over night, and very early in the morning of the 25th set off with his suite, sending word that they would breakfast with Arnold at Robinson's house. When nearly opposite West Point he turned his horse down a lane, when La Fayette reminded him that he was taking the wrong road and that Mrs. Arnold was no doubt waiting breakfast for them. "Ah," replied Washington, smiling. "I know you young men are all in love with Mrs. Arnold, and wish to get where she is as soon as possible. You may go and take your breakfast with her, and tell her not to wait for me, for I must ride down and examine the redoubts on this side of the river and will be there in a short time."

His officers, however, declined to leave him, and two of his aids-de-camp were sent forward to explain the cause of the delay. On learning that Washington and his suite would not be there for some time, Arnold and his family set down to breakfast with the aids. While they were yet at the table Lieutenant Allen came in and presented the letter from Jameson giving the intelligence of Andre's capture. By a powerful effort, which long practice in dissimulation enabled him to make, Arnold read the letter, arose in some hurry, and informing the company that his presence was urgently needed at West Point, went up to his wife's chamber, and sent to call her. In a few words he explained to her that he must fly for his life, and leaving her in a swoon on the floor he rode hastily to the river side, entered a six-oared barge, stimulated the men by promises of drink to extra exertion, held up a white handkerchief as he passed Verplanck's Point, and was soon in safety on board the English sloop of war Vulture. Washington, shortly after Arnold's escape, reached headquarters at Robinson's house, and being told that Arnold had crossed the river, determined to hurry breakfast and to follow him as soon as possible. As the whole party glided across the river, surrounded by the majestic scenery of the Highlands, Washington said, "Well, gentlemen, I am glad on the whole that General Arnold has gone before us for we shall now have a salute, and the roaring of the cannon will have a fine effect among these mountains." The boat drew near to the beach but no cannon were heard and there was no appearance of preparation to receive them. "What," said Washington, "do they not intend to salute us?" As they landed an officer descended the hill, and in some confusion apologized for not being prepared to receive such distinguished visitors. "How is this, sir," said Washington; "is not General Arnold here?" "No, sir," replied the officer; "he has not been here these two days, nor have I heard from him within that time." "This is extraordinary," said Washington; "we were told that he had crossed the river and that we should find him here. However, our visit must not be in vain, since we have come, although unexpectedly, we must look around a little and see in what state things are with you." An hour or two spent in this examination, and then the commander-in-chief with his officers in company returned to the Robinson house in the afternoon. Hamilton, who had remained behind, met Washington on his return, and in great agitation placed in his hands the papers which had just arrived by the express sent by Jameson, together with the letter of Andre. Although shocked by the discovery of Arnold's base treason, Washington did not lose his self command for a moment. "Whom can we trust now?" were his words, addressed to La Fayette; and with great caution he kept the matter quiet for a time. Hamilton was sent down to Verplanck's Point, but too late to prevent Arnold's escape.

The wife of the traitor was frantic with grief and excitement, and the sympathies of Washington and his officers were bestowed upon the unhappy woman. Not long after a letter was sent in which Arnold had written on board the Vulture, asking for protection to his wife and child, asserting that Mrs. Arnold was wholly innocent of any knowledge or complicity in his guilt, and with unblushing effrontry boasted of his love to his country which prompted his present conduct. Beverly Robinson also sent from on board the Vulture a letter to Washington claiming that Andre was under protection of a flag, and ought to be set at liberty immediately. Washington promptly took measures to defeat any designs which Clinton might have in view, and although it was impossible to tell how many or how few were concerned in Arnold's guilt, the commander-in-chief did not withdraw his confidence from any of his officers, but treated them all as innocent of any knowledge or share in so black a crime. To the honor of the Ameircan name be it recorded, that not a single man in any station, high or low, took any part in the "bad pre-eminence" of Benedict Arnold.

Andre on the 26th arrived at Robinson's house in the custody of Major Tallmadge. On the 28th he was sent down the river to Stony Point and thence under escort of cavalry to Tappan. Andre, not unnaturally, was inquisitive about Major Tallmadge's opinion as to the result of his capture. "When I could no longer evade his importunity," says the major in a very interesting letter quoted by Mr. Sparks, " I remarked to him as follows: I had a much loved classmate in Yale College by the name of Nathan Hale, who entered the army in 1775. Immediately after the battle of Long Island General Washington wanted information respecting movements of the enemy. Captain Hale tendered his services, went over to Brooklyn, and was taken just as he was passing the outposts of the enemy on his return. Said I, with emphasis, 'Do you remember the sequel of this story?' 'Yes,' said Andre, 'he was hanged as a spy. But you surely do not consider his case and mine alike?' I replied, 'Yes, precisely similar, and similar will be your fate.' He endeavored to answer my remarks, but it was manifest he was more troubled in spirit than I had ever seen him before."

The next day a court martial was appointed by the commander-in-chief, of which General Greene was president, and La Fayette, Steuben, and others, were members, to inquire into the case of Major Andre and to pronounce upon the punishment which he deserved. On being examined he gave a candid recital of the circumstances of his case, as he had already stated them in his letter to Washington. He concealed nothing that regarded himself, but steadily avoided all disclosures inculpating others. He acknowledged everything that was recorded essen-

CAPTURE OF MAJOR ANDRE, BY PAULDING, VAN WART AND WILLIAMS.

In the following Congress, the faithful services of these three brave and true men was duly acknowledged on November 3. It was resolved: "that Congress have a high sense of the virtuous and patriotic conduct of John Paulding, David Williams and Isaac Van Wart; in testimony whereof, ordered, that each of them receive annually, $200 in specie or an equivalent in the current money of these States, during life, and that the Board of War be directed to procure for each of them a silver medal, on one side of which shall be a shield, with this inscription, Fidelity, and on the other the following motto: *Vincit Amor Patriæ*, and forward them to the Commander-in-Chief who is requested to present the same with a copy of this resolution, and the thanks of Congress for their fidelity, and the eminent service they have rendered their Country."

tial to his condemnation, and the board of general officers to whom his case was referred, without calling any witnesses, considered merely that he had been within their lines in disguise, and reported that in their opinion Major Andre was a spy, and ought to suffer death as a spy.

Washington communicated the result to Sir Henry Clinton and Andre was allowed to write a letter to the British general in regard to his personal affairs. Indirectly efforts were made by Washington to effect an exchange for Andre, in hope that Clinton might be induced to give up the traitor Arnold, and allow him to be hung instead of Andre; but much as Arnold was despised and scorned by his new associates, Clinton declined to surrender him to the vengeance of his countrymen. The British commander, to whom Andre was especially dear, opened a correspondence with Washington, and urged every consideration of justice, policy and humanity, in favor of Andre. Finding that his letters were ineffectual, he dispatched General Robertson and two other gentlemen on the 1st of October to confer with Washington, or army officers whom he might appoint. Robertson was met by General Greene at Dobb's Ferry, and every possible reason was urged by the British officer to induce the belief that Andre was not a spy, but entreaties and threats were alike of no avail. Robertson presented an impudent letter from Arnold which was effective in a high degree, and could not help the case of the prisoner, and the conference ended without effect so far as Andre was concerned.

The execution had been appointed to take place at five o'clock on the afternoon of October 1, but owing to the length of the interview with Robertson it was postponed till the next day at twelve o'clock. Andre had entreated that he might be shot as a soldier instead of being hung as a malefactor, but the request was not granted; it could not be granted consistently with the customs of war, and the established facts in regard to his case.

We give the conclusion of this distressing scene in the words of Dr. Thatcher, who presents a vivid picture of the last hours of the hopeless Major Andre: "October 2d. Major Andre is no more among the living. I have just witnessed his exit. It was a tragical scene of the deepest interest. During his confinement and trial he exhibited those proud and elevated sensibilities which designate greatness and dignity of mind. Not a murmur, not a sigh, ever escaped him, and civilities and attentions bestowed on him were politely acknowledged. Having left a mother and two sisters in England, he was heard to mention them in terms of the greatest affection, and in his letters to Sir Henry Clinton he recommends them to his particular attention. The principal guard officer, who was constantly in the room with the prisoner relates that when the hour of his execution was announced to him in the morning he received it without emotion, and while all present were affected with a silent gloom, he retained a firm countenance, with calmness and composure of mind. Observing his servant enter his room in tears, he exclaimed, 'Leave me till you can show yourself more manly!' His breakfast being sent him from the table of General Washington, which had been done every day of his confinement he partook of it as usual, and having shaved and dressed himself he placed his hat on the table and cheerfully said to the guard officer, 'I am ready at any moment, gentlemen, to wait on you.' The fatal hour having arrived, a large detachment of troops were paraded, and an immense concourse of people assembled. Almost all our general and field officers, excepting his excellency and his staff, were present on horseback: melancholy and gloom prevailed all ranks and the scene was effectingly awful. I was so near during the solemn march to the fatal spot as to observe every movement and participate in every emotion which the melancholy scene was calculated to produce. Major Andre walked from the stone house in which he had been confined between two of our subaltern officers, arm in arm; the eyes of the vast multitude were fixed on him, who, rising superior to the fears of death, appeared as if conscious of the dignified deportment which he displayed. He betrayed no want of fortitude, but retained a complacent smile on his countenance, and politely bowed to several gentlemen whom he knew, which was respectfully returned. It was his earnest desire to be shot, as being the mode of death most conformable to the feelings of

MAJOR-GENERAL NATHANIEL GREENE.

Born in Warwick, R. I., 1740. Was an anchor-smith when the Revolution broke out. He hastened to Boston after the Lexington engagement, and was one of the most useful officers in the army to the close of the war, receiving the rank of Major-General from Congress. He was President of the Court Martial that tried and convicted Major Andre. Died June, 1786.

a military man, and he had indulged the hope that his request would be granted.

At the moment, therefore, when suddenly he came in view of the gallows, he involuntarily started backward and made a pause. 'Why this emotion, sir?' said an officer by his side. Instantly recovering his composure, he said, 'I am reconciled to my death, but I detest the mode.' While waiting and standing near the gallows I observed some degree of trepidation, placing his foot upon a stone and rolling it over and choking in his throat as if attempting to swallow. So soon, however, as he percieved that things were in readiness he stepped quickly into the wagon, and at this moment he appeared to shrink, but instantly elevated his head; with firmness, he said, 'It will be but a momentary pang;' and taking from his pocket two white handkerchiefs, the provost-marshall, with one loosely pinioned his arms, and with the other the victim, after taking off his hat and stock bandaged his own eyes with perfect firmness, which melted the hearts and moistened the cheeks not only of his servant but of the throng of spectators.

The rope being appended to the gallows he slipped the noose over his head and adjusted it to his neck without the assistance of the awkward executioner. Colonel Scammel now informed him that he now had an opportunity to speak if he desired it. He raised his hanckerchief from his eyes and said, 'I pray you to bear me witness that I meet my fate like a brave man.' The wagon being now removed from under him, he was suspended, and instantly expired. It proved, indeed, but a momentary pang. He was dressed in his royal regimentals and boots, and his remains in the same dress were placed in an ordinary coffin and interred at the foot of the gallows, and the spot was consecrated by the tears of thousands."

BENEDICT ARNOLD'S ADDRESS.

An Historical Treasure found after an Obscurity of over a Century. Published in Full.

After Benedict Arnold had betrayed his country to the British, he issued an address, on October 7, 1780, to the American people in vindication of his course. That address, in the traitor's own handwriting, was found, this afternoon, Nov. 13, 1886, in a barrel of old papers, in Kingston. The precious document is now in the possession of *The Freeman*, who very kindly favored us with a true copy. For over a century it has "laid around anywheres," and it has finally been discovered by the merest accident. The document was found in the same loft where the Aaron Burr letters and the secret ciphers were discovered, recently. The Arnold letter is reproduced here, as near as it is possible to do so—the capitalization, punctuation and paragraphing having been followed closely, as follows:

To the Inhabitants of America:—I should forfeit in my opinion, the place I have so long held in yours, if I could be indifferent to your own approbation, and silent on the motives which have induced me to join the King's Arms. A very few words, however, shall suffice upon a subject so personal, for to the Thousands who suffer under the tyranny of usurpers, in the Revolted Provinces, as well as to the great multitude who have long wished for its subversion; this instance of my conduct can want no Vindication, and as to that Class of Men who are criminally protracting the War from Sinister Motives at the Expense of the Public Interest, I prefer their Enmity to their Applause. I am therefore only concerned in this address to Explain myself to such of my Countrymen, as want abilities or Opportunities, to detect the artifices by which they are duped.

Having fought by your sides, when the Love of our Country animated our Arms, I shall Expect from your Justice and Candour what

BENEDICT ARNOLD.

Born in Norwich, Conn., Jan. 3, 1740. He fought in the Revolutionary War until 1778, when he was courtmartialed. His sentence was to be reprimanded by Washington, after which he was put in command at West Point and vicinity. He then bargained for the surrender of West Point to the British. The capture of Major Andre prevented the betrayal. Died in London, June 14, 1801.

your deceivers with more Art and less honesty, will find it Inconsistent with their own Views to Admit.

When I quitted domestic Happiness for the Perils of the Field, I conceived the rights of my Country in danger and that duty and honor called me to her defence, A redress of grevience was my only object and aim. However I acquiesced in a Step which I thought precipitate, The Declaration of Independence. To justify this measure many plausible Reasons were urged which could no longer Exist, when Great Britain with the Open Arms of a Parent offered to Embrace us as Children and grant the wished for Redress,

And now that her worst Enemies are in her own Bosom I should change my principles if I conspired with their designs, Yourselves being Judges, was the War less Just because fellow Subjects were Considered as Foes you have felt the Tortures in which was raised our Arms against A Brother! God Incline the Guilty protractors of these unnatural dissentions, to Resign their Ambition and cease from their delusions in Compassion to kindred blood.

I anticipate your question, was not the War a defensive one, Until the French joined in the Combination? I answer that I thought so. You will add was it not afterwards necessary till the separation of the British Empire was Compleat? By no means in contending for the welfare of my Country I am free to declare my opinion, that this End attained, all Strife should have ceased. I lamented therefore the Impolicy, tyranny, and injustice, which with a Sovereign contempt of the people of America, Studiously neglected to take their collective Sentiments, of the British Proposals of Peace, and to negotiate under a suspension of Arms for an adjustment of differences, as a dangerous sacrifice of the great interests of this Country to the partial views of a proud, antient and Crafty foe. I had my suspicions of some Imperfections in our Councils, as proposals prior to the Parliamentary Commission of 1778, but having then less to do in the Cabinet than the Field, (I will not pronounce premptorily as some may, and perhaps justly) that Congress have Veiled them from the public Eye) I continued to be guided in the negligent confidence of a Soldier. But the whole world saw, and all America Confessed that the overtures of the Second Commission exceeded our Wishes and expectations, and if there was any suspicion of the National liberalty it was from its Excess—Do any believe we were at that time really entangled by an Alliance with France, unfortunate Deception? and thus they have been duped, by a Virtuous Credulity in the precautious moments of intemperate passion to give up their felicity, to save a Nation wanting both the Will and the Power to protect us; and aiming at the destruction both of the Mother Country and the Provinces, in the plainness of Common Sense for I pretend to no casnistry, did the pretended treaty with the Court of Versailes amount to more than an Overture to America? Certainly not because no Authority has been given by the people to Conclude it. Nor to this very Hour have they Authorized its Ratification, the Articles of Confederation Remain still unsigned.

In the firm perswasion therefore, that the private Judgment of any Individual Citizen of this Country is as free from all conventional restraints since as before the insiduous offer of France I preferred those from Great Britian, thinking it infinitely wiser and safer, to cast my confidence upon his justice and generosity, than to trust a Monarchy too feeble to Establish your Independency so perilous to her distant dominions, the Enemy of the Protestant Faith, and fraudently avowing an Affection for the liberties of Mankind while she holds her Native Sons in Vassalage and Chains.

I Affect no disguise, and therefore frankly declare, that in these principles I had determined to Retain my Arms and Command for an Opportunity to Surrender them to Great Britain, and in Concoting the measures for a purpose in my Opinion, as grateful as it would have been beneficial to my Country, I was only Solicitions to Accomplish an Event of decisive Importance, and to prevent as much as possible, in the Execution of it the Effusion of Blood.

With the highest satisfaction I bear testimony to my Old fellow Soldiers and Citizens, that I find solid Grounds to rely upon the clemency of our Sovereign, and abundent conviction that it is the Generous Intention of Great Britain, not only to leave the Rights and privileges of the Colonies unimpaired together with their perpetual Exemption from taxation, but to superadd such further benefits as may consist with the common prosperity of the Empire. In short, I fought for much less than the Parent Country is as willing to grant to her Colonies as they can be to receive or Enjoy.

Some may think I continued in the Struggle of these unhappy days too long, and others that I quitted too soon. To the first I reply, that I did not see with their Eyes, nor perhaps had so favorable a situation to look from, and that to our Common Master I am willing to stand or fall—in behalf of the candid among the latter—some of whom I believe serve blindly but honestly in the bonds I have left, I pray God to give them all the light Requisite to their own Safety before its too late, (and with Respect to that hord of Censurers—whose enmity to me Originates in their hatred to the principles by which I am now led to devote my life to the Reunion of the British Empire, as the best, and only means to dry up the Streams of Misery that have deluged this Country, they may be assured that conscious of the Rectitude of my pretentions, I shall treat their malice and Calumnies with contempt and Neglect.

New York, 7th Oct. 1780.　　　　　　　　　　　　　　　B. ARNOLD.

NOTE.—It is self evident that Arnold's gall must have been great when he took upon himself to write the above address to his countrymen, attempting to vindicate his designs to defeat the will of his country, and forever blast the hopes of enjoying the liberty of free and independent people. His address was simply "adding insult to injury."

THE HISTORICAL SCHUYLER MANSIONS, AT ALBANY, N. Y.

THE BIRTH PLACE AND BRIEF SKETCH OF GEN. PHILIP SCHUYLER AND THE SCHUYLER FAMILY, ALSO OTHER NOTED COLONIAL AND REVOLUTIONARY SOLDIERS IN THE DAYS THAT NOT ONLY TRIED MEN BUT WOMEN'S SOULS.

None of the historic buildings of Albany, unless it be the Van Rensselaer manor, has attracted more attention or possesses greater interest for citizens than the Schuyler mansion. This house, its exterior at least, is familiar to all Albanians, standing as it does on a commanding elevation at the head of Schuyler street. Its exterior is imposing and beautiful, and the most casual beholder can readily believe that romance and history have strange tales to tell concerning it. The most romantic episode in the history of the house, the attempted capture of Gen. Philip Schuyler by Tories and Indians, and the brave rescue of an infant by his daughter Margaret, who afterwards became the wife of the last patroon. The Schuyler family are at all points identified with the city and country's history, and the records of this one mansion would form no mean chronicle of the old Dutch burgh.

There are no less than three Schuyler houses known to history, and all of them are now standing. The first, and perhaps the most interesting, is the one at the "Flats," just south of West Troy, on the banks of the Hudson river.

The old homestead—the family mansion—I could not but recall some of the many interesting historical incidents connected with the place. Here, in 1677, a party of Mohawks attacked the Mohegans and took many prisoners. About the same time, four Mohawk warriors routed eighty "Uncasmen," Connecticut Indians. To this place General Fitz John Winthrop, in 1690, sent the first detachment of his army from Albany for the invasion of Canada. Here, in 1690, John, the youngest son of Peter Schuyler, conceived the design of attacking La Prairie on the St. Lawrence, with a company of thirty whites and one hundred and twenty Indians. Here, his eldest brother, Major Peter Schuyler, formed his plans for the invasion of Canada, the next year, and gathered his dusky warriors. Between this door and the river marched for the next seventy years the several armies against the French and here many of their officers found entertainment. Here the gallant Lord Howe spent the night, and ate his breakfast on the march under Abercrombie to attack Ticonderoga. Here the "American Lady" of Mrs. Grant, "Aunt Schuyler," presided as mistress for thirty years after her husband's death, extending a generous hospitality. Under the shade of the trees before the door she sat one summer's afternoon, when the alarm of fire was raised. In yonder graveyard lies her dust with no stone to mark the spot.

It is not probable that Philip Schuyler built the house. Arent Van Curler, a cousin of the first Patroon Van Rensselaer, came with the first colonists of the manor, 1630, and was soon after made superintendent. He married in 1643, and on his return from Holland, where he had gone on his "bridal tour," he removed to his farm on the Flats. After him, Richard Van Rensselaer, a son of the patroon, occupied it.

A deed in the county clerk's office, recites that K. V. Rensselaer sold the property to Philip Schuyler on the 22d of June, 1672, for five thousand Holland guilders.

The second is at Schuylerville, which was known as Gen. Schuyler's country place in Saratoga Co. The original house belonged to an uncle of the general's, who was burned in the house by the French and Indians, under Marin. This uncle bequeathed his estate to General Philip Schuyler of Revolutionary fame of whom we give a portrait of, and who also came into possession of several parts of other estates in that locality: A new house was erected near the site of the one that was burned, and the water-power was used by the construction of saw and grist mills. When Burgoyne swept down from the

PHILIP SCHUYLER.

Born in Albany, N. Y., November 22, 1733. Entered the army, 1775, serving three years. Was in expedition against Ticonderoga and Crown Point, as Colonel. Member of the second Continental Congress. One of the four Major-Generals appointed to command the army, 1775. Twice U. S. Senator. Died July, 1804.

north, Gen. Schuyler had already taken out 6,000 logs, which were directly in the path of the invader, and were lost by fire, together with the mills and the new residence. The fact that logs were there is claimed by some to prove that Burgoyne was not expected to advance so far to the southward before being stopped. Just after the surrender, General Schuyler built the present edifice, of wood, but it is not occupied to-day by any of his descendants or relatives.

The third "Schuyler house" is the one best known by the name, and the subject of our illustration. When the mansion was built it stood half a mile from the stockade, but now it is in the center of our densest population. During the revolution Albany was a stockaded city. The "flats" were at the north, and the "pastures," where the city herdsmen cared for the cattle, were at the south. Just beyond the pastures the mansion was built, immediately preceding the revolution, like most of the structures of the time, with a frame of timber and a veneered front of bricks brought from Holland. There were no Buddensieks in those days, and the house is as substantial to-day as when the Indians forced its gates, and it gives promise of lasting for centuries to come. The mansion was built by General Bradstreet, about the time of his success at Fort Frontenac, and not by Mrs. Schuyler, during the absence of her husband in Europe, as one account confidently states. General Schuyler was born in the old house at the corner of South Pearl and State streets, where his father lived, and where the earlier part of his married life was passed. He bought the Schuyler mansion of the Bradstreet estate, of which he was the executor. Various romantic stories have been related of the old structure; that the grounds extended to the river, and that a subterranean passage ran from the house thither, a quarter of a mile away. Neither of these is probable. A terrace runs abruptly from the street and this is crowned with a noble row of huge horse-chestnut trees, and fringed with lilacs. The main part of the house is about sixty feet square, with the front entrance on the east. A hexagon, of later date than General Schuyler's time, forms a vestibule or outer hall. The contour of the roof is of the "double-hip" pattern, pierced with small dormers and two square chimneys. Balustrades are carried all about the roof and across the dormers. A row of seven large windows with larger panes of glass than was common in those days, have a place in the front wall above. The main hall is thirty feet long, twenty feet wide, and twelve feet high. There is a rear hall containing the historic stairway which still bears the mark of the tomahawk thrown at the brave girl heorine, Margaret Schuyler, by the blood-thirsty and cruel savage. A large room on the north of the main hall was evidently used as a sitting room, while the one on the south is a drawing room in which General Schuyler's second daughter Elizabeth, married Alexander Hamilton, then the aid and military secretary of General Washington. In this room, also, ex-President Fillmore married Mrs. McIntosh, a subsequent owner of the property. The interior decoration of the house is very artistic, and of the genuine, solid quality in which our forefathers delighted. In the rear of the drawing room is the private room of Gen. Schuyler, which is connected with a retiring room. Accurate measurements have shown that a space of about four feet square close to one of the great chimneys cannot be accounted for in any other way than that it forms the access to a concealed way that led underground to the barracks, or fortified house, about fifteen rods distant. The recent caving in of this covered way has revealed its location and direction, but the secret passage in the house cannot be explored without materially damaging the building.

The house, at various times, sheltered many noted guests, and the host was famous for his generous hospitality. In the large and beautiful dining room General Burgoyne was entertained after his surrender, and his treatment called forth the spontaneous tribute: "You show me great kindness, though I have done you much injury." One of the large and generous chambers upstairs is famed as that in which General Burgoyne and several of his officers slept when they were prisoners of war. Here, during the earlier part of the revolution, were entertained

SCHUYLER MANSION.
At the head of Schuyler Street, Albany, N. Y.

VAN RENSSELAER MANOR HOUSE.
At Greenbush, Rensselaer Co., N. Y. On the bank of the Hudson River opposite Albany. Erected 1642.

Benjamin Franklin, Samuel Chase and Charles Carroll, of Carrolton, delegates from congress with a mission to persuade the Canadians to join the Americans. Carroll gave a Marylander's view of Gen. Schuyler in these words: "He behaved to us with great civility; lives in pretty style; has two daughters (Betsey and Peggy), lively, agreeable, black-eyed girls." When Lady Harriet Ackland and the Baroness Riedesel, with her children, had nowhere to go after the defeat of Burgoyne, General Schuyler sent Col. Varick to Mrs. Schuyler to announce their arrival as guests. The ladies were captivated by the charming hospitality of the Schuyler mansion. The generosity of the host broke over all petty opposition and welcomed Gen. Gates, even when the latter was ready to remove him by all the arts in his power. La Fayette, Baron Steuben, Rochambeau and a long list of eminent Americans enjoyed the genial disposition of the host, and shared his bounty. Thither came Aaron Burr, with a letter of introduction from New York; and he, too, became a guest of the General before undertaking the practice of law in Albany. Washington, also, in the closing months of the war, came hither with Governor Clinton and was entertained on his way to view the northern battle fields and to examine the remarkable topography of the country.

OLDEST AMERICAN HOMESTEAD.

THE VAN RENSSELAER HOUSE AT GREENBUSH—BRIEF HISTORICAL EVENTS CONNECTED WITH IT.

There is an old mansion in Greenbush, the subject of our illustration, nearly opposite Arch street, Albany, near the river, that would seem to be older than any house in that country. The evidence of its age is not quite conclusive, but the inscription found in the cellar on one of the stones of the foundation wall reads: "K. V. R. 1642. Anno Domini." From this it would seem that the actual age of the house is clearly defined. But what are claimed to be complete records of that time made no mention of this manor. Bricks taken from its walls have been found to bear the date, 1629. While there is not much evidence in this alone, taken with many other things, it goes to prove that the house was erected in 1642. On another stone of the foundation wall is found this: "D. J. Megapalensis." This was the first preacher to come to Albany, influenced to do so by Killian Van Rensselaer.

The old port holes are of great interest. These were made of a block of sandstone about a foot square each way. Into one side was dug out a comical shaped hole extending nearly through the centre, then from the other side was pierced a hole about the shape of a modern keyhole. The whole thing was then set into the wall of the building, the keyhole shaped aperture on the outside. There are yet two of them seen in the front wall of the house. There were nine all told, beside one recently found in the cellar wall. The one seen shows the works plainly, of the glancing bullets fired against it. This is said to be the only house in the United States that still retains these port holes.

In the floor of the main hall there is a trap door, which opened downward into the cellar. Tradition says that this was used to entrap unfriendly Indians. They were lured into the house, and when they stepped on this trap, down they went to the cellar where the men awaited them. There is one port hole opening from the cellar. This was but recently discovered.

There is nothing special about any of the rooms to be seen now, they having all been modernized. The linen room is interesting from the fact connected with it. The aristocracy of the old manor were so dependent upon the mother country "Holland," that they even had to have their linen washed there. For that purpose, once a year, it was all sent over and laundried. In the meantime, the soiled linen was kept stored in this linen room. In the "tile room" were formerly above fifty scenes from Scripture, in old Dutch tiles, on one of the walls. These tiles, as were also the brick and timbers from which the house was built, were all brought from Holland. There has never been many relics found in or about the house. One—and the only interesting one—is a weapon, evidently intended as a instrument of war. This is about five feet long, an inch wide at the handle and running out to a sharp point, of wrought iron. It was probably used in the same manner swords are used now. There are many legends connected with the old mansion, which for want of space, will render them out of place here. One only will suffice. A Gertrude Von Tzilier and her brother Walter were visiting the manor one time. At evening, the young girl went down to the river's bank and sat down. She was approached from behind by Indians, and suddenly seized. She gave a scream, but was forcibly borne away, and never heard from again. This scream is said to have been heard for years about the halls of the house. It was in the rear of this mansion that "Yankee Doodle" was composed. While Abercrombie's army was encamped there, by the old sweep well at the rear of the house, waiting for reinforcements, the country people came straggling in in all manner of costumes and dress. Their ludicrous appearance so excited the humor of a British surgeon that he, while sitting by the bed (now to be seen) composed the original version of "Yankee Doodle," words and music both.

PART XXIV.

THE INAUGURATION OF WASHINGTON,

The First President of the United States of America, in New York, April 30, 1789.

At an expense of fifteen thousand florins, Columbus gave to the world America, out of which has grown the United States, whose population exceeds fifty-five millions, which with its yearly influx of from three to four hundred thousand immigrants, coupled with its native increase, invites the prediction that during the next twenty years her population will approximate one hundred million.

Its constitution, which declares that "We, the people of the United States, in order to form a more perfect union, establish justice, insure domestic tranquility, provide for the common defence, promote the general welfare, and secure the blessings of liberty to ourselves and our posterity, do ordain and establish this Constitution for the United States of America," is the base stone upon which our Republican form of government was reared, and has been perpetuated. To insure the faithful implanting and exercise of such constitutional provisions, George Washington, "the father of his country," was selected and inaugurated first President of these United States, on the 30th of April, 1789, while standing on the balcony in front of the Senate Chamber, in the old court house in Wall street, fronting Broad street, the site now occupied by the sub-treasury, in full view of the multitude on the streets, roofs, and in the windows of neighboring buildings. The balcony where Washington stood was supported by lofty columns, and upon the conclusion of the reading of the oath of office, Washington, with his hand resting upon the Bible, audibly responded, "I swear, so help me God." This declaration was the signal for "Long live George Washington, President of the United States." A flag was hoisted amid the plaudits of the people and boom of cannon. Thus began the life of a government which today has no equal on earth.

THE PRESIDENTIAL VOTE FROM 1789 TO 1884.

YEAR.	CANDIDATES.	PARTY.	POPULAR VOTE.	Elect'l vote
1789	George Washington		Elec'd by St'e Leg	Unani.
1796	John Adams	Federal.		71
1796	Thomas Jefferson	Democrat.		69
1800	Thomas Jefferson	Democrat.	Elect'd by vote of	73
1800	Aaron Burr	Democrat.	Reps on 36th ballot	73
1800	John Adams	Federal.		65
1804	Thomas Jefferson	Democrat.	Elect'd by St'e Leg	118
1804	C. C. Pinckney	Federal.	" "	24
1808	James Madison	Democrat.		122
1808	C. C. Pinckney	Federal.	" "	47
1812	James Madison	Democrat.		284
1812	DeWitt Clinton	Federal.	" "	89
1816	James Monroe	Democrat.		184
1816	Rufus King	Federal.		34
1820	James Monroe	Democrat.	But one Elec'l vote in oppo.	
1824	Andrew Jackson	Democrat.	152,827	Adams 99
1824	John Q. Adams	Federal.	105,321	elec by st
1824	W. H. Crawford	Republican.	44,282	House 41
1824	Henry Clay	Republican.	46,587	Reps. 37
1828	Andrew Jackson	Democrat.	617,231	178
1828	John Q. Adams	Federal.	509,097	83
1832	Andrew Jackson	Democrat.	687,502	219
1832	Henry Clay	Nat.Repub'c'n.	530,189	49
1832	John Floyd	Whig.		11
1832	William Wirt	Whig.		7
1836	Martin Van Buren	Democrat.	761,549	170
1836	W. H. Harrison	Whig.		73
1836	Hugh L. White	Whig.	736,656	26
1836	Daniel Webster	Whig.		14
1836	W. P. Mangum	Whig.		11
1840	Martin Van Buren	Democrat.	1,128,702	48
1840	W. H. Harrison	Whig.	1,275,017	234
1840	J. G. Birney	Liberty.	7,059	
1844	James K. Polk	Democrat.	1,337,243	170
1844	Henry Clay	Whig.	1,299,068	105
1844	James G. Birney	Liberty.	62,300	
1848	Zachary Taylor	Whig.	1,360,101	163
1848	Lewis Cass	Democrat.	1,222,544	127
1848	Martin Van Buren	Free Soil.	291,263	
1852	Franklin Pierce	Democrat.	1,601,474	254
1852	Winfield Scott	Whig.	1,380,578	42
1852	John P. Hale	Free Soil.	156,149	
1856	James Buchanan	Democrat.	1,838,169	174
1856	John C. Fremont	Republican.	1,341,262	114
1856	Millard Fillmore	American.	874,534	8
1860	Abraham Lincoln	Republican.	1,866,352	180
1860	Stephen A. Douglas	Democrat.	1,375,157	12
1860	John C. Breckenridge	Democrat.	845,763	72
1860	John Bell	Union.	589,581	39
1864	Abraham Lincoln	Republican.	2,216,067	212
1864	George B. McClellan	Democrat.	1,808,725	21
1868	Ulysses S. Grant	Republican.	3,015,071	214
1868	Horatio Seymour	Democrat.	2,709,613	80
1872	Ulysses S. Grant	Republican.	3,597,070	286
1872	Horace Greeley	Liberal & Dem	2,834,079	47
1872	Charles O'Connor	Democrat.	29,408	
1872	James Black	Temperance.	5,608	
1876	R. B. Hayes	Republican.	4,033,950	185
1876	Samuel J. Tilden	Democrat.	4,284,885	184
1876	Peter Cooper	Greenback.	81,740	
1876	G. C. Smith	Prohibition.	9,522	
1876	Scattering		2,636	
1880	James A. Garfield	Republican.	4,449,053	214
1880	Winfield S. Hancock	Democrat.	4,442,035	155
1880	James B. Weaver	Greenback.	307,306	
1884	Grover Cleveland	Democrat.	4,913,901	219
1884	James G. Blaine	Republican.	4,847,669	184
1884	B. F. Butler	Peoples'.	133,889	
1884	St. John	Prohibition.	150,633	
1884	Belva Lockwood	Wom'n's Rig'ts	Scattering.	

NOTE 1. No returns of the popular vote for President are presented with any accuracy prior to 1824. During the earlier elections the majority of the states chose the Presidential electors by their legislatures, and not by popular vote. Even as late as 1824 six states thus voted, while the state of South Carolina continued to choose Presidential electors by her legislature until 1868.

G Washington

John Adams.

Th. Jefferson

James Madison

James Monroe

J. Q. Adams

Andrew Jackson

M Van Buren

W. H. Harrison

John Tyler

James K. Polk

Zachary Taylor

Millard Fillmore

Franklin Pierce

James Buchanan

Your friend, as ever
A. Lincoln

Andrew Johnson

U. S. Grant

Sincerely
R. B. Hayes

J. A. Garfield

C. A. Arthur

Grover Cleveland

TO OUR PRESIDENTS.

THE name of Washington, like a fragrant rose,
    Wafts its perfume where'er it goes;

If all the Presidents will follow in the path he trod,
They'll be beloved by the American people and the people's God.

They should know no north, south, east or west;
To secure the nation's interests they should do their best;

Let all issues tending to party strife sink and pass away,
And the perpetuation of this Union be the order of the day.

Then your name will go to posterity crowned with as great a fame,
Immortal! as that of Washington, our great father's name!

CAPITAL OF THE UNITED STATES,
In the City of Washington, District of Columbia.

PART XXV.

CONSTITUTION OF THE UNITED STATES.

PREAMBLE. We, the people of the United States, in order to form a more perfect union, establish justice, ensure domestic tranquility, provide for the common defence, promote the general welfare, and secure the blessings of liberty to ourselves and our posterity, do ordain and establish this Constitution for the United States of America:

ARTICLE I.

SECTION 1. All legislative powers herein granted shall be vested in a congress of the United States, which shall consist of a senate and house of representatives.

SEC. 2. The house of representatives shall be composed of members chosen every second year by the people of the several states; and the electors in each state shall have the qualifications requisite for electors of the most numerous branch of the state legislature.

No person shall be a representative who shall not have attained to the age of twenty-five years, and been seven years a citizen of the United States, and who shall not, when elected, be an inhabitant of that state in which he shall be chosen.

Representatives and direct taxes shall be apportioned among the several states which may be included within this Union, according to their respective numbers, which shall be determined by adding to the whole number of free persons, including those bound to service for a term of years, and excluding Indians not taxed, three-fifths of all other persons. The actual enumeration shall be made within three years after the first meeting of the Congress of the United States, and within every subsequent term of ten years, in such manner as they shall by law direct. The number of representatives shall not exceed one for every thirty thousand, but each state shall have at least one Representative; and until such enumeration shall be made, the state of New Hampshire shall be entitled to choose three; Massachusetts, eight; Rhode Island and Providence Plantations, one; Connecticut five; New York, six; New Jersey, four; Pennsylvania, eight; Delaware, one; Maryland, six; Virginia, ten; North Carolina, five; South Carolina, five; and Georgia, three.

When vacancies happen in the representation from any state, the executive authority thereof shall issue writs of election to fill such vacancies.

The House of Representatives shall choose their speaker and other officers, and shall have the sole power of impeachment.

SEC. 3. The Senate of the United States shall be composed of two senators from each state, chosen by the legislature thereof for six years; and each senator shall have one vote.

Immediately after they shall be assembled in consequence of the first election, they shall be divided as equally as may be, into three classes. The seats of the senators of the first class shall be vacated at the expiration of the second year; of the second class at the expiration of the fourth year; of the third class at the expiration of the sixth year, so that one-third may be chosen every second year; and if vacancies happen by resignation or otherwise during the recess of the legislature of any state, the executive thereof may make temporary appointments until the next meeting of the legislature, which shall then fill such vacancies.

No person shall be a senator who shall not have attained to the age of thirty years and been nine years a citizen of the United States, and who shall not, when elected, be an inhabitant of that state for which he shall be chosen.

The Vice-President of the United States shall be president of the

FIRST PRESIDENT.

Born in Westmoreland county, Va., Feb. 22, 1732. Began surveying the Virginia Valley, 1748. Appointed Major in the army 1751. Promoted to colonel, 1754. Married Mrs. Martha Custis, 1759. Member House of Burgesses of Virginia 1759. Delegate to the first Continental Congress, 1774. Elected Commander-in-Chief, by the Congress, June 15, 1775. Salary fixed at $6000 per year, but he declined to receive any compensation. War ended by surrender of Cornwallis at Yorktown, Va., Oct. 19, 1781. Treaty of Peace signed in Paris, Sept. 3, 1783. Resigned his commission Dec. 23, 1783. Presided over the Convention which framed the Constitution Philadelphia 1787. Inaugurated first President of the United States, New York, April 30, 1789. Elected for a second term, 1793. Declined a third term. Issued his "Farewell Address," Sept. 19, 1796. Believing a French invasion contemplated, he was again summoned to take the field, May, 1798. Died Dec. 14, 1799. Vice President, John Adams.

senate, but shall have no vote unless they be equally divided.

The Senate shall choose their own officers, and also a president pro tempore, in the absence of the vice-president, or when he shall exercise the office of President of the United States.

The Senate shall have the sole power to try all impeachments. When sitting for that purpose they shall be on oath or affirmation. When the President of the United States is tried the chief justice shall preside; and no person shall be convicted without the concurrence of two-thirds of the members present.

Judgment in cases of impeachment shall not extend further than to removal from office, and disqualification to hold and enjoy any office of honor, trust or profit under the United States; but the party convicted shall nevertheless be liable and subject to indictment, trial, judgment and punishment, according to law.

SEC. 4. The times, places and manner of holding elections for senators and representatives shall be prescribed in each state by the legislature thereof; but the Congress may at any time by law make or alter such regulations, except as to the place of choosing senators.

The Congress shall assemble at least once in every year, and such meeting shall be on the first Monday in December, unless they shall by law appoint a different day.

SEC. 5. Each house shall be the judge of the elections, returns and qualifications of its own members, and a majority of each shall constitute a quorum to do business; but a smaller number may adjourn from day to day, and may be authorized to compel the attendance of absent members, in such manner and under such penalties as each house may provide. Each house may determine the rules of its proceedings, punish its members for disorderly behavior, and with the concurrence of two-thirds expel a member.

Each house shall keep a journal of its proceedings, and from time to time publish the same, excepting such parts as may in their judgment require secrecy; and the yeas and nays of the members of either house on any question shall at the desire of one-fifth of those present be entered on the journal.

Neither house during the session of Congress shall, without the consent of the other, adjourn for more than three days, nor to any other place than that in which the two houses shall be sitting.

SEC. 6. The senators and representatives shall receive a compensation for their services, to be ascertained by law and paid out of the treasury of the United States. They shall in all cases except treason, felony and breach of the peace, be privileged from arrest during their attendance at the session of their respective houses, and in going to and returning from the same; and for any speech or debate in either house they shall not be questioned in any other place.

No senator or representative shall, during the time for which he was elected, be appointed to any civil office under the authority of the United States which shall have been created, or the emoluments whereof shall have been increased during such time; and no person holding any office under the United States shall be a member of either house during his continuance in office.

SEC. 7. All bills for raising revenue shall originate in the House of Representatives, but the Senate may propose or concur with amendments, as on other bills.

Every bill which shall have passed the House of Representatives and the Senate, shall, before it becomes a law, be presented to the President of the United States; if he approve, he shall sign it; but if not, he shall return it, with his objections, to that house in which it shall have originated, who shall enter the objections at large on their journal, and proceed to reconsider it. If, after such reconsideration, two-thirds of that house shall agree to pass the bill, it will be sent, together with the objections, to the other house, by which it shall likewise be reconsidered, and, if approved by two-thirds of that house, it shall become a law. But in all cases the votes of both houses shall be determined by yeas and nays, and the names of the persons voting for and against the bill shall be entered on the journal of each house, respectively. If any bill shall not be returned by the President within ten days (Sundays excepted) after it shall have been presented to him, the same shall be a law in like manner as if he had signed it, unless the Congress by their adjournment prevent its return; in which case it shall not be a law.

Every order, resolution or vote to which the concurrence of the Senate and House of Representatives may be necessary (except on a question of adjournment) shall be presented to the President of the United States, and before the same shall take effect, shall be approved by him, or being disapproved by him, shall be repassed by two-thirds of the Senate and House of Representatives, according to the rules and limitations prescribed in the case of a bill.

SEC. 8. Congress shall have power

To lay and collect taxes, duties, imposts and excises, to pay the debts and provide for the common defence and general welfare of the United States; but all duties, imposts and excises shall be uniform throughout the United States;

To borrow money on the credit of the United States;

To regulate commerce with foreign nations, and among the several states, and with the Indian tribes;

To establish an uniform rule of naturalization, and uniform laws on the subject of bankruptcies throughout the United States;

To coin money, regulate the value thereof and of foreign coin, and fix the standard of weights and measures;

To provide for the punishment for counterfeiting the securities and current coin of the United States;

SECOND PRESIDENT.

Born in Quincy, Mass., Oct. 19, 1735. Graduate at Harvard College, 1755. Admitted to the bar, 1758. Commissioner to France, 1778. Author of Constitution of Massachusetts, 1779. Minister to negotiate peace with Great Britain, 1779; sent to Holland, 1780; summoned to Paris to consult on the general peace, which was signed, 1783. Appointed Minister Plenipotentiary to Great Britain, 1785. Resigned 1788, and was elected Vice-President. Elected President of the United States, 1796, defeating Thomas Jefferson. Died July 4, 1826. Vice-President, Thomas Jefferson.

To establish post offices and post roads;

To promote the progress of science and useful arts, by securing for limited times to authors and inventors, the exclusive right to their respective writings and discoveries;

To constitute tribunals inferior to the Supreme Court;

To define and punish piracies and felonies committed on the high seas, and offences against the law of nations;

To declare war, grant letters of marque and reprisal, and make rules concerning captures on land and water;

To raise and support armies; but no appropriation of money to that use shall be for a longer term than two years;

To provide and maintain a navy;

To make rules for the government and regulation of the land and naval forces;

To provide for calling forth the militia to execute the laws of the Union, suppress insurrections and repel invasions;

To provide for organizing, arming and disciplining the militia, and for governing such part of them as may be employed in the service of the United States, reserving to the states, respectively, the appointment of the officers, and the authority of training the militia according to the discipline prescribed by Congress;

To exercise exclusive legislation in all cases whatsoever over such district (not exceeding ten miles square) as may, by cession of particular states and the acceptance of Congress, become the seat of the government of the United States; and to exercise like authority over all places purchased by the consent of the legislature of the state in which the same shall be, for the erection of forts, magazines, arsenals, dock-yards, and other needful buildings; and

To make all laws which shall be necessary and proper for carrying into execution the foregoing powers, and all other powers vested by this Constitution in the government of the United States, or in any department or officer thereof.

Sec. 9. The migration or importation of such persons as any of the states now existing shall think proper to admit, shall not be prohibited by the Congress prior to the year one thousand eight hundred and eight; but a tax or duty may be imposed on such importation, not exceeding ten dollars for each person.

The privilege of the writ of *habeas corpus* shall not be suspended unless when, in cases of rebellion or invasion, the public safety may require it.

No bill of attainder, or *ex post facto* law, shall be passed.

No capitation or other direct tax shall be laid unless in proportion to the census or enumeration hereinbefore directed to be taken.

No tax or duty shall be laid on articles exported from any state. No preference shall be given by any regulation of commerce or revenue, to the ports of one state over those of another; nor shall vessels bound to or from one state be obliged to enter, clear or pay duties in another.

No money shall be drawn from the treasury but in consequence of appropriations made by law; and a regular statement and account of the receipts and expenditures of all public money shall be published from time to time.

No title of nobility shall be granted by the United States, and no person holding any office of profit or trust under them shall, without the consent of the Congress, accept of any present, emolument, office, or title of any kind whatever, from any king, prince or foreign state.

Sec. 10. No state shall enter into any treaty, alliance or confederation; grant letters of marque and reprisal; coin money; emit bills of credit; make anything but gold and silver coin a tender in payment of debts; pass any bill of attainder, or *ex post facto* law, or law impairing the obligation of contracts, or grant any title of nobility.

No state shall, without the consent of Congress, lay any imposts or duties on imports or exports, except what may be absolutely necessary for executing its inspection laws; and the net produce of all duties and imposts laid by any state on imports or exports, shall be for the use of the treasury of the United States; and all such laws shall be subject to the revision and control of the Congress.

No state shall, without the consent of Congress, lay any duty of tonnage, keep troops or ships of war in time of peace, enter into any agreement or compact with another state or with a foreign power; or engage in war, unless actually invaded or in such imminent danger as will not admit of delay.

ARTICLE II.

Section 1. The executive power shall be vested in a President of the United States of America. He shall hold his office during the term of four years, and, together with the Vice-President, chosen for the same term, be elected as follows:

Each state shall appoint, in such manner as the legislature thereof may direct, a number of electors equal to the whole number of Senators and Representatives to which the state may be entitled in the Congress; but no Senator or Representative, or person holding an office of trust or profit under the United States, shall be appointed an elector.

[The electors shall meet in their respective states, and vote by ballot for two persons, of whom one at least shall not be an inhabitant of the same state with themselves. And they shall make a list of all the persons voted for, and of the number of votes for each; which list they shall sign and certify and transmit sealed to the seat of the government of the United States, directed to the president of the Senate. The president of the Senate shall, in the presence of the Senate and House of Representatives, open all the certificates, and the votes shall then be counted. The

THIRD PRESIDENT.

Born in Shadwell, Va., April 2, 1743. Received a classical education in William and Mary College. Admitted to the bar, 1767. Member House of Burgesses, Va., 1769. Elected to the Colonial Congress, 1775. Chosen to prepare the Declaration of Independence, adopted, July 4, 1776. Elected Governor of Va., 1779. Member of Congress, 1783. Appointed Minister to France, to succeed Benjamin Franklin, 1784. Appointed Secretary of State by President Washington, 1789. Elected Vice-President, 1796. Elected President of the United States, 1801, and re-elected for second term. Founder of the University of Virginia. Died July 4, 1826. Vice-President, Aaron Burr.

person having the greatest number of votes shall be the President, if such number be a majority of the whole number of electors appointed; and if there be more than one who have such a majority, and have an equal number of votes, then the House of Representatives shall immediately choose, by ballot, one of them for President; and if no person have a majority, then from the five highest on the list the said house shall, in like manner, choose the President. But in choosing the President the votes shall be taken by states, the representation from each state having one vote; a quorum for this purpose shall consist of a member or members from two-thirds of the states, and a majority of all the states shall be necessary to a choice. In every case after the choice of the President the person having the greatest number of votes of the electors shall be the Vice-President. But if there should remain two or more who have equal votes, the Senate shall choose from them by ballot, the Vice-President.]*

The Congress may determine the time of choosing the electors, and the day on which they shall give their votes, which day shall be the same throughout the United States.

No person, except a natural born citizen, or a citizen of the United States at the time of the adoption of this Constitution, shall be eligible to the office of President; neither shall any person be eligible to that office, who shall not have attained to the age of thirty-five years and been fourteen years a resident within the United States.

In case of the removal of the President from office, or of his death, resignation, or inability to discharge the powers and duties of the said office, the same shall devolve on the Vice-President; and the Congress may by law provide for the case of removal, death, resignation or inability both of the President and Vice-President, declaring what officer shall then act as President, and such officer shall act accordingly until the disability be removed or a President shall be elected.

The President shall at stated times receive for his services a compensation which shall neither be increased nor diminished during the period for which he shall have been elected; and he shall not receive within that period any other emolument from the United States, or any of them.

Before he enters upon the execution of his office, he shall take the following oath or affirmation:

"I do solemnly swear (or affirm) that I will faithfully execute the office of President of the United States, and will, to the best of my ability, preserve, protect and defend the Constitution of the United States."

SEC. 2. The President shall be commander-in-chief of the army and navy of the United States, and of the militia of the several states when called into the actual service of the United States; he may require the opinion in writing of the principal officer in each of the executive departments, upon any subject relating to the duties of their respective offices;

---

* The portion in brackets has been superseded by the 12th Amendment.

and he shall have power to grant reprieves and pardons for offences against the United States, except in cases of impeachment.

He shall have power, by and with the advice and consent of the Senate, to make treaties, provided two-thirds of the Senators present concur; and he shall nominate, and by and with the advice and consent of the Senate shall appoint ambassadors, other public ministers and consuls, judges of the Supreme Court, and all other officers of the United States whose appointments are not herein otherwise provided for, and which shall be established by law. But the Congress may, by law, vest the appointment of such inferior offices as they think proper, in the President alone, in the courts of law, or in the heads of departments.

The President shall have power to fill up all vacancies that may happen during the recess of the Senate, by granting commissions which shall expire at the end of their next session.

SEC. 3. He shall from time to time give to Congress information of the state of the Union, and recommend to their consideration such measures as he may judge necessary and expedient. He may, on extraordinary occasions, convene both houses, or either of them; and in case of disagreement between them with respect to the time of adjournment, he may adjourn them to such time as he may think proper; he shall receive ambassadors and other public ministers. He shall take care that the laws be faithfully executed, and shall commission all the officers of the United States.

SEC. 4. The President, Vice-President, and all civil officers of the United States, shall be removed from office on impeachment for, and conviction of, treason, bribery, or other high crimes and misdemeanors.

ARTICLE III.

SECTION 1. The judicial power of the United States shall be vested in one Supreme Court, and in such inferior courts as the Congress may from time to time ordain and establish. The judges both of the supreme and inferior courts shall hold their offices during good behavior, and shall at stated times recieve for their services a compensation which shall not be diminished during their continuance in office.

SEC. 2. The judicial power shall extend to all cases in law and equity, arising under this Constitution, the laws of the United States, and treaties made, or which shall be made, under their authority; to all cases affecting ambassadors, other public ministers and consuls; to all cases of admiralty and maritime jurisdiction; to controversies to which the United States shall be a party; to controversies between two or more states, between a state and the citizens of another state, between citizens of different states, bstween citizens of the same state claiming lands under grants of different states, and between a state, or the citizens thereof, and foreign states, citizens or subjects.*

---

* See the 11th Amendment.

FOURTH PRESIDENT.

Born in King George, Orange county, Va., March 16, 1751. Graduate at Princeton College, N. J., 1771. Elected to the General Assembly of Virginia, 1776; to the Executive Council of the State, 1778, and to the Congress, 1779, holding his seat until 1783. Member of the Virginia Legislature, 1784, '85, 86, and of the Convention which framed the Constitution, 1787. Elected a Member of the first Congress, 1789, continuing as such until 1797. Appointed Secretary of State by President Jefferson, 1801. Elected President of the United States, 1808, and re-elected for a second term. Died June 28, 1836. Vice-President, first term, George Clinton; second term, Elbridge Gerry.

In all cases affecting ambassadors or other public ministers and consuls, and those in which a state shall be a party, the Supreme Court shall have original jurisdiction. In all other cases before mentioned, the Supreme Court shall have appellate jurisdiction both as to law and fact with such exceptions and under such regulations as the Congress shall make.

The trial of crimes, except in cases of impeachment, shall be by jury, and such trial shall be held in the state where the said crimes shall have been committed; but when not committed within any state, the trial shall be at such place or places as the Congress may by law have directed.

SEC. 3. Treason against the United States shall consist only in levying war against them, or in adhering to their enemies, giving them aid and comfort. No person shall be convicted of treason unless on the testimony of two witnesses to the same overt act, or on confession in open court.

The Congress shall have power to declare the punishment of treason; but no attainder of treason shall work corruption of blood, or forfeiture, except during the life of the person attained.

ARTICLE IV

SECTION 1. Full faith and credit shall be given in each state to the public acts, records, and judicial proceedings of every other state. And the Congress may by general laws prescribe the manner in which such acts, records and proceedings shall be proved, and the effect thereof.

SEC. 2. The citizens of each state shall be entitled to all privileges and immunities of citizens in the several states.

A person charged in any state with treason, felony or other crime, who shall flee from justice, and be found in another state, shall, on demand of the executive authority of the state from which he fled, be delivered up, to be removed to the state having jurisdiction of the crime.

No person held to service or labor in one state under the laws thereof, escaping into another, shall, in consequence of any law or regulation therein, be discharged from such service or labor, but shall be delivered up on claim of the party to whom such service or labor may be due.

SEC. 3. New states may be admitted by the Congress into this Union; but no new states shall be formed or erected within the jurisdiction of any other state, nor any state be formed by the junction of two or more states or parts of states, without the consent of the legislatures of the states concerned, as well as of the Congress.

The Congress shall have power to dispose of and make all needful rules and regulations respecting the territory or other property belonging to the United States; and nothing in this Constitution shall be so construed as to prejudice any claims of the United States, or of any particular state.

SEC. 4. The United States shall guarantee to every state in this Union a Republican form of government; and shall protect each of them against invasion, and on application of the legislature or the executive (when the legislature cannot be convened) against domestic violence.

ARTICLE V.

The Congress, whenever two-thirds of both houses shall deem it necessary, shall propose amendments to this Constitution; or, on application of the legislatures of two-thirds of the several states, shall call a convention for proposing amendments, which, in either case, shall be valid to all intents and purposes, as part of this Constitution, when ratified by the legislatures of three-fourths of the several states, or by conventions in three-fourths thereof, as the one or the other mode of ratification may be proposed by the Congress: *provided*, that no amendment which may be made prior to the year one thousand eight hundred and eight shall in any manner affect the first and fourth clauses in the ninth section of the first article; and that no state, without its consent, shall be deprived of its equal suffrage in the Senate.

ARTICLE VI.

All debts contracted and engagements entered into before the adoption of this Constitution, shall be as valid against the United States under this Constitution, as under the Confederation.

This Constitution, and the laws of the United States which shall be made in pursuance thereof, and all treaties made or which shall be made under the authority of the United States, shall be the supreme law of the land; and the judges in every state shall be bound thereby, anything in the Constitution or laws of any state to the contrary notwithstanding.

The Senators and Representatives before mentioned, and the members of the several state legislatures, and all executive and judicial officers, both of the United States and of the several states shall be bound by oath or affirmation to support this Constitution; but no religious test shall ever be required as a qualification to any office or public trust under the United States.

ARTICLE VII.

The ratification of the conventions of nine states shall be sufficient for the establishment of this Constitution between the states so ratifying the same.

FIFTH PRESIDENT.

Born in Westmoreland county, Va., April 28, 1758. Graduate at William and Mary College, 1776. Served that year in the Continental Army with Washington, and was Aide to Lord Sterling at Brandywine. Studied law with Thomas Jefferson. Elected to the State Legislature, 1782; to Congress, 1783, and the Legislature, 1786. Elected United States Senator, 1790. Envoy Extraordinary to the Court of Versailles, where he bought the Louisiana tract from Napoleon for $15,000,000. 1794. Served a short time as Minister to England. Elected Governor of Virginia, 1810, and held the office until appointed Secretary of State by President Madison. Elected President of the United States, 1817; re-elected, 1821. Died July 4, 1831. Vice-President, D. D. Tompkins.

ARTICLES

In addition to, and amendment of the Constitution of the United States of America, proposed by Congress and ratified by the Legislatures of the several States, pursuant to the fifth article of the original Constitution.

ARTICLE I.

Congress shall make no law respecting an establishment of religion or prohibiting the free exercise thereof, or abridging the freedom of speech, or of the press, or the right of the people peaceably to assemble, or to petition the government for a redress of grievances.

ARTICLE II.

A well regulated militia being necessary to the security of a free state, the right of the people to keep and bear arms shall not be infringed.

ARTICLE III.

No soldier shall, in time of peace, be quartered in any house without the consent of the owner, nor in time of war but in a manner to be prescribed by law.

ARTICLE IV.

The right of the people to be secure in their persons, houses, papers and effects, against unreasonable searches and seizures, shall not be violated, and no warrant shall issue but upon probable cause, supported by oath or affirmation, and particularly describing the place to be searched and the persons or things to be siezed.

ARTICLE V.

No person shall be held to answer for a capital or otherwise infamous crime, unless on a presentment or indictment of a grand jury, except in cases arising in the land or naval forces, or in the militia, when in actual service, in time of war or public danger; nor shall any person be subject for the same offence to be twice put in jeopardy of life or limb; nor shall be compelled in any criminal case to be witness against himself, nor be deprived of life, liberty or property without due process of law; nor shall private property be taken for public use without just compensation.

ARTICLE VI.

In all criminal prosecutions the accused shall enjoy the right to a speedy and public trial by an impartial jury of the state and district wherein the crime shall have been committed, which district shall have been previously ascertained by law, and to be informed of the nature and cause of the accusation; to be confronted with the witnesses against him; to have compulsory process for obtaining witnesses in his favor, and to have the assistance of counsel for his defence.

ARTICLE VII.

In suits at common law, where the value in controversy shall exceed twenty dollars, the right of trial by jury shall be preserved, and no fact tried by a jury shall be otherwise re-examined in any court of the United States, than according to the rules of the common law.

ARTICLE VIII.

Excessive bail shall not be required, nor excessive fines imposed, nor cruel and unusual punishments inflicted.

ARTICLE IX.

The enumeration in the Constitution of certain rights shall not be construed to deny or disparage others retained by the people.

ARTICLE X.

The powers not delegated to the United States by the Constitution, nor prohibited by it to the states, are reserved to the states respectively, or to the people.

ARTICLE XI.

The judicial power of the United States shall not be construed to extend to any suit in law or equity, commenced or prosecuted against one of the United States by citizens of another state, or by citizens or subjects of any foreign state.

ARTICLE XII.

The electors shall meet in their respective states and vote by ballot for President and Vice-President, one of whom at least shall not be an inhabitant of the same state with themselves; they shall name in their ballots the person voted for as President, and in distinct ballots the person voted for as Vice-President; and they shall make distinct lists of all persons voted for as President and of all persons voted for as Vice-President, and of the number of votes for each; which lists they shall sign and certify

J. Q. Adams

SIXTH PRESIDENT.

Born in Quincy, Mass., July 11, 1767. Son of the second President. Entered Harvard College, 1786, and on graduating studied law. Appointed Minister to the Hague, 1794; transferred to Berlin, 1797; recalled, 1801. Elected State Senator, 1802. Appointed United States Senator, 1803, and resigned 1808. Appointed Minister to Russia, 1809. Assisted in negotiating the Treaty of Ghent, 1815. Appointed Minister to Great Britain same year. Secretary of State under President Monroe, 1817, both terms. Chosen President of the United States by the Congress, there being no choice by the people, 1824. Elected Member of Congress, 1830; held the position to his death, which occurred Feb. 23, 1848, two days after being stricken with paralysis while arising to address the House. Vice-President, John C. Calhoun.

and transmit, sealed, to the seat of the government of the United States, directed to the president of the Senate. The president of the Senate shall, in the presence of the Senate and House of Representatives, open all the certificates, and the votes shall then be counted; the person having the greatest number of votes for President shall be President, if such number be a majority of the whole number of electors appointed; and if no person have such majority, then from the persons having the highest numbers, not exceeding three, on the list of those voted for as President, the House of Representatives shall choose immediately, by ballot, the President. But in choosing the President, the votes shall be taken by states, the representation from each state having one vote; a quorum for this purpose shall consist of a member or members from two-thirds of the states, and a majority of all the states shall be necessary to a choice. And if the House of Representatives shall not choose a President whenever the right of choice shall devolve upon them, before the fourth day of March next following, then the Vice-President shall act as President, as in the case of the death or other constitutional disability of the President.

The person having the greatest number of votes as Vice-President shall be the Vice-President, if such number be a majority of the whole number of electors appointed; and if no person have a majority, then from the two highest numbers on the list, the Senate shall choose the Vice-President; a quorum for the purpose shall consist of two-thirds of the whole number of Senators, and a majority of the whole number shall be necessary to a choice.

But no person constitutionally ineligible to the office of President shall be eligible to that of Vice-President of the United States.

ARTICLE XIII.

SECTION 1. Neither slavery nor involuntary servitude, except as a punishment for crime whereof the party shall have been duly convicted, shall exist within the United States, or any place subject to their jurisdiction.

SEC. 2. Congress shall have power to enforce this article by appropriate legislation.

ARTICLE XIV.

SECTION 1. All persons born or naturalized in the United States, and subject to the jurisdiction thereof, are citizens of the United States and of the state wherein they reside. No state shall make or enforce any law which shall abridge the privileges or immunities of citizens of the United States; nor shall any state deprive any person of life, liberty or property, without due process of law, nor deny to any person within its jurisdiction the equal protection of the laws.

SEC. 2. Representatives shall be appointed among the several states according to their respective numbers, counting the whole number of persons in each state, including Indians not taxed. But when the right to vote at any election for the choice of electors for President and Vice-President of the United States, Representatives in Congress, the executive and judicial officers of a state, or the members of the legislature thereof, is denied to any of the male inhabitants of such state being twenty-one years of age and citizens of the United States, or in any way abridged, except for participation in rebellion or other crime, the basis of representation therein shall be reduced in the proportion which the number of male citizens shall bear to the whole number of male citizens twenty-one years of age in such state.

Sec. 3. No person shall be a Senator or Representative in Congress or elector of President and Vice-President, hold any office, civil or military, under the United States or under any state, who having previously taken an oath as a member of Congress, or as an officer of the United States, or as a member of any state legislature, or as an executive or judicial officer of any state to support the Constitution of the United States, shall have engaged in insurrection or Rebellion against the same, or given aid and comfort to the enemies thereof. But Congress may by a vote of two-thirds of each house, remove such disability.

Sec. 4. The validity of the public debt of the United States, authorized by law, including debts incurred for payment of pensions and bounties for services in suppressing insurrection or rebellion shall not be questioned. But neither the United States nor any state shall assume or pay any debt or obligation incurred in aid of insurrection or rebellion against the United States, or any claim for the loss or emancipation of any slave; but all such debts, obligations and claims shall be held illegal and void.

Sec. 5. The Congress shall have power to enforce, by appropriate legislation, the provisions of this article.

ARTICLE XV.

Section 1. The right of the citizens of the United States to vote shall not be denied or abridged by the United States, or by any state, on account of race, color, or previous condition of servitude.

Sec. 2. The Congress shall have power to enforce this article by appropriate legislation.

Note.—The Constitution was adopted September 17th, 1787, by the unanimous consent of the states present in the convention appointed in pursuance of the resolution of the Congress of the Confederation, of the 21st of February, 1787, and was ratified by the conventions of the several states, as follows, viz.: By convention of Delaware, December 7th, 1787; Pennsylvania December 12th, 1787, New Jersey, December 18th, 1787; Georgia, January 2d, 1788; Connecticut, January 9th, 1788; Massachusetts, February 6th, 1788; Maryland, April 28th, 1788; South Carolina, May 23d, 1788; New Hampshire, June 21st, 1788; Virginia, June 26th, 1788; New York, July 26th, 1788; North Carolina, November 21st, 1789; Rhode Island, May, 29th, 1790.

SEVENTH PRESIDENT.

Born in Mecklenburg county, N. C., March 15, 1767. Enlisted in the Revolutionary army, 1781, and was a prisoner of war. Admitted to the bar, 1786; began practice at Nashville, Tenn., 1788. Elected as first Representative from Tennessee in Congress, 1796. U. S. Senator, 1797. General of the army, 1812. Made the memorable defence of New Orleans, 1815. Expelled the Seminoles from Florida. Appointed Governor of Florida, 1821. U. S. Senator, 1823. Elected President of the United States, 1828; re-elected, 1832. Died at the "Hermitage," June 8, 1845. Vice-President, first term, John C. Calhoun; second term, Martin Van Buren.

The first ten of the amendments were proposed at the first session of the first Congress of the United States, September 25th, 1787, and were finally ratified by the constitutional number of states, December 15th, 1791. The eleventh amendment was proposed at the first session of the third Congress, March 5th, 1794, and was declared in a message from the President of the United States to both houses of Congress, dated January 8th, 1798, to have been adopted by the constitutional number of states. The twelfth amendment was proposed at the first session of the eighth Congress, December 12th, 1803, and was adopted by the constitutional number of states in 1804, according to a public notice thereof by the Secretary of State, dated September 25th, 1804.

The thirteenth amendment was proposed at the second session of the thirty-eighth Congress, February 1st, 1865, and was adopted by the constitutional number of states in 1865, according to a public notice thereof by the Secretary of State, dated December 18th, 1865.

The fourteenth amendment took effect July 28th, 1868.

The fifteenth amendment took effect March 30th, 1870.

SIGNERS OF THE CONSTITUTION.

List of the members of the Federal Convention which formed the Constitution of the United States, and who did and who did not sign the Constitution, for ratification by the thirteen original states.

GEORGE WASHINGTON — President.

Attended.

NEW HAMPSHIRE.
1787.
1 John Langdon.........July 3.
* John Pickering........
2 Nicholas Gilmore......July 23.
* Benjamin West........

MASSACHUSETTS.
* Francis Dana..........
† Elbridge Gerry........May 29.
3 Nathaniel Gorham.....May 28.
4 Rufus King...........May 25.
† Caleb Strong.........May 28.

CONNECTICUT.
5 William Samuel Johnson June 2.
6 Roger Sherman........May 30.
† Oliver Elsworth......May 29.

Attended.

NEW YORK.
1787.
† Robert Yates..........May 25.
7 Alexander Hamilton...May 25.
† John Lansing.........June 2.

NEW JERSEY.
8 William Livingston....June 5.
9 David Brearly........May 25.
† William C. Houston....May 25.
* John Neilson..........
10 William Patterson.....May 25.
* Abraham Clark........
11 Jonathan Dayton......June 21.

RHODE ISLAND.
(*No appointment.*)

Attended.

PENNSYLVANIA.
1787.
12 Benjamin Franklin....May 28.
13 Thomas Mifflin........May 28.
14 Robert Morris.........May 25.
15 George Clymer........May 28.
16 Thomas Fitzsimons....May 25.
17 Jared Ingersoll........May 25.
18 James Wilson.........May 25.
19 Gouverneur Morris....May 25.

VIRGINIA.
20 George Washington....May 25.
* Patrick Henry (declined)
† Edmund Randolph.....May 25.
21 John Blair............May 25.
22 James Madison, Jr.....May 25.
† George Mason.........May 25.
† George Wythe.........May 25.
† James M'Clurg in place of
   P. Henry............May 25.

GEORGIA.
23 William Few..........May 25.
24 Abraham Baldwin.....June 11.
† William Pierce........May 31.
* George Walton........
† William Houstoun.....June 1.
* Nathaniel Pendleton...

Attended.

MARYLAND.
1787.
25 James M'Henry.......May 29.
26 Daniel, of St. Thomas Jenifer..
   ....June 2.
27 Daniel Carroll.........July 9.
† John Francis Mercer....Aug. 6.
† Luther Martin.........June 9.

NORTH CAROLINA.
* Richard Caswell........
28 William Blount ......June 20.
† Alexander Martin......May 25.
† William R. Davie......May 25.
29 Richard D. Spraight...May 25.
30 Hugh Williamson......May 25.
* W. Jones...............

SOUTH CAROLINA.
31 John Rutledge.........May 25.
32 Charles C. Pinckney....May 25.
33 Charles Pinckney......May 25.
34 Pierce Butler..........May 25.

DELAWARE.
35 George Read..........May 25.
36 Gunning Bedford, Jr...May 28.
37 John Dickinson.......May 28.
38 Richard Bassett.......May 25.
39 Jacob Broom..........May 25.

Those with numbers before their names, signed the Constitution..... 39
Those designated by an asterisk (*) never attended.................. 10
Members who attended, but did not sign the Constitution, are designated by a dagger (†) 16

Total.. 65

Attested.
        WILLIAM JACKSON,
              Secretary.

EIGHTH PRESIDENT.

Born in Kinderhook, N. Y., Dec. 5, 1782. Admitted to the bar, 1803. Appointed Surrogate of Columbia Co., 1808. Elected State Senator, 1812; continuing such until 1820, and acting as Attorney-General a part of the period. Elected U. S. Senator, 1821; re-elected, 1827. Elected Governor of New York, as a Democrat, 1828, but resigned shortly after inauguration to become Secretary of State in President Jackson's Cabinet. Resigned, 1831, and was appointed Minister to England, but the Senate refused to confirm him. Elected Vice-President, 1832. Elected President of the United States, 1836. Nominated for President and defeated, 1840, (Gen. Harrison), 1844, (James K. Polk), 1848, (Gen. Taylor). Made a tour of Europe, 1853, '55. Died July 24, 1862. Vice-President, (elected by Senate) R. M. Johnson.

OUR NATIONAL GOVERNMENT AND HOW IT IS ADMINISTERED.

Government is necessary for the restraint of disorderly persons and for the security of justice. It is the manifestation of organized social power. Its primary and necessary functions are to maintain the peace and to execute justice between different members of society.

Where there is no transgression there is no necessity for law. Every citizen has a natural right to defend his life and property from injury. The collective body of citizens have the right to organize power for the general good—in other words, to create a government which, therefore, justly derives its powers from the will and consent of the governed—THE PEOPLE.

According to this fundamental principle the people of the United States, in representative convention assembled, established a national government in Republican form, having its functions prescribed by a written declaration adopted by the people and known as the "Constitution of the United States."

THE GOVERNMENT.

The national government is composed of three co-ordinate departments, namely:

1. The Legislative, or that which makes the laws.
2. The Executive, or that which enforces the laws.
3. The Judicial, or that which interprets the laws and administers justice.

These powers are lodged in different hands. The body which makes the laws has nothing to do with the enforcement of them, while the judicial department is independent of the legislative and executive departments.

LEGISLATIVE DEPARTMENTS.

The legislative power is vested in a Congress of representatives of the people. It consists of a Senate and House of Representatives. The members of the former are chosen by the several state legislatures, and those of the latter are chosen directly by the people by secret ballots.

REPRESENTATIVES.—A representative, when chosen, must be twenty-five years of age, a citizen of the United States six years, and an inhabitant of the state in which he is chosen.

The number of representatives of each state is determined by the population of the state. In order to keep the number of the members of the House of Representatives about the same the ratio of representatives is changed from time to time. For example, in 1792 the apportionment was 33,000 inhabitants to every representative; in 1870 the number was 138,000 inhabitants to every representative.

When a vacancy happens in the representation of a state, the executive authority of such state issues writs of election to fill such vacancy.

The representatives choose their own presiding officer (the Speaker) and others, and have the sole power of impeachment.

SENATE.— A Senator, when chosen, must be thirty years of age, nine years a citizen of the United States, and an inhabitant of the state for which he is chosen.

Each state is entitled to two senators, without regard to its population. They are chosen for a term of six years. Each Senator has one vote.

The Vice-President of the United States is President of the Senate, but has no vote unless they be equally divided.

The Senate has the sole power to try all impeachments. When sitting as such high court it is the duty of the chief justice of the United States to preside, and no person may be convicted without the concurrence of two-thirds of the members of the Senate present.

BOTH HOUSES.—The two Houses of Congress meet at the same time and place, in separate chambers. Each House is the judge of the elections, returns and qualifications of its own members. A majority in each House constitutes a quorum.

Each House determines its own rules of proceeding, may punish its members, and, with the concurrence of two-thirds of the members present, may expel a member.

Neither House during the session of Congress may, without the consent of the other, adjourn for more than three days, nor to any other place than that in which the two Houses may be sitting.

Members of both houses are privileged from arrest (except in cases of treason, felony or breach of peace) during their attendance at the sessions of their respective Houses, or going to or returning from the same. Nor may they be questioned in any other place for any speech or words in debate in either House.

No person holding office under the United States may be a member of either House during his continuance in office.

The existence of each Congress is limited to two years.

POWERS OF CONGRESS.

Congress is vested with sovereign powers to levy and collect taxes, and provide for the national defence; to borrow money; to regulate commerce with foreign nations and among the several states; to coin money; to punish counterfeiters; to establish post-routes and post-offices; to grant

NINTH PRESIDENT.

Born in Berkeley, Charles City Co., Va., Feb. 2, 1773. Educated at Hampton Sidney College and studied medicine. Joined the Northwestern army 1792, serving against the Indians. Secretary of the Northwestern territory, 1797, and delegate to Congress, 1799. First territorial governor of Indiana, 1800, serving twelve years, and concluding eighteen Indian treaties. Gained the celebrated battle of Tippecanoe over the Indians, Nov. 7, 1811. Commander of the Northwestern army during war of 1812. Elected to Congress from Ohio, 1816. Minister to the Republic of Columbia, S. A., 1828. Elected President of the United States, 1840. Died April 4, 1841, one month after inauguration. Vice-President, John Tyler.

paténts and copyrights; to declare war, carry it on on land and sea (but not to make appropriations for the purpose for a longer time than for two years) and conclude peace; to create and maintain a navy; to call forth the militia of the several states in certain contingencies, and to enact all laws necessary for the execution of the powers granted them. But Congress may not suspend the privilege of the writ of *habeas corpus* unless where the public safety may require it; pass a bill of attainder or *ex post facto* law; lay a tax or duty on inter-state exchanges of commodities; give commercial preference to any port; subject vessels bound to or from one state to enter, to clear, or pay duties in another state; cause money to be drawn from the public treasury, excepting appropriations made by law; grant any title of nobility, nor allow any person holding any office of profit or trust under the United States, without the consent of Congress, to accept any gift from any foreign power while holding such office.

MODE OF PASSING LAWS.

All bills for raising revenue must originate in the House of Representatives. Every bill must have the concurrence of both Houses, and then be presented to the President of the United States. If approved by him he signs it and it becomes a law; if not approved he returns it with his written objections. This is called a *veto*. Then it may be reconsidered, and if passed by a vote of two-thirds of each House, it becomes a law without the signature of the President.

Every order, resolution or vote to which the concurrence of the two Houses may be necessary (excepting on a question of adjournment) is presented to the President of the United States, and may take the course of a bill.

The enumerated powers vested in Congress are denied to the several states which compose the Republic.

THE STATES.

The several states of the Republic are independent in a degree, but not sovereign. By the provisions of the National Constitution they are denied the exercise of the functions of sovereign power.

Originally there were thirteen states in the Union. Since then the process of forming a new state is by erecting a prescribed domain of the Republic into a territory and organizing a territorial government, administered by a chief magistrate and other officers appointed by the President of the United States, by and with the consent of the Senate. The territory has a legislature to enact laws of local application, but Congress may reject any of them. The inhabitants elect a delegate who represents them in Congress, tells that body what the territory needs, but has no vote. The people of a territory do not vote for President of the United

States. When a territory contains a specified number of inhabitants a convention may be called, a state constitution formed and adopted, and application be made to Congress for the admission of the territory into the Union as an independent state. The application may be rejected, and there is no appeal but to another Congress. If permitted to become a state it immediately assumes state powers and takes its position as an equal of the other states according to its ability.

NAVIGATION WITH STEAM.

Its History Traced Back for Several Centuries—Early Experiments and Partial Successes—Fulton's Clermont—Some Famous Old Steam Vessels—The First Steam Railroad Train in America and the First in the World.

The history of steam navigation starts back of the Christian era. Attempts were made as early as 1544, as set forth in the most authentic records, to propel a small boat by steam paddles. This was followed by many other machines and devices, applied either directly or indirectly to the propulsion of boats by steam. The idea of the method in which they were to proceed, seems to have been crude in the extreme in the minds of the old experimenters. The idea was to propel the boat by means of paddles, erected either at the sides or a small crude wheel behind. The paddles resembled in a manner the oars used in modern row boats, and the motion aimed at was to imitate a man rowing.

The steps in the progress of the steamboat are briefly followed: Belasco de Garey, in 1543, is said to have made the first attempt at steam navigation. This was so unsuccessful that for many years little attention was paid to it. Papin tried in 1707, on the Fulda at Cassel, to demonstrate the value of his engine. In 1736, Jonathan Hulls took out a patent for a marine

TENTH PRESIDENT.

Born in Charles City Co., Va., March 29 1790. Graduated at William and Mary College, 1807. Admitted to the bar when 19 years old, and elected to the Legislature when 21. Elected to Congress, 1816. Elected Governor of Virginia, 1826, and sent to the U. S. Senate the following year, resigned in 1836. Elected Vice-President, 1840. Became President of the United States by the death of President Harrison, April 4. 1841. Presiding officer of the the Peace Congress, Washington, D. C., Feb., 1861. Member of Virginia Convention which decided to secede, April, 1861. Elected Member of Confederate Senate. Died Jan. 17, 1862. President U. S. Senate, William R. King.

engine. The next year he issued a pamphlet, containing a description of this engine: "a system of counterpoises, ropes, rachets and grooved wheels, giving a continuous motion." A man named William Chester, of Pennsylvania, in 1763, tried his model boat. A Frenchman next attempted the solution of the puzzle in 1774.

Success in a small degree awaited the Marquis de Jouffray, who, in 1776 to 1783, worked on a larger scale. The first attempt that met any success in America was that of James Rumsey in 1784. John Fitch was working at the same time with Rumsey. He made an experimental trip on his steamer in 1786, on the Delaware. This boat was about sixty feet long. His idea was to use the paddles, worked by cranks. A vessel which followed this in 1790 reached as high a speed as seven and a half miles per hour. It was abandoned in 1792. The first screw used was by Fitch, who returned from England to continue his experiment in New York in 1796.

A party of Scotch experimenters conceived the idea of placing two long, narrow boats a short ways apart, and connecting them in a parallel position, and propelling the two by a paddle wheel between them. Symington, in 1801, constructed the Charlotte Dundas, for Lord Dundas, for towing on a canal. It had a wheel on the stern, driven by an engine of twenty-two inches diameter of cylinder and four feet stroke. It drew vessels of one hundred and forty tons burden three and a half miles per hour. This was soon afterward laid away, the reason assigned being that the waves would injure the banks of the canal.

Robert Fulton, the famous engineer who built the Clermont, which made her first tirp to Albany, built a boat on the Seine in 1803. He seems to have been familiar with the attempts of Henry in America and of the prominent English experiments. Fulton studied the problem at home and abroad and returned to the United States in 1806. The dimensions of the Clermont, the result of his labor on the question, were as follows: One hundred and thirty feet long, eighteen feet beam, seven feet deep, one hundred and sixty tons burden. Charles Brown of New York, built the hull. The engine had a steam cylinder twenty-four inches in diameter and a stroke of four feet. The boiler was twenty feet long, seven feet deep and eight feet wide. The wheels were fifteen feet in diameter, floats four feet long, two feet deep. The trip was made in 1807, leaving New York at 1 P. M., Monday, August 7. The average speed was nearly five miles an hour. This was the first steamboat ever made commercially successful. At almost the same time Stevens produced the Phœnix, another side-wheel steamer.

Fulton held a monopoly of the steam navigation of the Hudson river, and so this boat could not ply on it, and it was taken around by sea to the Delaware river. This was, therefore, the first trip on the ocean of any steam vessel. The steamboat now rapidly progressed; men saw it was a financial success, and it was rapidly introduced.

In 1811, Fulton and Livingston commenced building steamers at Pittsburg. The Comet, built by Henry Bull, opened steam navigation on the Clyde, in Scotland. Compound engines were introduced in 1825 by Thomas Allaire of New York. With engines of this manufacture a speed of twelve hours and eighteen minutes was made for a trip between New York and Albany.

Ocean navigation by steam was opened by Stevens in 1808. He sent a vessel from Savannah, Ga., to Russia *via* England. When she came back she made the trip from St. Petersburg to New York in twenty-six days. From this the progress of ocean steam navigation is easily followed. The screw is now used almost entirely and much more successfully. The first steamer that ever arrived in Troy, N. Y., was the Fire Fly, in 1814, Capt. Keller.

The Chancellor Livingston was the first steamer to provide a ladies' cabin, two smoke stacks, and was steered with a wheel with ropes from the head of the rudder attached. This was the first steamer to take a tow on a canal, and was at the celebration of the authorization of the canal project in 1817. Her officers were as follows: Captain, Samuel Wiswell; pilot, David Mandeville; engineer, H. Maxwell.

The steamer Olive Branch, in 1824, was the first to have steam guards around her. She used a bell to call passengers, instead of the bugle used on the old boats. Her officers were: Captain, James Moore; pilot, Thomas Hope; engineer, Philip

ELEVENTH PRESIDENT.

Born in Mecklenberg Co., N. C., Nov. 2, 1795. Graduate at the University of North Carolina, 1815. Admitted to the bar 1820. Elected Representative to the Tennessee Legislature 1823. Elected to Congress, 1825, and held his seat until 1839, being Speaker 1835-'37. Elected Governor of Tennessee, 1839. Elected President of the United States 1844. The Mexican War occurred during his administration. Retired from the Presidency, March, 1849. Died June 15, 1849. Vice-President, George M. Dallas.

Vermeder. In 1825 the Constitution first used an iron boiler. She also had a boiler on her deck. Officers of the Constitution: Captain, W. J. Wiswell, clerk, ———— Tuttle; pilot, Thomas Acker; second pilot, A. Bice; engineer, Job Fish; second engineer, J. Allen.

Two years following, the steamer North America was the first to have two engines, also hog frame and masts. Captain, Walter Cochrane; pilots, John Gould, John Dunbar; engineers, C. Whitbeck, John King, James King. The glass pilot house was introduced in 1837 by the Dewitt Clinton. She was also first to furnish state-rooms. Captain, S. R. Roe; pilots, James Havens, James Gibson; engineers, ———— Sewell, Peter Patchey. The North America, in 1840, successfully used coal in her engines. The Confidence first used a whistle in 1848. Captain St. John commanded the Westchester, the first steamer with a round stern.

The first railroad in the world was completed from Stockton to Darlington, in England, on September 27, 1825, which was the birthday of railroads. The first locomotive engine was built and driven by George Stephenson, called the Rocket, who took the first train from Darlington to Stockton, and Mr. Stephenson was declared the smartest man in all England and all the world. In 1826 a charter was granted to the Mohawk & Hudson Railroad Company for a railroad to run from Albany to Schenectady, N. Y.— sixteen miles.

In 1830 work was commenced on the road, and finished in 1831. Both locomotive engines and horses were used on the road, and the tickets were sold at stores or shops or by the conductor and the trains proceeded at a very slow rate of speed. Stationary engines had to be used, and were at the top of the hills, and the train was hauled up hill or let down by a strong rope with balance cars on the other track loaded with stone. The brakeman used hand levers to stop or check the train. The first locomotive engine was the "John Bull," which was shipped to America from Liverpool, England. Its weight was four tons; the engineer, John Hampson, was an Englishman. The first steam passenger excursion train in America was run on this road on August 9, 1831. There were fifteen passengers on the train of two coaches; the whole train only consisted of three cars, one being used for fuel. The passengers were as follows: Captain R. G. Crittenden, S. Wilcox, Lewis Benedict, Joseph Alexander, president Commercial Bank, Albany, Charles E. Dudley, Jacob Hayes, John Meiggs, sheriff of Albany; Edwin Crosswell, Billy Winne, John Townsend, Thurlow Weed, Erastus Corning, Albany; John I. Degroff, mayor of Schenectady; Josiah Snow, Ex-Governor I. C. Yates, William Marshall, Schenectady, conductor; John Hampson engineer. The Mohawk & Hudson railroad was the first link in what is now the great New York Central, and in the chain of railroads from Albany to Chicago, St. Louis, the Southwest, West and the Northwest.

Out of the primitive methods of railroading fifty-five years ago has grown the grand palatial system of the present day. Also the gigantic and rich corporations, owning or controlling a vast number of miles and lines of railroads throughout the United States. It was the outgrowth of civilization and of quick transit, and has therefore opened to the world the rich prairie lands and the products of the far West, and also untold millions of mineral wealth. It has built up large cities, towns and villages. It was, and is, the great motive power that has principally caused the advancement and the outgrowth of our country.

TWELFTH PRESIDENT.

Born in Orange Co., Va., Sept. 24, 1784. Commissioned as Lieut. in the Seventh Infantry, 1808. Brevetted Major for heroic defense of Fort Harrison against Indians, June 19, 1812. From this period until 1840 he was engaged in almost constant warfare with the Indians in the West. Was in command of Army of the Rio Grande, at opening of Mexican War. Won the great battles of Palo Alto, Resaca de la Palma, Monterey and Buena Vista. Elected President of the United States 1848. Died July 9, 1850.
Vice-President, Millard Fillmore.

PART XXVI.

PREFATORY.

In presenting to our readers the following pages containing the settlement, population, area, boundary and growth of the United states of America from 1790 to 1880, the date of the organization of each territory and the admission of each state, together with the territories and their capitals, including the District of Columbia and Alaska, the publishers do this believing that the reader will get a much more correct idea of that vast portion of our country than can be elsewhere obtained. The early explorers in America consisted of English, Spanish, Russian, French, Dutch, Swedes and Americans. And the events connected with the history of them date back to the years that are now historical in the pages of our country, and at the same time when the great Northwestern territory stretched from the mouth of the Mississippi river to the British possessions at the north, and to Russian America on the extreme northern Pacific coast, now Alaska. This vast domain, "as it were," empire, then was known as the territory of Louisiana. But the steady advancing columns of civilization has at last driven before them almost to extermination, the numberless roving bands and tribes of savages that for ages were the sole occupants of this immense tract of country, and out of which a number of territories were created, and afterwards some as states were admitted into the Union. Thus the "star of empire takes its way," the causes of which are probably due to the blessings of a free government. The remaining territories are still advancing in wealth and population, and the historical reminiscences connected with those that first explored the wild frontier from the Atlantic to the Pacific, as well as the interior portion of this vast country, deserves a more lengthy mention, perhaps, than the one we have at this time given, but we hope our readers will excuse the brevity, and feel amply paid for their time.

G. B. H.

STATISTICS OF THE UNITED STATES.

A Chronological, Statistical Discussion of our Population and Area from 1790 to 1880.---Official.

The first census of the United States, taken as of the first Monday in August, 1790, under the provisions of the second section of the first article of the Constitution, showing the population of the thirteen states then existing, and of the unorganized territory, to be in the aggregate 3,929,214. This population was distributed almost entirely on the Atlantic seaboard, extending from the eastern boundary of Maine nearly to Florida, in the region known as the Atlantic Plain. Only a very small proportion of the inhabitants of the United States, not, indeed, more than five per cent., was then found west of the system of the Appalachian mountains. The average depth of settlement in a direction at right angles to the coast was two hundred and fifty-five miles. The densest settlement was found in eastern Massachusetts, Rhode Island and Connecticut, and about New York city, whence population had extended northward up the Hudson, and was already quite dense as far as Albany, N. Y. The settlements in Pennsylvania, which had started from Philadelphia, on the Delaware, had extended northeastward and formed a solid body of occupation from New York through Philadelphia, down to the upper part of Delaware.

The Atlantic coast, as far back as the limits of tide-water, was well settled at the time from Casco bay southward to the northern border of North Carolina. In what was then the dis-

THIRTEENTH PRESIDENT.

Born at Summer Hill, N. Y., Jan. 7, 1800. Learned the clothier's trade; bought his time when 19, and began a course of legal study under Judge Wood, who defrayed all his expenses. Admitted to the bar at Aurora, 1823, as an attorney, 1827, and as a councilor in the Supreme Court, 1829. Elected to the Legislature, 1829. Elected to Congress, 1832, 1836. Defeated in the Gubernatorial election, 1844. Elected Comptroller of the State, 1847. Elected Vice-President, 1848. Became President of the United States by the death of President Taylor July 9, 1850. Died March 8, 1874.

trict of Maine, sparse settlement extended along the whole seaboard. The southern two-thirds of New Hampshire and nearly all of Vermont were covered by population. In New York, branching off from the Hudson from the mouth of the Mohawk, the line of population followed up a broad gap between the Adirondacks and the Catskills, and even reached beyond the center of the state, occupying the whole of the Mohawk valley and the country about the interior of New York lakes. In Pennsylvania population had spread northwestward, occupying not only the Atlantic plain, but with sparse settlements, the region traversed by the numerous parallel ridges of the eastern portion of the Appalachians. The general limit of settlement was, at that time, the southeastern edge of the Allegheny plateau, but beyond this, at the junction of the Allegheny and Monongahela rivers, a point early occupied for military purposes, considerable settlements had been established prior to the war of the Revolution. In Virginia the settlements had extended westward beyond the Blue ridge and into what is now West Virginia, on the western slope of the Allegheny mountains, though very sparsely. From Virginia also, a narrow tongue of settlement had penetrated down to the head of the Tennessee river, in the great Appalachian valley.

In North Carolina the settlements were abruptly limited by the base of the Appalachians. In South Carolina there was evidence of much natural selection, apparently with reference to the character of soil. Charleston was then a city of considerable magnitude, and about it was grouped a comparatively dense population. At this date settlements were almost entirely agricultural, and the causes for variations in their density were general ones. Outside the area of continuous settlement, which we have attempted to sketch, were found, in 1790, a number of smaller settlements of greater or less extent. The principal of these lay in northern Kentucky, bordering upon the Ohio river, and one upon the Cumberland, comprising an area of 12,850 square miles. In addition to this there were a score or more of small posts, or incipient settlements, scattered over what was then an almost untrodden wilderness, such as Detroit, Vincennes, Kaskasia, Prairie du Chien, Mackinac and Green Bay, besides the humble beginnings of Elmira and Binghamton, in New York, which, even at that time, lay outside the body of continuous settlement. In 1790 the district of Maine belonged to Massachusetts. Georgia comprised not only the present state of that name, but nearly all of what are now the states of Alabama and Mississippi. The states of Kentucky and Tennessee were then known as the " territory south of the Ohio river," and the present states of Ohio, Indiana, Illinois, Michigan, Wisconsin, and part of Minnesota, as the " territory northwest of the Ohio river." Spain claimed possession of what is now Florida, with a strip along the southern border of Alabama, Mississippi, and all of the region west of the Mississippi river.

In 1800, in Maine and New Hampshire there is apparent only a slight northward movement of settlement. In Vermont, its density has become greater. Massachusetts shows but little change, but in Connecticut the settlements have appreciably increased. In New York settlement has poured up the Hudson to the mouth of and beyond the Mohawk to Schenectady, and thence through the great natural roadway westward, and down the St. Lawrence and along the northern border of the state to Lake Champlain, completely surrounding what may be defined as the Adirondack region. In Pennsylvania settlements have extended up the Susquahana and joined the New York groups, and the population has streamed across the southern half of the state and settled in a dense body about the forks of the Ohio river at the present site of Pittsburg, and thence extended slightly into the state of Ohio. In Virginia we note but little change, although there is a general extention of settlement, with an increase in density along the coast. In North and South Carolina there is a general increase in density of settlement. The incipient settlements in northern Kentucky have spread southward across the state and into Tennessee, on the Cumberland river, and across the Ohio into the present state of Ohio, where we note the beginning of Cincinnati. Other infant settlements appeared at this date in Mississippi along the bluffs below the Yazoo bottom. Beside the settlement on the present site of St. Louis, there was not a settlement in what is now the state of Illinois.

FOURTEENTH PRESIDENT.

Son of General Benjamin Pierce, of the Revolutionary Army. Born at Hillsboro, N. H., Nov. 23, 1804. Graduate at Bowdoin College, Me., 1824. Admitted to the bar, 1827. Elected to State Legislature, 1829, remaining four years, and being Speaker two. Elected to Congress, 1833; to the U. S. Senate, 1837; and re-elected 1841. Resigned 1842 and resumed practice of law at Concord, N. H. Declined appointment as Attorney-General by President Polk. Enrolled himself for the Mexican War as a private, but received a Brig-General's commission from the President before his departure, March, 1847. Resigned his commission after the war, resuming his law practice. Elected President of the United States, 1852. Resumed his profession at close of term. Died Oct. 8, 1869. Vice-President, William R. King. Died before taking his seat.

It appears from the region embraced between the frontier line and Atlantic, that the total area of settlement is 305,708 square miles, and an aggregate of population of 5,308,483. During the decade just passed Vermont, formed from a part of New York, had been admitted to the Union, also Kentucky and Tennessee, formed from the "territory south of the Ohio river."

In 1810 the occupation of the Ohio river had now become complete from its head to its mouth, with the exception of small gaps below the mouth of the Tennessee; and the Kentucky settlements covered almost the entire state to the Tennessee river in northern Alabama. In Ohio the settlements had worked their way northward and westward until two-thirds of the area of the state was covered. St. Louis, from a fur trading post, had become an important center of settlement, the population having spread above the mouth of the Missouri, and southward along the Mississippi to the mouth of the Ohio. At the mouth of the Arkansas, in what is now the state of Arkansas, was a similar body of settlements. The transfer of the territory of Louisiana to our jurisdiction in 1803 brought in the country a large population along the Mississippi river. The purchase of Louisiana added 1,124,685 square miles to the United States, and gave to us the control of the Mississippi and its navigable tributaries. Georgia, during the same period, ceded to the United States that portion of its territory which now constitutes the larger part of the states of Alabama and Mississippi. The state of Ohio had been formed from what was known as the "territory north of the Ohio river." Michigan territory had been erected. Indiana territory became restricted to the present limits of the state of that name. Illinois territory, comprised of the present state of Illinois and Wisconsin, and part of Minnesota. The Louisiana purchase had been carved under the name of the "territory of Orleans," and all that part of the present state of Louisiana west of the Mississippi river, the name of "Louisiana territory." The total area of settlement in 1810 was 408,945 square miles, the aggregate population being 7,239,881.

The decade from 1810 to 1820 had witnessed several territorial changes. Alabama, Mississippi, Indiana, Illinois, Louisiana and Maine, had all been erected as states. The Indian territory had been constituted to serve as a reservation for the Indian tribes. Michigan territory had been extended to include the present states of Michigan, Wisconsin and part of Minnesota. The Arkansas territory was cut from the southern portion of the territory of Louisiana, and that part of territory remaining recieved the name of "Missouri territory." The great increase of population of central New York swept up the Mohawk valley to Lake Ontario, and along its shores nearly to the Niagara river. A similar increase was seen on the Ohio river, and northward and westward the population spread from Kentucky and Ohio into Indiana, covering sparsely the lower third of the state. The groups of population around St. Louis were enjoying a rapid growth and had extended widely, making a junction with the settlements of Kentucky and Tennessee, along a broad belt in southern Illinois, following the main water courses up the Mississippi and the Missouri rivers. The frontier line now had a length of 4,200 miles, and in the aggregate we have a total settled area of 608,717 square miles, and a population of 9,633,822.

In the early part of the decade of 1830 the final transfer of Florida from Spanish jurisdiction was effected and became a territory of the United States. During this period the Indians especially in the south delayed settlement to a great extent through Georgia, Alabama, Mississippi and Florida, extending even to the gulf coast. In Missouri the principle extension of settlement had been a broad belt up the Missouri river, reaching to the present site of Kansas City at the mouth of the Kansas or Kaw river, where quite a dense population appeared. Settlements had progressed in Illinois from the Mississippi eastward, in Indiana it had followed up the Wabash river, and thence had spread until it reached nearly to the north line of the state. But little of Ohio remained unsettled. The sparse settlements about Detroit, in Michigan territory, had broadened out, extending into the interior of the state. At this date the frontier line had a length of 5,300 miles, making a total settled area of 632,717 square miles, and an aggregate population of 12,866,020.

During the decade ending in 1840, the state of Michigan had been created with its present limits, the remainder of the old

FIFTEENTH PRESIDENT.

Born in Franklin county, Pa., April 23, 1791. Graduate at Dickinson College, 1809. Admitted to the bar, 1812. Elected to the State Legislature, 1814; re-elected, 1816. Elected to Congress, 1820; resigned March, 1831. Appointed Minister to Russia, May, 1831. Returned 1834, and elected to U. S. Senate for an unexpired term; re-elected for full terms, 1836, 1842. Secretary of State during President Polk's administration. Appointed Minister to England 1853. Returned 1856. Elected President of the United States, 1856. The Civil War broke out in the closing months of his administration. Died June 1, 1868. Vice-President, John C. Breckenridge.

territory being known as Wisconsin territory. Iowa territory had been created from a portion of Missouri territory, embracing the present state of Iowa and the western part of Minnesota, and Arkansas had been admitted to the Union. In Georgia, Alabama and Mississippi, the Cherokee, Creek, Choctaw and Chickasaw Indians, who occupied large areas in these states and formed a serious obstacle to the settlement, were removed to the Indian territory, and their country was opened up to settlement. In northern Illinois the Sac and Fox and Pottowatomie tribes having been removed to the Indian territory, their country had been promptly taken up, and we find new settlements carried over the whole extent of Indiana, Illinois, and across Michigan and Wisconsin, as far north as the forty-third parallel. The greater part of Florida remained without settlement. This is doubtless due greatly to the Seminole Indians, who still occupied nearly all of the peninsula. The frontier line in 1840 had a length of 3,300 miles. This shrinking in its length is due to its rectification on the northwest and southwest, owing to the filling out of the entire interior. Total entire settled area, 807,292 square miles, the aggregate population being 17,069,463.

Between 1840 and 1850 the limits of our country had been further extended by the annexation of the state of Texas and of the territory acquired from Mexico from the treaty of Guadalupe Hidalgo. The states of Iowa, Wisconsin and Florida had been admitted to the Union, and the territories of Minnesota, Oregon and New Mexico had been created. In Iowa settlements had made some advance, moving up the Missouri, the Des Moines, and other rivers. The settlements in Minnesota at and about St. Paul, St. Anthony and other localities, greatly extended up and down the Mississippi river, and scattering bodies of population appeared in northern Wisconsin. In southern Georgia and Florida, settlements had already reached southward, being now free to extend without fear of hostile Seminoles who had been removed to the Indian territory. The frontier line now extended around a considerable part of Texas, and issues on the gulf coast at the mouth of the Nueces river, and is 4,500 miles in length. The total area of settlement is at this date 979,249 square miles, and the aggregate population, 23,191,876.

Between the years 1850 and 1860 the territorial changes are as follows: The strip of Arizona and New Mexico south of the Gila river had been acquired from Mexico by the Godsden purchase (1853); Minnesota territory had been admitted as a state; Kansas and Nebraska territories had been formed from parts of Missouri territory; California and Oregon had also been admitted as states. In the unsettled parts of the Cordilleran region two new territories—Utah and Washington—were formed out of the parts of that *terra incognita*, which we bought from France as a part of Louisiana, and which we acquired by conquest from Mexico. The incipient settlements in the vicinity of St. Paul and the Falls of St. Anthony, in Minnesota, had grown like Jonah's gourd, spreading in all directions and forming a broad band of union down the shores of the Mississippi river. In Iowa, settlements had crept steadily northwestward until the state is nearly covered. Following up the Missouri river the population had reached into the southeastern corner of the present area of Dakota. Wisconsin settlements had moved at least one degree further north, while in the lower peninsula of Michigan they have spread up the lake shores, nearly encircling it on the side next to Lake Michigan. On the upper peninsula the little settlements that appeared in 1850 in the copper region on Keeweenaw point have extended and increased greatly as the mining interest was developed in value. Along the gulf coast there is little or no change. Our frontier line now measures 2,300 miles; the total area of settlement in 1860 is 1,194,754 square miles, and the aggregate population 31,443,321.

During the decade from 1860 to 1870 a number of territorial changes had taken place in the extreme west. Arizona, Colorado, Dakota, Idaho, Montana, Nevada and Wyoming, were organized as territories. Kansas, Nebraska and Nevada were admitted as states. West Virginia had been cut off from the mother commonwealth and made a separate state. The settlements in the extreme west beyond the frontier line, had arranged themselves mainly in three belts. The most eastern of these is located in central Colorado, New Mexico and Wyoming along the eastern base of and among the Rocky Moun-

SIXTEENTH PRESIDENT.

Born in Hardin County, Ky., Feb. 12, 1809. Removed to Illinois, 1830, and worked at rail-splitting, flat-boating and clerking. Was Captain in the Black Hawk War, 1832. Studied law; began practice, 1836; settled in Springfield, 1837. Elected to State Legislature, 1836, 1838; to Congress, 1846. Republican candidate for U. S. Senator in opposition to Stephen A. Douglas, with whom he canvassed the State, 1858. Elected President of the United States, 1860; re-elected 1864. A war measure, his Emancipation Proclamation, taking effect Jan. 1, 1863, put an end to slavery forever in the United States. Shot by John Wilkes Booth, April 14, 1865, at Washington, D. C., and died the following day. Vice-President, first term, Hannibal Hamlin; second term, Andrew Johnson.

tains. To this region settlers were first attracted in 1859 and 1860 by the discovery of mineral deposits, and has since been retained on account of the richness of the soil and for the abundance of water for irrigation, which have promoted the agricultural industry.

The second belt of settlement is that of Utah, settled by Mormons in 1847.

The third belt or strip is that of the Pacific states and territories, extending from Washington territory southward to southern California and eastward to the system of "sinks" in Nevada. This group of population owes its existence to the mining industry which originated in 1849 by a stampede, the like of which the world had never before or since seen. It had grown by successive impulses as new fields for rapid money getting have been developed. Latterly, however, the value of this region to the agriculturist has become recognized, and the character of the occupations of the people is undergoing a marked change. These three great western groups comprise nine-tenths of the population west of the frontier line. The remainder is scattered about in the valleys and the mountains of Montana, Idaho and Arizona, at military posts, isolated mining camps, and on cattle ranches. The total settled area (1870) embraces 1,272,239 square miles, and the aggregate population is 38,538,371.

In tracing the history of our country's growth we are now brought down to the latest census—that of 1880. But during the decade just passed, Colorado has been added to the sisterhood of our states. And not only has the population spread westward, but the isolated settlements of the Cordilleran region and of the Pacific coast show enormous accessions of occupied territory. The settlements in Kansas and Nebraska have made great strides over the plains, reaching at several points the boundary of the humid region, so that their westward extension beyond this point is to be governed hereafter by the supply of water in the streams. As a natural result we will see settlements follow these streams in long ribbons of population. Minnesota, Nebraska, Kansas, Arkansas and Texas have all made great strides both in the extension of the frontier line of settlement also in the increase in the density of the population, which is due both to the building of railroads and to the development of the cattle, sheep and agricultural interests. In Minnesota the increase has been large, especially in the cities of Minneapolis and St. Paul, and along the water-ways. The heavy population in the prairie portions of the states is explained by the railroads which now traverse them. Dakota, besides her great agricultural population in the eastern and northern part of the territory, has a large body of settlements in the Black Hills, in the southwest corner, which in 1870 formed a part of the Souix Indian reservation. These settlements were the result of the discovery of valuable gold deposits. Of all the states and territories of the Cordilleran region, Colorado has made the greatest stride during the last decade. This increase is the result of the discovery of very extensive and very rich mineral deposits about Leadville, producing a stampede second only to that of 1849 and 1850 to California. New Mexico shows but little change. Arizona, too, although its extent of population has increased somewhat, is but just commencing to enjoy a period of rapid development, owing to the extension of railroads and to the extermination of the hostile Apache Indians. Utah presents to us a case dissimilar to any other territory—a case of steady, regular growth, due almost entirely to its agricultural capabilities. Nevada also shows a sleight extension of population. In California, as the attention of the people has become more and more adapted to the agricultural pursuits, at the expense of the mining and cattle industries, the population shows an increase. In Oregon the increase has been slow but sure. In Washington territory, in the settled portions along the Columbia, into the valleys of Walla Walla and the Snake rivers here spoken of, irrigation is not necessary for the cultivation of crops; the population in the past decade has been wonderful. The length of the frontier line in 1880 was 3,337 miles, and the total settled area 1,269,570 square miles, and a population of 50,155,783, and the average density of settlement thirty-two to the square mile.

NOTE.—In all the discussion regarding the population and the area of the United States, Alaska is intentionally omitted. It is not as yet constituted even a territory of the United States, and its area remains a matter of conjecture. The population and resources of this latest addition to our domain are now the subject of a special investigation by the census office of the United States government.

SEVENTEENTH PRESIDENT.

Born at Raleigh, North Carolina, Dec. 29, 1808. Never attended school. Instructed wholly by his wife. In 1826 he emigrated to Greenville, Tennessee, and began business as a tailor. Elected Alderman of the town, 1828. Mayor 1830-34. Elected to State Legislature, 1835; re-elected 1839. Elected to State Senate 1841. Elected member of Congress 1843-53. Elected Governor of Tennessee, 1853, and U. S. Senator, 1857. He was a strong Union man at the opening of the Civil War. Appointed Military Governor of Tennessee, 1862-64. Elected Vice-President, 1864. Became President of the United States, April 15, 1865, on the assassination of President Lincoln by J. Wilkes Booth. The hostility between the President and the party that elected him began in 1866, and resulted in his being impeached, Feb. 1868. However on his trial before the High Court of Impeachment, the votes of the Court were taken in May on three of the eleven articles, which resulted in 35 for conviction to 19 against. He was therefore acquitted on these, a two-thirds vote being necessary to convict, and the vote on the remainder was indefinitely postponed. He was again elected United States Senator from Tennessee in 1874. Died July 31, 1875. President of the Senate, L. S. Foster.

DISTRIBUTION OF THE POPULATION.

STATISTICS OF IMMIGRATION, AND THE GROWTH AND DISTRIBUTION OF THE POPULATION.

We have no direct official information respecting the constituents of the population of the United States, as regards the place of birth, at any period prior to 1850. We have not even adequate information prior to 1820 respecting the arrivals at our ports of persons of foreign birth. The results of a rapid survey to the settlements of the English-American colonies may be of sufficient interest to justify their insertion here. The substance of the following is taken from official resources of the "Statistics of Immigration, and the Growth and Distribution of the population."

In one sense, substantially, all the white inhabitants within the present United States were at one time foreigners. But in the days when the population was mainly recruited by immigration, the word "foreigner" was never applied to an Englishman, nor generally to a Scot or Welshman, nor always to an Irishman. Thus we find it recorded of the Rhode Island colony in 1680: " We have lately had few or no new-comers, either of English, Scotch, Irish or foreigners." The population of the thirteen states was mainly composed of Englishmen. Mr. Bancroft (Vol. VII., 355) speaks of the colonies in 1775 as inhabited by persons "one-fifth of whom had for their mother tongue some other language than English." The order in which other nationalities contributed to the numbers of that population, the same writer indicates as follows: " Intermixed with French, still more with Swedes, and yet more with Dutch and German." The French were mainly Protestant refugees. After the revocation of the edict of Nantes, William III. dispatched to the colonies large numbers of those who had sought a home in England. A few of these came to Massachusetts (Holmes' Annals, 441). In 1690 a large number of these refugees were sent out to Virginia, and in the same year many arrived in Carolina. In 1698 another considerable body arrived in Virginia. Even prior to these dates the French had appeared in New York. "When the Protestant churches in Rochelle were razed," says Mr. Bancroft, (II., 302) " the colonists of that city were gladly admitted and the French Protestants came in such numbers that the public documents were sometimes issued in French as well as in Dutch and English."

The persons of Swedish stock referred to by Mr. Bancroft as found in the colonies in 1775, were largely the descendants of those who settled in Delaware. The descendants of the colonists in the course of generations widely scattered and blended with emigrants of other lineage, constitute probably more than one part in two hundred of the present population of our country. At the time of the surrender they did not much exceed seven hundred souls. The fecundity which Mr. Bancroft thus assigns these Swedes is only surpassed by that which Mr. Hildreth (I., 267) assigned to the twenty-five thousand, or fewer, original emigrants into New England prior to 1640: "A primitive stock, from which has been derived not less, perhaps, than a fourth part of the present population of the United States."

"But of all the European nations outside the British Isles, the chief migration," says Bancroft, "was from that Germanic race most famed for love of personal independence."

The commercial enterprise of Holland had already planted many thousands of her subjects in the "New Netherlands" when the dominion of the last of the colonies passed to England; nor did Dutch or German emigration cease, but it rather increased, when New York lost scout, burgomaster and schepens, to gain mayor, aldermen and sheriff.

We have said that South Carolina in its earliest settlement recieved accessions of Dutch both from New York and Holland. Before the downfall of the power of Holland on the continent, the Dutch had also appeared in Connecticut and for a time dis-

EIGHTEENTH PRESIDENT.

Born at Point Pleasant, Ohio, April 27, 1822. Graduate at U. S. Military Academy, 1843. Served in the Mexican War. Ordered to Oregon, 1852. Captain 1853. Resigned his commission, 1854. Removed to Galena where he engaged in the tanning business. Colonel 21st Ill. Vols. and Brig.-Gen., July 1861. Received surrender of Confederate Gen. Pemberton, of Vicksburg, Miss., July 4, 1863. Appointed Lieut.-General, March, 1864. Received surrender of Confederate General Lee, April 9, 1865. Commissioned General, a grade created for him by Congress, July 25, 1866. Elected President of the United States, 1868, 1872. Started on a tour of the world from Philadelphia, May 17, 1877, returning via San Francisco, Sept. 20, 1879. Died, July 23, 1885. Vice-President, first term, Schuyler Colfax; second term, Henry Wilson.

puted with the English the sovereignty of the soil even to the Connecticut river, but their few colonists were overwhelmed by the rapid invasion of the English.

To Pennsylvania the Germans resorted, until in 1764, Durand, in a report to Choiseul wrote that "Germans, weary of subordination to England and unwilling to serve under English officers, openly declared that Pennsylvania would one day be called Little Germany. Like Pennsylvania and the Carolinas, New York, in 1749, contained a great admixture, but those of Dutch origin still constituted a majority of all the German states, the misfortunes of the Palatinate made it the largest contributor to the population of the New World. When Hunter came out in 1710 as governor of New York, we find notice of his bringing with him 2,700 of these unfortunate people. Large numbers of the Palatines settled also in Carolina, upon the Roanoke and Pamlico, and many were cut off by the Tuscaroras in the savage war of 1712. "We shall soon have a German colony," wrote Logan, of Pennsylvania, in 1726, "so many thousands of Palatines are already in the country." Even after the adoption of the Constitution and the removal of the seat of government to the banks of the Potomac, we find a proposition seriously entertained for bringing over Germans to furnish the labor for building up Washington city (Washington's Works, 305). The Swiss also appeared in considerable force among the early settlers of America. Newbern, (as we now write it) on the Neuse, speaks of old Bern, on the Tar.

In 1730 Swiss immigrants founded Purysburg, the first town on the Savannah; and Grahame speaks of considerable accessions to the same state from the same source in 1733. "Asylum for the oppressed" of all nations and all religions as America had become, the Moravians found their way in large numbers to our shores. Of Oglethorpe's three hundred recruits in 1726 more than one-half were of this faith, to which their brethren who preceded them had already witnessed by raising their "Ebenezar" on the banks of the Savannah. Pennsylvania, however, was their chosen country of refuge during the eighteenth century.

The first colonial naturalization act of which we find notice was that of Maryland in 1666. Virginia followed in 1671. Pennsylvania naturalized the Swedes, Fins and Dutch of Delaware. Carolina naturalized the French refugees she received in 1696. The English privy council was long troubled by the scope and effect given to the colonial acts of naturalization by which aliens were vested with the power of exercising functions which they were disabled from performing by the navigation acts. At last, by act of Parliament in 1746, a uniform system of naturalization was established on the basis of seven years' residence, an oath of allegiance and profession of the Protestant faith. Of the inhabitants of the British Isles, by far the largest contribution next to that of England, was from Ireland.

This immigration, though somewhat spasmodic, had reached a vast but indeterminate total before the Revolution. The Irish settled all the way from New Hampshire, where Londonderry was founded in 1719 by a colony of about one hundred families from Ulster to Carolina, where a colony of five hundred arrived as early as 1715. However, Bancroft says that a small colony under Ferguson had preceded them, arriving as early as 1683. Burke speaks of the population of Virginia in 1750-54 as "growing every day more numerous by the emigration of the Irish, who, not succeeding so well in Pennsylvania as the more industrious and frugal Germans, sell their lands in that province to the latter and take up new ground in the remote counties of Virginia, Maryland and North Carolina, especially in the northwestern counties." "Hildrith these," he adds, "are chiefly Presbyterians from the north of Ireland, who in America are generally called the Scotch-Irish. It is probably to some colony thus planted that Jefferson referred when he wrote (Op. VI., 485) of the wild Irish, who had gotten possession of the valley between the Blue Ridge and the North mountains, forming a barrier over which none ventured to leap, and could still less venture to settle among." But Pennsylvania was still the especial center of attraction to the Irish before the Revolution.

In 1729 there was a large Irish migration to Pennsylvania. The years 1771-73 appears also to have witnessed a wholesale movement of population from Ireland, especially the northern

*Sincerely
R. B. Hayes*

NINETEENTH PRESIDENT.

Born in Delaware, Ohio, Oct. 4, 1822. Graduate of Kenyon College. Began practice of law in Cincinnati, 1856. Elected City Solicitor, 1858. Appointed Major 23d Ohio Inf., at opening of Civil War. Brevetted Major-General for bravery at Fisher's Hill and Cedar Creek. Elected to Congress, Oct., 1865; re-elected 1866. Elected Governor of Ohio, 1867 1869, 1875. Republican candidate for President, 1876. The adherents of Governor S. J. Tilden, the Democratic candidate, claimed the election for him. Owing to the extraordinary complication in several States, an Electoral Commission was authorized by Congress, consisting of five members of the Senate, five of the House and five Associated Justices of the Supreme Court. By a vote of 8 to 7 the Commission counted 185 votes of States for Hayes and Wheeler to 184 for Tilden and Hendricks. Messrs. Hayes and Wheeler were accordingly inaugurated, March 4, 1877. According to the official returns, Governor Tilden had a popular majority over all others, of 157,397 votes. Vice-President, William A. Wheeler.

counties, into this province. Of these, large numbers found their way to the region of the Monongahela and the Allegheny, and formed the pioneers of a vast population in western and southwestern Pennsylvania; we get a lively impression of the importance of this element a little later, when we find in the letters of that vehement Federalist, Oliver Walcott, Jr., the formidable "whiskey insurrection" of 1794, attributed almost wholly to the Irish of Pittsburg and vicinity, thus: "The Irishmen in that quarter have at length proceeded to great extremities." The Scotch were then as they are now, everywhere, though not largely in New England, nor generally in the colonies any where. In New Jersey, Georgia and North Carolina, we find, perhaps, the most prominent mention of the Scotch as a distinct element of the population. One exception to the rule that the Scotch did not tend to settle in colonies was found in the case of Highland soldiers of the British army, discharged in a body from service in America.

New York, as the only considerable state of the thirteen which was originally formed under any other flag than that of England might be supposed to have possessed the largest foreign element, proportionately, of all; and, indeed, from the first not only was New York a "city of the world," with a citizenship chosen from the Belgic provinces and England, from France and Bohemia, from Germany and Switzerland, from Piedmont and the Italian Alps, but the banks of the Hudson from the bay to Albany, was settled with a most motly population. But Pennsylvania long disputed with New York the honor of having the most curiously and variously composed population, and at the date of the Revolution indisputably carried off the palm. Chalmers says that Penn found the banks of the Delaware inhabited by three thousand persons—Swedes, Dutch, Finlanders and English. Those he brought with him and drew after him were only more widely assorted. "The diversity of people, religion, nations and languages," says the author of "European Settlements," "here is prodigious. Upward of two hundred and fifty thousand people," is his summary for 1750, "half of whom are Germans, Swedes or Dutch." At a little later date, within the century, General Washington wrote: "Pennsylvania is a large state, and from the policy of its founder and especially from the great celebrity of Philadelphia, has become the general receptacle of foreigners from all countries and of all descriptions." On the other hand, of all the colonies, those of New England received the smallest proportional accessions from nationalities other than pure English, and earliest experienced the cessation of immigration even from England. "The policy of encouraging immigration from abroad," says Hildreth, "which contributed so much to the rapid advancement of Pennsylvania and Carolina, never found favor in New England. Even the few Irish settlers at Londonderry became objects of jealousy,"

In 1796 we find Washington writing to Sir John Sinclair concerning the same section as follows: "Their numbers are not augmented by foreign emigrants; yet from their circumscribed limits, compact situation and natural population, they are filling the western parts of the state of New York, and the country on the Ohio with their own surplusage." It is to this long cessation of immigration into New England that Madison refers, when, writing after the fourth census (1820), he says: "It is worth remarking that New England, which has sent out such a continued swarm to other parts of the Union for a number of years, has continued at the same time, as the census shows, to increase in population, although it is well known that it has received but comparatively few emigrants from any quarter." The immigration into the United States from the close of the Revolutionary war to the year 1820 can hardly be estimated. It can only be conjectured from very few and partial data.

A recent report, March 31, 1882, of the Bureau of Statistics places the number at 250,000. No correct official statistics of immigration can be obtained prior to 1820. The following statistics of the nationality of aliens from 1821 to 1850 is as given in the report of the Bureau of Statistics: Countries, 1821 to 1830. British Isles, 75,823; total Europe, 98,815; all other countries aggregate 143,439; from 1831 to 1840, aggregate 599,125; from 1841 to 1850, aggregate 2,244,602; from and after 1850 the statistics relating to the nativities of the population of the United States, available for the uses of the student

TWENTIETH PRESIDENT.

Born in the town of Orange, Ohio, Nov. 19, 1831. Graduate at Williams College, 1856. Became Professor of Latin and Greek in Hiram College, O. Elected State Senator, 1859. Appointed Colonel 42d Ohio Vols., 1861. Nominated for Congress while in the field, 1862, but continued in service until 1863. Member of the 38th, 39th, 40th, 41st, 42d, 43d, 44th, 45th and 46th Congresses. Elected U. S. Senator, Jan. 1880. Elected President of the United States, Nov., 1880. Shot by Charles J. Guiteau, in B. & P. R. R. depot, Washington, D. C., July 2, 1881. Died at Elberon, N. J., Sept. 19, 1881. Vice-President, Chester A. Arthur.

of politics or economics, have been of vastly wider range and of far greater accuracy. It should be remembered that all children born on the soil of the United States are known and ranked as Americans. Regarding the French Canadians, who are found in such large numbers throughout the New England and other states, notably Michigan, bordering the British Dominions, not unfrequently these people by reason of their language, are called Frenchmen, though in this case not even coming from a country under French rule.

By the census of 1850 it was ascertained that persons of foreign birth constituted 9.68 per cent. of the total population. By 1860 the proportion had risen to 13.16 per cent.; by 1870 this had increased to 14.44 per cent., while the census of 1880 found this element of the population to be but 13.32 per cent. The following shows the total population of the United States and the total number of persons of foreign birth with the proportion subsisting between the two numbers, at each of the four censuses taken since this class of statistics has been collected: The year 1850, total population, 23,191,876; persons of foreign birth, 2,244,602; per cent. of foreign born, 9.68; the year 1860, total population, 31,443,321; persons of foreign birth 4,138,697; per cent. of foreign born, 13.16; the year 1870, total population, 38,558,371; foreign birth, 5,567,229; per cent. of foreign born, 14.44; the year 1880, total population, 50,155,783; by foreign birth, 6,679,943; per cent. of foreign born, 13.32.

Between 1870 and 1880 the foreign born elements of the country fell back nearly to the position, in relation to the total population, which they had occupied in 1860. In conclusion, we will append the rate of standing of the more different foreign born population, in some of the larger states. Thus New York, which stands first in aggregate foreign born, is first also in Irish, German and English, though only third in British American, and seventh in Scandinavian population. Illinois, which is third in aggregate foreign born, is third in English and Scandinavian, fourth in Irish and second in German, while in British Americans it is only fifth. Iowa, which is tenth in aggregate foreign born, is tenth in Irish, English and British American population, eighth in German and fourth in Scandinavian.

Kansas, which is sixteenth in aggregate, is eighteenth in Irish, seventeenth in German and fifteenth in British Americans, though thirteenth in English and ninth in Scandinavian.

On the other hand, Pennsylvania is second in aggregate foreign born, and is second in Irish and in English, is only fifth in German, twelfth in Scandinavian and sixteenth in British American population. Massachusetts, which is fourth in aggregate foreign born, is second in British American, third in Irish, fifth in English, thirteenth in Scandinavian and nineteenth in German. Minnesota, which is ninth in aggregate foreign born, is first in Scandinavian, sixth in British American, tenth in German, fourteenth in Irish and eighteenth in English. Texas presents the following contradiction: Though fifteenth in aggregate foreign born, it ranks as high as fourteenth in one only of the five elements specified, viz., the German. In Scandinavian population it is only nineteenth; in English, twentieth; in Irish, twenty-fifth, and in British American only twenty-seventh. The explanation is found in the large number of Mexicans reported, being over 48,000—about two-thirds of all reported in the United States—and also has a large representation in the state of Austrians, Bohemians, Swiss and French. In like manner California, though put down as the eighth in aggregate of foreign population, ranks as high as eighth in respect to only one of the five specified nationalities, the large number of Chinese in this state (being seventy per cent. of the total number in the country) serving to make up its relative deficiency in the enumerated elements. The concentration of the British American population in the New England states and in Michigan, are due in the former case equally to the lumber interest and the factory industries, and in the latter case to the lumber interest mainly, and the settlement of the Scandinavian population to the west and north of Michigan are notable features due to the latitude of the climate. The Swiss are mainly found in California, Illinois, Iowa, Missouri, New York, Ohio, Wisconsin and Pennsylvania; total population of 88,621 souls.

The Bohemians are found mainly in Illinois, Minnesota, Nebraska, New York, Ohio and Wisconsin. A majority of the Poles are found in Illinois, Michigan, New York and Wiscon-

TWENTY-FIRST PRESIDENT.

Chester Alan Arthur was the son of an Irishman named William Arthur, who was a Baptist Minister, and was born at Fairfield, Franklin Co., Vt., on the 5th of October 1830. While his father was preaching in Schenectady, N. Y. he entered Union College in 1845 in that city, and graduated in 1848. Went to New York City, studied law and was admitted to the bar. Appointed Engineer-in-Chief by Governor Morgan, Jan. 1861, and Quartermaster-General on his Staff, Jan. 1862. The rapid despatch of New York troops to the seat of war was due almost exclusively to his tact and energy. Appointed Collector of the Port of New York, Nov. 20, 1871; re-appointed Dec. 1875. Removed by President Hayes, July 21, 1878. Elected Vice-President 1880. Became President of the United States by the death of President Garfield, Sept. 19, 1881. Died in New York City at his residence after a long illness, Nov. 18, 1886.

sin. Of the 35,722 Russians (predominately Mennonites) in the country, a large majority are found in three states and territories, as follows: Kansas, 8,032; New York, 5,438; Dakota, 6,493. One-third of the 15,535 Belgians in the United States are found in Wisconsin. More than one-half of the Portuguese and almost one-half of the natives of the Portuguese Atlantic Islands are found in California. Massachusetts is the only other state in which these elements appear in an appreciable degree.

The Austrians are found principally in Illinois, Minnesota, Nebraska, New York, Pennsylvania, Texas and Wisconsin, and the French are chiefly inhabitants of California, Illinois, Indiana, Louisiana, Missouri, New York, Ohio and Pennsylvania. The Chinese are found in considerable numbers in the following states and territories: California, Nevada, Oregon, Idaho and Washington territory.

The natives of Holland resident in the United States number 58,090. Of these 17,177 are found in Michigan, 8,399 in New York, 5,698 in Wisconsin, 5,012 in Illinois and 4,743 in Iowa, leaving 17,061 in all other states and territories.

Thus we have a total population of Swiss, 88,621; of Bohemians, 85,361; of the Poles, 48,557; of the Russians, 35,722; of the Austrians, 38,663; of the French, 106,971; of the Chinese, 104,468; of the Hollanders, 58,090; making a sum total of 550,731 souls of these nationalities, included in the population of the United States, but principally located in the western states and territories.

DISTRICT OF COLUMBIA.

The territory embracing our national capital, the District of Columbia, was organized March 3, 1791. At that time it was composed of lands on both sides of the Potomac river. But on July 9, 1846, all that portion of the District of Columbia south of the Potomac river, was retroceded to Virginia. The city of Washington is on the north side of the Potomac and occupies a tract of land taken from Maryland, which comprises a territory of ten miles square. In 1874 the county government was abolished and the present form of government established, under the charge of the President and Congress. Washington city, where the capital is established, is a city of about two hundred thousand people, and is handsomely laid out with broad streets and avenues. All the government buildings are located there—the White House or Presidential mansion, the treasury, general post-office, patent office, pension office and interior department; also all other departments, consisting of justice, agriculture, printing and engraving, the navy yard and arsenal, and all the general offices belonging to the United States governmental machinery. Washington is a city of palatial residences, principally owned by government officials and members of Congress and United States Senators.

It has many important attractions, fine hotels and boarding houses. The churches are a predominent feature, and consists in all denominations. The school system is one of rare excellence. The city government is conducted upon a first-class basis, and Washington without doubt is, and is destined to be, the handsomest metropolis in the United States, and perhaps the world. The first Congress that assembled in Washington in the capitol building was the second session of the sixth Congress, November 17, 1800.

TWENTY-SECOND PRESIDENT.

Born in Caldwell, N. J., March 18, 1837. Educated at Clinton Seminary, Oneida Co., N. Y. until 16. Went to New York City and taught for a while in the Asylum for the Blind. Then went to Buffalo, N. Y., studied law and was admitted to the bar 1859. Appointed Assistant District Attorney of Erie Co., 1863. Drafted into the army while Assistant District Attorney and furnished a substitute. In 1870, elected Sheriff of Erie Co., N. Y. Elected Mayor of Buffalo, 1881. Nominated in 1882 for Governor of New York and elected by a majority of nearly 200,000. Received the nomination for President in 1884 as a Democrat and elected by less than 1,200 majority in New York. Vice-President Hon. Thomas A. Hendricks, of Indiana.

GENERAL JOHN A. LOGAN.

A Short Biographical Sketch of the Eventful Life of the Dead Statesman, Citizen, Soldier and Comrade.

Among the last of the long procession of great men who have disappeared forever from the arena of human affairs in the past two years, is Senator John Alexander Logan, of Illinois. Born in Jackson county, February 9, 1826, the Celt and Scot were united in his parentage, and the sterling and sagacious qualities of both were evident. He served through the Mexican war, graduated at Louisville Law School, Kentucky, 1851. Member of Illinois legislature four years. Prosecuting attorney, 1853-57. Presidential elector, 1856. Elected to the Thirty-seventh Congress and resigned to enter the Union army. Attained the rank of major-general. Declined appointment as Minister to Mexico, 1865. Elected to the Fortieth and Forty-second Congress. Before he could take his seat in the Forty-second Congress he was elected United States Senator, 1871, 1879, 1885, and was Republican candidate for Vice-President of the United States in 1884. Died after a short illness at Washington, D. C., December 26, 1886. General Logan's services in the war were signal and brilliant. He fought first as a private in the first Bull's Run and then returned home to resign his seat, stay the tide of secession sentiment that was arising in "Egypt" in southern Illinois, and raise a regiment — of which he was made colonel — for the Union service. At Belmont he left his horse dead on the field; at Fort Henry he was at the head of his command; at Fort Donelson he was badly wounded; and at Pittsburg Landing he was made a brigadier-general. Refusing a re-election to Congress with the memorable words: "I have entered the field to die, if need be, for this government." His bravery and skill led in 1862 to his appointment as major-general, as which he fought at Port Gibson, Raymond, Jackson and Champion Hill. At Vicksburg his column was the first to enter the city, and he became its military governor. In November, 1863, General Logan succeeded General Sherman in command of the fifteenth army corps, and the following May he joined Sherman as the Georgia campaign was opening. General Logan led the advance of the army of the Tennessee at the battles of Resaca, Dallas and Kenesaw Mountain. July 22 he was in the fierce battle before Atlanta, which cost the gallant McPherson his life. In his report of the battle General Sherman said: "General Logan succeeded him (McPherson)." He accompanied Sherman in his "march to the sea," and continued with him until the surrender of General Joseph E. Johnston, April 26, 1865. President Johnson quickly tendered him the mission to Mexico which he declined. During his congressional life, the soldier showed himself a statesman and an orator, and his speeches gave him a more than national reputation. In the Republican convention of 1880 at Chicago, General Logan was one of the famous triumvirate which stood out for Grant's nomination, and four years later was a prominent candidate himself. Gracefully acquiescing in Blaine's nomination, he took the second place on the ticket. In 1888 he would have been at least a leading candidate, and many of his friends predicted that he would lead the Republican hosts. But death has stepped in and once more set at naught human speculations.

General Logan was married at Shawneetown, Illinois, in 1855, to Miss Mary S. Cunningham, and much of his success in life was due to his noble wife. A great and good feature of General Logan's later life has been his prominence in G. A. R. matters and his untiring zeal for the unfortunate soldiers. He was a true friend to their interests, and has always advocated their cause at all times and upon all occasions; and without doubt it is the universal feeling of all his comrades that they have lost a true friend and the nation a brave and faithful defender. "When the last reveille has been beaten, and the last bugle call sounded, then the immortal command is given —'Surrender!'"

JOHN A. LOGAN.

The citizen, soldier and statesman. Born February 9, 1826. Died December 26, 1886.

THE TERRITORY OF UTAH.

The capital of Utah, Salt Lake City, is situated near a lake of the same name, in Salt Lake county. It has a population of 21,000. The inhabitants are composed of Mormon and Gentile people. The city is well laid out and shows a very business-like appearance, and is reached by railroads in two directions. The principal attractions of the city are the Mormon temple and tabernacle. Utah was settled in 1847 by the Mormons fleeing from Nauvoo, Illinois. This community then differed, and still differs, radically from that of the Rocky Mountains, being essentially agricultural, mining having been discountenanced from the first by the church authorities, as tending to fill the "Promised Land" with Gentile adventurers, and thereby imperil Mormon institutions. The increase in population from 1870 to 1880 was sixty per cent., and rating higher by a steady growth than any of the other territories from first settlement. The settlements of Utah extend from southern Idaho southward through central Utah, and along the eastern base of the Wahsatch range into northern Arizona. They consist mainly of scattered hamlets and small towns, about which are grouped the farms of the communities. Utah has an area of 88,056 square miles, and a population of 143,906.

THE TERRITORY OF NEW MEXICO.

The capital of New Mexico, Santa Fe, is situated in Santa Fe county, and has a population of about ten thousand inhabitants. The government officials have their headquarters there, and is also military headquarters of the army for that district. It is now reached by rail, and shows a marked sign of improvement since the bugle of the iron horse was first sounded in its limits. Santa Fe has the oldest record of any city now in the United States, as it dates back to 1580, when it was founded by Antonio de Espejo. The territory of New Mexico was created in 1850 and comprises an area of 121,201 square miles, and in 1880 had a population of 119,565; this shows an increase since 1870 of thirty per cent. New Mexico was acquired by treaty of Guadalupe Hidalgo from Mexico in 1845, on account of the Mexican war. Tradition says, that some four hundred years ago, in Montezuma's reign, New Mexico was a part of his empire, and was inhabited by Spanish and Indians. Whether this be so or not, it is to this day in some parts of the territory, and especially at Taos, a small domain in the interior, self evident that Montezuma was held in high favor over four hundred years ago as his memory is still kept alive by a continually burning fire in an old cathedral at Taos, which the followers and believers in the chief or king, Montezuma, have kept burning for a period of four hundred years. In New Mexico it is not an uncommon thing to find large land owners, as large tracts were held as Spanish claims, which was recognized by the treaty of the United States. New Mexico belongs to the Cordilleran belt, known as the "mineral or irrigating range."

ROBERT FULTON.

Born in Little Britain, Pa., 1765. At the age of 21 he began studying with West, the painter, but gradually developed a genius for mechanics, and became a civil engineer. He made a voyage from New York to Albany in the Clermont, his first experimental steamboat in 36 hours, 1807. Successfully constructed submarine batteries, and built the first steam man-of-war for the Government. Died Feb. 24, 1815.

THE TERRITORY OF WYOMING.

Cheyenne, the capital of Wyoming, is situated in Laramie county on the Union Pacific Railroad, and has a population of about 7,000. It is a flourishing city, nicely laid out, and has first-class railroad facilities. It was for a number of years the outfitting post for the northwestern frontier and still retains a good share of this business. It was for a long time the military headquarters for Fort De Russe. It has fine hotel accommodations, good churches and school system, and does the chief merchandizing for the territory. Chyenne is where most all of the first Black Hills' outfitting trains was supplied, and from where the first start was made by prospecters for that part of the uninhabited frontier. The territory of Wyoming belongs to the same range or belt as Utah, Colorado, Arizona and New Mexico. It has an area of 93,107 square miles and a population in 1880 of 20,788, and makes a showing of 128 per cent. increase since 1870. Wyoming abounds in mineral wealth of all kinds; however. stock and sheep raising is the chief business, which is conducted on a large scale mostly by eastern capitalists, who own large herds of cattle or sheep.

THE TERRITORY OF IDAHO.

The territory of Idaho was first traversed by white men in 1804, when the party of explorers under Lewis and Clarke passed through this region. It was then a part of the great territory known as Louisiana, which had just previously been purchased from France by the United States government. Many years before this time the existence of one or more large rivers west of the great water-shed of the Rocky Mountains was considered very probable by geographers, including Thomas Jefferson, afterwards President of the United States. Search for this superstitious river was vigorously prosecuted by various explorers and others. In 1793 Captain Gray, who had been sent out to buy furs in the interest of Boston merchants, made the discovery of the mightiest river of the Pacific slope, and named it the Columbia, after the vessel of which he was master. Not long afterward Captain Gray, in company with Captain Vancouver, an Englishman, sailed some distance up the Columbia, but they made no overland explorations of the country, and consequently did not penetrate as far as the limits of what is now Idaho. Vancouver formally claimed the country for his sovereign, King George III., "by right of discovery and explorations," while at the same time Gray laid claim to it for the United States.

Under the provisions of the treaty of 1818, the country north of the forty-second parallel of latitude and west of the Rocky Mountains was occupied jointly by Great Britian and the United States. To this whole region was given the name of Oregon (from an Indian word signifying wild marjoram). The international line by the terms of the treaty was made the forty-ninth parallel of north latitude, so that the territory of Oregon embraced all the vast region west of the Rocky Mountains and between the forty-second and forty-ninth parallels of latitude. Congress, in 1847, offered rich bounties in land to those who would take up their residence in Oregon, and in 1849, when the California gold discoveries were made, it had a population of several thousand.

Idaho was created a territory by act of Congress of March 3, 1863, from portions of Washington, Dakota and Nebraska territories, comprising an area of 326.373 square miles and em-

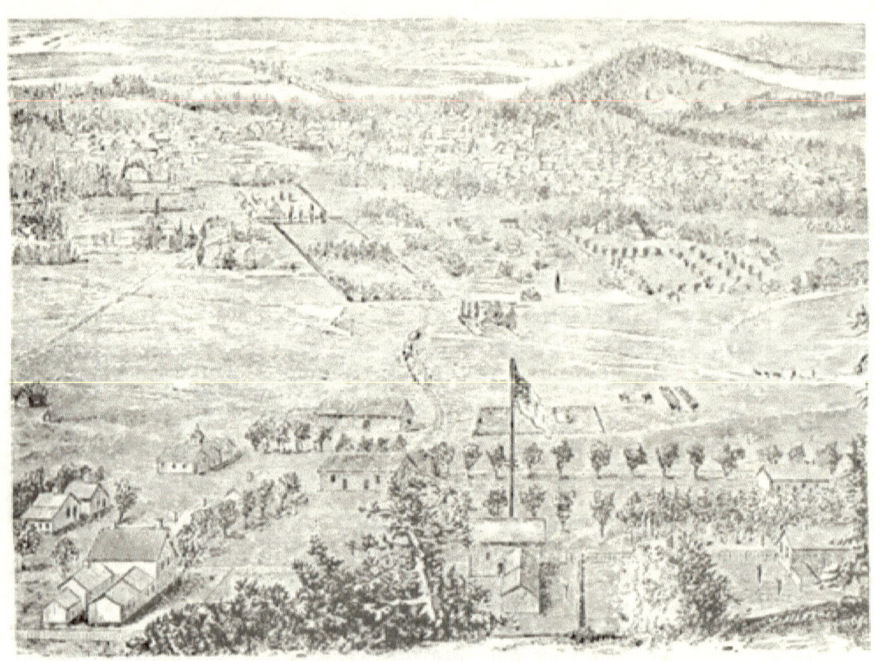

BOISE CITY AND VALLEY, FROM FORT BOISE.

bracing the present state of Nebraska and nearly all of Wyoming. The name Idaho is a corruption of the Indian word *E-dah-hoe*, which has been translated "Gem on the Mountains." In 1868, the territories of Montana and Wyoming, having been called into existence, Idaho embraced its present area. It extends from latitude 42° to 49°, has the British possessions on the north, Montana and Wyoming on the east, Utah and Nevada on the south, and Oregon and Washington on the west. The length of the territory is 410 miles, and its width from 257 miles in the extreme south to 60 miles at its northern limit.

Boise City, the capital of Idaho, is located in the Boise valley, on the Boise river, in the county of Ada, on a line of the Union Pacific Railroad, in latitude 33° 37′ north, and longitude 116° 12′ west, 2,880 feet above the sea level, on a beautiful plateau, near Fort Boise. It has a population of about 2,500 inhabitants. A United States Government general land office and United States troops are located there.

THE TERRITORY OF ARIZONA.

HISTORICAL AND MODERN.

With a history older than that of any other political division of the American Union, Arizona still remains comparatively unknown. The Pacific coast of northern México was explored by Spanish adventurers early in the sixteenth century, and in the spring of 1540, Vasquez de Coronado led an expedition through the wilds of Arizona. This was twenty-five years before the founding of San Augustine, sixty-seven years before the settlement of Jamestown, and eighty years before the Mayflower cast Anchor at Plymouth Rock. Like other daring spirits who followed in the wake of Columbus, Coronado was a soldier of fortune who sought wealth and fame in the New World. Glowing reports had reached New Spain of the existence, far to the north, of seven cities called "Cibola, or Cities of the Bull." They were said to be large and populous, magnificently built, and fabulously rich in the precious metals.

Sallying out of Culiacan early in April, 1540, at the head of nearly 1,000 men, mostly Indians, the Spanish cavalier turned his face to the north, eager to reap the golden harvest that awaited him in the Seven Cities. Through the rugged defiles of the Sierra Madre and the parched plains of Sonora, by the valley of the Santa Cruz, and past the present site of Tucson, where an Indian village was encountered, Coronado reached the Pima towns on the Gila.

After visiting the ruins, which he named "Casa Grande," and of whose origin and history the Indians knew nothing, he pursued his way to the San Francisco Mountains, and from thence to the valley of the Colorado *Chiquito*. Two days' journey northeast from this point and forty-five from Culiacan, brought the expedition in sight of the long sought "Cities of Cibola."

Bitter was the disappointment of the Spanish leader and his deluded followers. Instead of rich and populous cities they found a collection of miserable Moquis villages, and instead of the stores of wealth they found semi-savage penury. The people were a primitive race, who tilled the soil in a crude way and had no knowledge of metals.

Many other towns of a similar character were encountered east and north, but in none was there an indication of that marvelous wealth for which the Spaniards and their dusky allies had journeyed so many weary leagues to find. A wiser, if not a richer man, Coronado turned his steps homeward, and the gorgeous myth of the "Cities of the Bull" was dissipated forever.

Forty years later, Antonio de Espejo, the founder of Santa Fe, visited the Moquis towns and northern Arizona; but as his expedition, like that which preceded it, was undertaken with the hope of acquiring sudden wealth, no effort was made to effect permanent settlements.

A century later another class of explorers visited Arizona. Animated by different motives, and inspired by loftier purposes, the mission fathers came to spread the doctrine of peace and good will to men. While Coronado and Espejo sought gold and glory, Father Kino and his companions were content to undergo poverty, suffering and self-denial. The founding of the Mission of Guevavi, south of Tucson, in 1687, marks the establishment of the first settlement by Europeans in what is now the territory of Arizona. Thirty years later there were nine missions south of the Gila, all in a prosperous condition. Large number of Indians were baptized, and instructed in the arts of peaceful industry. The rich mineral deposits in the surrounding mountains were worked in a primitive way by the neophytes, under the direction of the *padres*. A number of *presidios* were established by the Viceroy of Spain, and many adventurers from Sinaloa and Sonora found their way to the new finds in the north. The only obstacle to prosperity was the Apache. That Ishmaelite of the hills frequently raided the settlements, carrying off what plunder he could secure. Incapable of civilization and disdaining peaceful labor, his delight was in deeds of rapine and murder. Despite his incursions, the missions grew and prospered, until their suppression by the Mexican government in 1828. For nearly one hundred and fifty years they kept ablaze the torch of civilization; when it dropped from their hands it was quenched in blood. With the abandonment of the missions the Apache swept down from his mountain strongholds, despoiled the churches, laid waste the fields, destroyed the mining plants, and reduced the country to its primeval savage condition.

At the close of the Mexican war, that portion of Arizona north of the Gila river was added to the United States. In 1854 that portion of the territory lying south of the Gila was acquired from Mexico by purchase. At that time the inhabitants of the entire region now known as Arizona numbered a few hundred Mexicans, huddled together in the wretched presidios of Tucson and Tubac. After the acquisition, the enterprising American soon made his appearance, and many of the abandoned mines were profitably worked. Capital sought investment, the country's wonderful resources were becoming known, and it seemed entering upon a career of lasting prosperity. From 1864 to 1874 civilization and savagery struggled for the mastery. More than a thousand men, women and children fell victims to Apache hate, while more than double that number of red demons bit the dust. The close of 1874 saw the last of the hostile Indians placed on reservations, and Arizona for the first time in its history enjoyed the blessings of peace. But the true era of Arizona's advancement dates from the hour when the iron horse crossed the Colorado river. This event occurred in the latter part of 1878. The shriek of the locomotive was the death-knell of savagery and isolation — the trumpet peal of progress and prosperity. Since then despite the spasmodic outbreaks of a small band of discontented Apaches, which are now entirely subdued, the country shows a steady growth in population and wealth.

This, in brief, is the history of Arizona, from the advent of the Spaniards to the present time. Through centuries of blood and fire the coming commonwealth faces the future, vigorous, confident and self-reliant. Possessed of all the resources that build up strong and prosperous states, she invites the immigrant and capitalist to share in their development. Untold millions are locked in her mountain ranges, and her smiling valleys offers homes for thousands.

Geographically, Arizona's position is the southwest corner of the United States. It extends from the 109th degree of longitude west to the Colorado river, and from 31 28' north latitude, to the 37th parallel. It is bounded on the north by Utah and Nevada, on the east by New Mexico, on the south by the Mexican state of Sonora, and on the west by California and Nevada. Its greatest length from north to south is 380 miles, and from east to west very nearly 350 miles. It is longer than all New England and Pennsylvania combined, having an area of 113,916 square miles, and had in 1880 a population of 40,440 inhabitants, and shows an increase in population since 1870 of 319 per cent.

The capital of Arizona, Prescott, and the county seat of Yavapai county, is situated on Granite creek, in a beautiful glade among the pine covered foot-hills of the Sierra Prieta range. It is handsomely built with mercantile establishments, mostly of brick, and on the hills about the plaza are many neat and comfortable homes. The religious societies have attractive places of worship. It also has two banks, a good hotel two daily and three weekly newspapers, and a good system of free schools, and has a population of about 2,000.

ALASKA.

Historical Sketch — Sitka, the Capital.

With the accession of Alaska, by purchase from Russia, by the United States in 1867, through the previous efforts of Secretary Seward and Senator Sumner, was the discovery of the Cassiar mines in British Columbia, but which must be reached through Alaska, and for other minor incentives, set many people to looking northward. They then found that they could continue their trips on a long inland salt water river, of which the well known Puget sound was a small part, (hardly the equivalent of Narragansett bay, taken from Long Island sound,) or Green bay, from Lake Michigan. Then Alaska was known only as Russian America, when it was spoken of at all, so seldom was it heard, and seemed to be as far away from the United States on that side of the continent, and as little thought of as Greenland or Iceland is today with our people of the Atlantic coast. Not that these were the first explorations and discoveries of importance in the inland passage and its surrounding woods and waters by any manner of means.

Cook and Clarke, as early as 1776; Dixon from 1785 to 1788; Langsdorff in 1803-8; La Perouse in 1785-8; Lisianski from 1803 to 1806; Meares, of the royal navy, from 1788 to 1789; and especially Vancouver from 1790 to 1795, but in 1799 Alaska was visited by a Russian named Baronoff, and upon an island by the same name he built a fort called the Archangel Gabriel, which after a number of rapidly recurring vicissitudes, was annihilated and its garrison massacred by the Sitka Indians. Three years later Baronoff re-established his power at the present site of Sitka, now the capital of Alaska, calling the new place Archangel Michael. Archangel Gabriel, having failed in his duty as a protector, and from this name it was called New Archangel, which changed to Sitka with the change of flags in 1867.

Sitka, the capital of Alaska territory, has about 3,000 inhabitants, and is most picturesquely located at the head of Sitka sound, through which, looking in a southwest direction, the Pacific Ocean is plainly visible. Almost directly west from Sitka, about fifteen miles distant, is Mount Edgecumbe, so named by Cook, it having previously been called Mount San Jacinto by Bodega in 1775, and Mount St. Hyacinth again by La Perouse. Tchirikov, before all others, I believe, got it chronicled as Mount St. Lazarus, and it looked as if it would go through the whole calender of the saints and their different national changes if it had not gotten pretty firmly rooted as Mount Edgecumbe. It is nearly 3,000 feet above the level of the sea, and looks like a peak of 5,000 feet cut off by a huge shaving plane at its present height. In the town proper the Greek church is the most conspicuous and interesting object, and especially those who have never seen one of this religion. It is built in the form of a Greek cross, in plan, and is surmounted by an oriental dome over the center, which has been painted an emerald green color.

One wing is used as a chapel and contains besides a curious font an exquisite painting of the Virgin and Child, copied from the celebrated picture at Moscow. All the drapery is of silver, and the halo of gold; so, of the painting itself, nothing is seen but the faces and background. The chancel, which is raised above the body of the church, is approached by three broad steps leading to four doors, two of which are handsomely carved and richly gilded, and contain four oval and two square *bas reliefs*. Above is a large picture of the Last Supper, covered, like that of the Madonna, with silver, as are two others, one on each side of the altar. Across the threshold of these doors no woman may set her foot, and across the inner ones to the innermost sanctuary none but the priest himself, or his superiors in the general Greek church, or the white czar, can enter. The doors, however, usually stand open; and the priest in residence, Father **Metropaulski**, is exceedingly courteous to visitors, showing them the

costly and magnificent vestments and the bishop's crown, almost covered with pearls and amethysts. The ornaments and the candelabra are all of silver, the walls are hung with portraits of princes and prelates, and the general effect is rich in the extreme.

Next to the church in interest—probably ranking before it—is the old Muscovite castle on the hill. Here in days gone by the stern Romanoff ruled this land, and Baron Wrangell, one of Russia's many celebrated Polar explorers, held sway. It is said that it has been twice destroyed, once by fire and then by an earthquake, but was again erected with such staunch belongings that it will probably stand for ages much as it is today. It is now used as an office for United States government officials, and it has a ballroom and theatre, with the same old brass chandiliers and huge bronze hinges that adorned it in its glory. The whole building has a semi-deserted and melancholy appearance; but it is of exceeding interest, speaking to us as it does of a grander history, when Sitka was the metropolis of the Pacific coast of North America, and it was the center from which such power emanated.

Of this country—the Chilkat and Chilkoot—Mrs. Eugene S. Willard, the wife of the missionary presiding at Haines Mission, Chilkoot Inlet, and who has resided here a number of years, writes in the *Century Magazine* of October, 1885: "From Portage Bay (of Chilkoot Inlet) west to the Chilkat river, and southward to the point, lies the largest tract of arable land, so far as my knowledge goes, in southeastern Alaska, while the climate does not differ greatly from that of Pennsylvania. Here summer reaches perfection, never sultry, rarely chilling. In May the world and the sun wake up together. In his new zeal, we find old Sol up before us at 2:15 A. M., and he urges us on until 9:45 at night. Even then the light is only turned down, for the darkest hour is like early summer twilight, not too dark for reading.

From our front door to the pebbly beach below the wild sweet pea runs rampant; while under, and in and through it, spring the luxuriant phlox, Indian rice, the white-blossomed 'yun-ate,' and wild roses which make redolent every breath from the bay. Passing out the back door, a few steps lead us into the dense pine woods, whose solitudes are peopled with great bears, and owls, and — T'linkit ghosts! while eagles and ravens soar without number. On one tree alone we counted thirty bald eagles. These trees are heavily draped with moss, hanging in rich festoons from every limb, and into the rich carpeting underneath one's foot may sink for inches. Here the ferns reach mammoth size, though many of fairy daintiness are found among the moss, and the devil's walking-stick stands in royal beauty at every turn, with its broad, graceful leaves, and waxen, red berries.

Out again into the sunshine and we discover meadows of grass and clover, through which run bright little streams grown over with willows, just as at home. And here and there are clumps of trees so like the peach and apple that a lump comes into your throat. But you lift your eyes, and there beyond is the broad shining of the river, and above it the ever present, dream-dispelling peaks of snow, with their blue ice sliding down and down.

The Chilkat people long ago gained for themselves the reputation of being the most fierce and warlike tribe in the archipeligo. Certian it is that between themselves and southern Hy-dah, there is not another which can compare with them in strength, either as to numbers, intelligence, physical perfection, or wealth. The children always belong to their mother, and are of her to-tem. This to-temic relation is considered closer than that of blood. If the father's and mother's tribes be at war, the children must take the maternal side, even if against their father. In very rare cases a woman has two husbands; oftener we find a man with two wives, even three; but more frequently met than either is the consecutive wife.

THE TERRITORY OF DAKOTA.

Dakota shows a remarkable growth in population, and by the development of only a small portion of its great agricultural resources shows a large increase in the number of farms, in the products of the soil, in the number of live stock, and in wealth. The returns of the territorial census taken in June, 1885, and the report of Governor Pierce to the Secretary of the Interior for 1885, compared with the returns of the United States census of 1880, show the growth of the territory, viz.: Population in 1880, 135,180; in 1885, 415,664. The reports from the United States General Land Office for 1883, 1884 and 1885, show that the total amount of government lands entered by settlers in the whole United States during the three years was 54,076,432 acres, of which 17,946,294 acres was entered by settlers in Dakota. This is thirty-three per cent., or within a fraction of one-third of the total amount of government lands taken up by settlers in the entire United States. Dakota has 147,490 square miles of area.

Bismarck, the capital of the territory, and the county seat of Burleigh county, is an active commercial city with a population of 4,000. Steamboats run from Bismarck up the Missouri river to the head of navigation, at Fort Benton, a distance of 1,200 miles, and down the river to Winona, Fort Yates, etc. Bismarck has five churches, five school buildings, four banks, twelve hotels, two daily and two weekly newspapers, a court house, a flouring mill, elevators and a brewery. The business portion is substantially built with brick. The Dakota Penitentiary, a large brick structure, is located about a mile east of the town. There is scarcely any waste land in Burleigh county, and the country tributary to Bismarck is destined to become a densely settled region of small farms. The Bismarck bridge, by which the Northern Pacific Railroad crosses the Missouri river, cost over a million dollars. The United States District Land Office is located at Bismarck.

BISMARCK, THE CAPITAL OF DAKOTA TERRITORY.

GENERAL VIEW OF HELENA, THE CAPITAL OF MONTANA.

THE TERRITORY OF MONTANA.

Montana is the third largest territory of the United States, being surpassed in size only by Alaska and Dakota. It has an area of 143,776 square miles, or 92,016,000 acres of land. Its average length from east to west is 500 miles, and its average width from north to south is 275 miles. Its greatest length is on its extreme northern boundary, which borders on the Canadian provinces of Assiniboine and Alberta. The southern boundary of the territory is in about the same latitude as middle Minnesota. Eastern Montana has an altitude of about 1,800 feet. The land gradually rises westward at an average of about eight feet per mile until a height of about 4,500 feet is reached at Livingston, at the eastern basis of the Belt Mountains. The average altitude of the territory is about 3,000 feet above the sea level. The highest mountain peaks in Montana have an altitude of 11,000 feet above the sea level. Montana was created a territory May 26, 1864, and has an estimated population of 45,000 souls. Helena, the capital of Montana, has a population of about 10,000, and is the important railroad, banking, commercial and political center. It is situated in what was formerly known as "Last Chance Gulch," from which over $30,000,000 worth of gold was taken during the early days of placer mining. Placers are still worked in this gulch. The site of the town is high and commands a view over the Prickly Pear valley as far as the Missouri river and the Belt Mountains. Helena has a United States assay office, United States land office, four national banks, four large, and numerous small, hotels, an opera house, two daily newspapers, and many large mercantile establishments. Some of the richest quartz mines in Montana are situated within a few miles of the city. Trains on the Wickes Branch of the Northern Pacific, and on the branch road running to the Ten Mile mining district, leave Helena. Stages connect with the Northern Pacific Railroad to all the towns and mining camps not reached by rail.

WASHINGTON TERRITORY.

Washington territory is about as large as the states of Pennsylvania and New York combined. It has a great variety of surface, soil, climate and scenery. The lofty range of the Cascade Mountains, running north and south, separates it into two natural grand divisions known as Eastern and Western Washington. There are numerous other mountain ranges, such as the Olympic range, a continuation of the Coast range of California and oregon; the Peshastin range, the Columbia river range, the Pend d'Oreille range and the Blue Mountains.

Hon. Watson C. Squire, governor of Washington territory, in his report to the legislative session of 1885-6, estimates the population of the territory at 175,000. The territory is free from debt, with $72,597.27 in the treasury, consequently, taxation is low with a low assessed valuation of taxable property. The assessed valuation for 1885 was $50,484,437, and the number of acres of land assessed was 3,754,564. The capital and surplus of the national banks in the territory is $1,120,000, and there are a number of private banking institutions. The territory enjoys good religious and educational advantages. Upwards of 2,000,000 acres of the public lands have been appropriated to the territory for public school purposes, which secures to it a large school fund. In addition to heavy shipments of the products of the territory to foreign and coastwise markets, via Portland and via Puget Sound, the shipments eastward via the Northern Pacific Railroad to the Atlantic and Western states and territories are growing to large proportions. Olympia, the capital, is a beautiful town at the head of Puget Sound, and has a population of 2,500. It has some lumber interests and considerable tributary farming country. A narrow guage railroad runs to Temno, on the Northern Pacific; steamboats to Tacoma and Seattle. Puget Sound has an extensive commerce. Lumber is exported to China, Japan, Australia, New Zealand, Mexico and South America. Coal is shipped to San Francisco. Daily steamers ply between Tacoma and Seattle, and Victoria, British Columbia.

SEATTLE, WASHINGTON TERRITORY.

PORTLAND, OREGON.

OREGON.

Portland is the commercial metropolis of the Pacific Northwest. The city is situated on the Willamette river, twelve miles above its confluence with the Columbia, and has now a population of about 40,000. It is a seaport, with ample wharf accommodation for large vessels. Portland is the seat of a steamship company which runs lines of ocean steamers to San Francisco, Puget Sound, British Columbia and Alaska, as well as a fleet of river boats. Railroads lead to Portland from each direction, making it a great railroad center. The buildings in the business thoroughfares would do credit to any city, and the same may be said of many churches, school houses, and other public buildings as well as private residences. Oregon became a st t February 14, 1859. Salem, the capital, is situated in Marion county, fifty-two miles from Portland. The population of Oregon in 1885 was estimated at 225,000. Oregon, in its climate and productions, resembles Washington territory in most respects, and, like Washington, it is divided into eastern and western divisions by the Cascade Mountains. The country in Oregon east of the Cascades, however, has less rainfall than that in Washington, and is principally valuable for grazing, although it contains some good farming districts. West of the Cascades is the Coast range; between these mountain ranges lies the productive Willamette valley, extending south from the Columbia river for a distance of about 200 miles, with an average width of about 30 miles. This is the oldest settled section of the Pacific Northwest, and the valley compares favorably with any in the world for fertility and scenic beauty. United States land offices are located at Oregon City, Roseburg, The Dalles and La Grande.

HISTORICAL AND STATISTICAL TABLE OF THE UNITED STATES.

Thirteen Original States.	Area in Sq. Miles.	Population Census 1880	Elect'l Vote.
New Hampshire	9,280	346,984	4
Massachusetts	7,800	1,783,012	14
Rhode Island	1,306	276,528	4
Connecticut	4,750	622,683	6
New York	47,000	5,083,810	36
New Jersey	8,320	1,130,983	9
Pennsylvania	46,000	4,282,786	30
Delaware	2,120	146,654	3
Maryland	11,124	934,632	8
Virginia, East and West	61,352	1,512,806	12
North Carolina	50,704	1,402,017	11
South Carolina	34,000	995,622	9
Georgia	58,000	1,539,048	12
Totals			158

Territories.	Act of Organization.	U. S. Statutes Vol.	U. S. Statutes Page.	Area in Square Miles.	Population Census 1880
Alaska	Purch'd 1867			Sup. 577,390	Not taken.
Arizona	Feb. 24, 1863	12	664	113,916	40,441
Dakota	Mar. 2, 1861	12	239	147,450	135,180
Idaho	Mar. 3, 1863	12	808	90,932	32,611
Indian Ter				68,991	6 tribes Ind'ns
New Mexico	Sept. 9, 1850	9	446	121,801	119,565
Montana	May 26, 1864	13	85	143,776	39,157
Utah	Sept. 9, 1850	9	453	80,056	143,906
Washington	Mar. 2, 1853	10	172	69,994	75,120
Wyoming	May 26, 1868			98,107	20,784
Dist. Columbia	July 16, 1790; Mar. 30, 1791	1 1	130 214	10 miles sq.	177,624
				1,192,413	1,381,356

NOTE.—The whole area of the United States, including water surface of lakes and rivers, is equal to three and a quarter million square miles. And it can be carefully approximated, according to the census of 1880, that the total population of the United States in 1886, may be set down in round numbers at fifty-five millions. The county government of the District of Columbia was abolished in 1871. That portion of the District of Columbia south of the Potomac river was retroceded to Virginia July 9, 1846.—[*United States Statutes, Vol. 9, Page 35.*] See balance of Electoral Vote on opposite page.

HISTORICAL AND STATISTICAL TABLE OF THE UNITED STATES.—(Continued.)

States Admitted.	Act Organizing Territories.	U. S. Statutes. Vol.	Page.	Act admitting States.	U. S. Statutes. Vol.	Page.	Area in Sq. Miles.	Population Census 1880	Elec'l Vote.
Kentucky				Feb. 4, 1791.	1	189	37,680	1,648,740	13
Vermont				Feb. 18, 1791.	1	191	10,212	332,286	4
Tennessee				June 1, 1796.	1	491	45,600	1,542,846	12
Ohio				April 30, 1802.	2	173	39,964	3,198,239	23
Louisiana	Ordinance of 1787.		331	April 8, 1812.	2	701	41,346	939,103	8
Indiana	May 7, 1800.	2	58	Dec. 11, 1816.	3	399	33,809	1,978,362	15
Mississippi	April 7, 1798.	1	549	Dec. 10, 1817.	3	472	47,156	1,131,592	9
Illinois	Feb. 3, 1809.	2	514	Dec. 3, 1818.	3	536	55,410	3,078,769	22
Alabama	March 3, 1817.	3	371	Dec. 14, 1819.	3	608	50,722	1,262,794	10
Maine				Mar. 3, 1820.	3	544	35,000	648,945	6
Missouri	June 4, 1812.	2	743	Mar. 2, 1821.	3	645	65,350	2,168,894	16
Arkansas	March 2, 1819.	3	493	June 15, 1836.	5	50	52,198	802,564	7
Michigan	Jan. 11, 1805.	2	309	Jan. 26, 1837.	5	111	56,451	1,636,331	13
Florida	March 30, 1822.	3	654	Mar. 3, 1845.	5	742	59,268	267,351	4
Iowa	June 12, 1838.	5	235	Mar. 3, 1845.	5	742	55,045	1,624,620	13
Texas				Dec. 29, 1845.	9	108	274,356	1,592,574	13
Wisconsin	April 20, 1836.	5	10	Mar. 3, 1847.	9	178	53,924	1,315,480	11
California				Sept. 9, 1847.	9	452	188,901	864,690	8
Minnesota	March 3, 1849.	9	408	Feb. 26, 1857.	11	166	83,531	780,806	7
Oregon	Aug. 14, 1848.	9	323	Feb. 14, 1859.	11	383	95,274	174,768	3
Kansas	March 30, 1854.	10	277	Jan. 29, 1861.	12	126	81,318	995,996	5
West Virginia				Dec. 31, 1862.	12	633	23,000	618,443	6
Nevada	March 2, 1861.	12	209	Mar. 21, 1864.	13	30	81,539	62,265	3
Colorado	Feb. 28, 1861.	12	172	Aug. 1, 1876.	32	32	104,500	194,649	3
Nebraska	May 30, 1854.	10	277	Mar. 1, 1867.	18	47	75,995	452,433	5
Totals							3,197,493	50,155,783	213 401

APPENDIX I.

THE FINANCIAL HISTORY, PUBLIC DEBT, REVENUE, EXPENDITURES, IMPORTS AND EXPORTS OF THE UNITED STATES.

In carrying forward the "Historical Sketches and the Outgrowth of the United States," we have endeavored, during its progress, to give all the needful facts and details respecting the discovery of America, its colonization and history, the commencement of the Federal Government, the growth of population and area, the immigration and the distribution of population, the territories and their capitals, and the historical tables of our country, date of the organization of each territory, and the admission of each state. It will, nevertheless, we think, be convenient to have brought together for the purpose of contrast as well as comparison, the more important statistics connected with our constitutional history from the first census, 1790 to 1885. The financial history of the United States from the year 1790 to 1885, showing the difference of the public debt, gross revenues, expenditures, imports and exports. In the years 1883 and 1885, the correct figures for exports and imports cannot be given with any accuracy, as is also the case in 1790 for public debt, revenue and expenditures.

APPENDIX I.

TABLE OF FINANCIAL HISTORY.

Presidents.	Yr.	Public debt	Revenue.	Expenditures.	Exports.	Imports.
Washington........	1789				20,205,156	23,000,000
Washington........	1791	75,463,476	10,210,025	7,207,539	19,012,041	29,200,000
John Adams........	1800	82,976,294	12,451,184	11,090,739	70,970,780	91,252,768
Madison...........	1810	53,173,217	12,144,206	13,319,026	66,657,970	85,400,000
Monroe............	1820	91,015,566	20,881,493	21,763,024	69,691,669	74,450,000
Jackson...........	1830	48,564,406	24,844,116	21,585,281	73,849,508	70,876,920
Van Buren	1840	3,573,343	25,032,193	28,226,533	132,085,946	107,641,519
Fillmore...........	1850	63,452,774	47,649,388	44,644,718	154,898,780	178,188,313
Buchanan..........	1860	64,842,287	76,841,407	76,981,848	400,122,297	362,166,254
Lincoln............	1865	2,680,647,869	1,805,939,345	1,907,171,306	201,558,372	248,555,652
U. S. Grant........	1870	2,480,672,427	696,729,973	702,907,842	499,092,143	462,377,587
R. B. Hayes........	1880	2,120,415,370	545,340,713	700,283,288	852,781,577	760,989,056
Arthur.............	1883	1,554,091,207	398,287,582	265,408,138	....	....
Cleveland..........	1885	1,451,050,100	398,297,582	260,432,120	....	....

NOTE.—The figures given from 1850 to 1880 are from the report of John Sherman, Secretary of the Treasury, to the Senate of the United States June 10, 1880, and can be relied upon as correct. The amounts given under head of Public Debt represent all outstanding principal. The cash in the Treasury has not been deducted from amount. Also the large increase from 1861 to 1865, under Mr. Lincoln, was due to the late civil war, but it has been gradually diminished each year since the close of hostilities in 1865.

APPENDIX II.

Astronomers, with some few exceptions, express the opinion that it is impossible for human beings to inhabit Mercury and Venus, because of the great heat generated upon these planets, by their proximity to the sun. They would have us believe that the globe upon which we live, having a mean distance from the sun of 91,500,000 miles, is the only planet inhabited; that Mars, Jubiter, Saturn, Uranus and Neptune, in consequence of their great distance from the sun, are so cold and dark as to be uninhabitable.

Can it be possible that our learned astronomers, in this age of intellectual progress, can reasonably reconcile themselves to believe that the Creator who has brought into existence our sun and her offspring, namely, the planets just named, besides ten thousand millions of other suns and their planets, did not possess the power to arrange their atmosphere so that the sun's light and warm rays could be refracted on all the other planets, as well as upon this earth?

For many centuries the people of our earth were taught to believe it was flat and that upon the yielding water of the sea rested the crystalline dome of the sky. The sun, moon and planets were of a subordinate nature, their use being simply to give light to man.

The discovery of America by Columbus in 1492 and the circumnavigation of the earth by Magellan in 1521 proved its sphericity and broke the chains that bound physical science and astronomy for thousands of years, and opened the way for the

APPENDIX L.   221

introduction of the Heliocentric system as taught by Pyshagoras six hundred years B. C.

Not until the sixteenth century was this theory restored to life by Copernicus, and it was quickly adopted by Kepler, Galileo and Newton.

In 1709 Galileo invented the telescope. This instrument had a magnifying power of thirty diameters, and it showed that each of the planets, like the earth, rotated on an axis in an eliptical orbit around the sun, which is the central attractive power of the system. The important discoveries made by Galileo demonstrated the correctness of the Copernicus theory.

Among the discoveries to which allusion has been made are the laws of refraction of heat and light; by these wonderful principles, all the planets are made inhabitible for human beings. We will now make this plain. The burning-glass is a double convex lens which brings the rays of solar heat to a focus at nearly the same point at which it collects the rays of light. These rays of heat and light are concentrated by refraction at a shorter or longer distance from the lens, according to the form of its opposite surfaces.

The eye of a youth as a refracting lens might be compared to the atmosphere of the planet Mercury, which is nearest the sun, and therefore the youngest of our system. Age flattens the eye and its focal distance is changed, but this distance is easily regulated by the aid of a ground glass lens, which brings the light to a focus at the requisite distance. With a proper glass a person, however old, may be enabled to see almost as well as a youth without a glass.

The atmosphere being collections of molecules of oxygen and nitrogen, are vast lenses, the great eye, so to speak, of each of the planets. Its refractive power is in operation on Mercury, whose distance from the sun is 40,000,000 miles, and on Neptune, which is at the vast distance of 3,000,000,000 miles.

As a matter of fact, the law of refraction applies equally to the atmospheric lenses of all the planets, doing its work as well, accomplishing its purpose as effectively for Mercury and Neptune as for the earth, on which we know human beings dwell. We can, therefore, conclude that all the planets are peopled with human beings. Under this view how blest must be the inhabitants of Saturn, with its eight satellites and grand system of rings, and all the other planets surrounded by their retinue of little worlds. Words cannot describe the grandeur of the scene and magnitude of the Creator's power.

> How beautiful is Nature, how great her creative power;
> Everything's so perfect, yet changing every hour.
> The trees and shrubs all dressed in robes so gay,
> Like man, all must wither, die and pass away.

But magnificent at these planets must be, which, by reason of certain well known facts, have advanced in their cosmical age say twenty thousand years beyond that of earth, we doubt if any of them have, since the establishment of the United States government, a more happy and prosperous country, or one so rich in agriculture, minerals, and the productions of mother earth; or one with such a free and independent government, of religious liberty, thought and action. Some learned philosophers declared after the Revolution that it would be impossible to maintain a free and independent government in America. But as these philosophers have been mistaken in regard to the inhabitability of all the members of the solar system so have these philosophers erred in regard to the freedom and prosperity of the United States and its free government, which was the outgrowth of the conquest of the Moors by the Spanish, and the discovery of America by Christopher Columbus.

www.ingramcontent.com/pod-product-compliance
Lightning Source LLC
Chambersburg PA
CBHW030012240426
43672CB00007B/915